T0340027

A THEORY OF ENVIRONMENTAL LEADERSHIP

In *A Theory of Environmental Leadership*, Mark Manolopoulos draws on his original model of leading outlined in his cutting-edge book *Following Reason* to derive and develop the first properly systematic model of eco-leadership.

Suppose humanity's relation with the Earth may be described in terms of leadership "stages" or modalities: once upon a time, the Earth led or ruled humanity, and now we humans rule or lead the Earth. When the Earth led, the Earth flourished; now that humankind leads, the Earth flounders – ecological crises multiply and intensify. However, there might be a third stage or modality of leadership: humanity leading *for* the Earth, leading in a way that allows the world, including humans, to re-flourish. What would be the nature of this truly *environmental* form of leadership? *A Theory of Environmental Leadership* identifies and critically analyzes the two basic and incompatible positions associated with the way we construe and interact with the non-human: anthropocentrism (human supremacism) and ecocentrism (ecological egalitarianism). By rigorously analyzing and leveraging this polarity, this book outlines an innovative theory of eco-leadership together with some of its confronting-but-necessary measures.

Expansive and incredibly timely, *A Theory of Environmental Leadership* is ideal for a range of audiences, from scholars and students of environmental leadership studies to activists and policymakers. The book's remarkable clarity and engaging character also makes it suitable for the general public.

Dr Mark Manolopoulos is a philosopher. He is a Monash Associate with the School of Languages, Literatures, Cultures and Linguistics at Monash University, and the author of *Following Reason: A Theory and Strategy for Rational Leadership* (2019), *Radical Neo-Enlightenment* (2018), and *If Creation is a Gift* (2009). He is the editor of *With Gifted Thinkers* (2009) and the author of several journal articles and op-ed pieces.

LEADERSHIP: RESEARCH AND PRACTICE SERIES

Series Editors

Georgia Sorenson

Møller Leadership Scholar and Møller By-Fellow, Churchill College, University of Cambridge, Founder of the James MacGregor Academy of Leadership at the University of Maryland, and co-founder of the International Leadership Association.

Ronald E. Riggio, Henry R. Kravis

Professor of Leadership and Organizational Psychology and former Director of the Kravis Leadership Institute at Claremont McKenna College.

For more information about this series, please visit: www.routledge.com/ Leadership-Research-and-Practice/book-series/leadership

A THEORY OF ENVIRONMENTAL LEADERSHIP

Leading for the Earth

Mark Manolopoulos

Routledge
Taylor & Francis Group

NEW YORK AND LONDON

First published 2021
by Routledge
605 Third Avenue, New York, NY 10017

and by Routledge
2 Park Square, Milton Park, Abingdon, Oxon, OX14 4RN

Routledge is an imprint of the Taylor & Francis Group, an informa business

© 2021 Taylor & Francis

Library of Congress Cataloging-in-Publication Data
Names: Manolopoulos, Mark, 1968– author.
Title: A theory of environmental leadership : leading for the earth / Mark Manolopoulos.
Description: New York, NY : Routledge, 2021. | Includes bibliographical references and index.
Identifiers: LCCN 2020043657 (print) | LCCN 2020043658 (ebook) | ISBN 9780367474010 (hardback) | ISBN 9780367474003 (paperback) | ISBN 9781003035350 (ebook)
Subjects: LCSH: Leadership. | Leadership—Environmental aspects. | Sustainability. | Environmentalism.
Classification: LCC BF637.L4 M2663 2021 (print) | LCC BF637.L4 (ebook) | DDC 158/.4—dc23
LC record available at https://lccn.loc.gov/2020043657
LC ebook record available at https://lccn.loc.gov/2020043658

ISBN: 978-0-367-47401-0 (hbk)
ISBN: 978-0-367-47400-3 (pbk)

Typeset in Bembo
by Apex CoVantage, LLC

For the Earth – but especially for Keysha,
and for Georgia Sorenson (1947–2020)

CONTENTS

SERIES FOREWORD

Of the many leadership challenges that we face, the biggest is the environmental degradation of the Earth. We are already seeing the devastating effects of human activity – the burning of fossil fuels, deforestation, and overpopulation. As we experience the effects of global warming and damage to the ecosystem, we throw up our hands because the problem seems insurmountable.

Building on his earlier book, *Following Reason: A Theory and Strategy for Rational Leadership* (2019), Mark Manolopoulos suggests that a shift in focus is needed, from the notion that the Earth is here for human use/consumption, to a more ecocentric, or Earth-centered view that recognizes that we must care for and limit human impact on the environment. He argues that this seemingly insoluble environmental problem is one that leadership can and should address. From this, a theory of environmental leadership is proposed and guidelines suggested for "leading for the Earth."

This book extends Manolopoulos earlier work and proposes that leadership is the key to the survival of the human race, and the Earth as we know/knew it. We look to leaders to provide answers, but leaders need frameworks and plans to work from. This extraordinary addition to the leadership literature is just such a valuable guide.

Ronald E. Riggio
Kravis Leadership Institute, Claremont McKenna College
Georgia Sorenson
Moller Center, Churchill College, Cambridge University

PREFACE

Suppose humanity's relation with the Earth may be described in terms of leadership "stages" or modalities: once upon a time, the Earth led or ruled over humanity, and now we humans rule or lead the Earth. When the Earth led, the Earth flourished; now that humankind leads, the Earth flounders – ecological crises multiply and intensify. There might be, however, a third stage or modality of human history: humanity leading *for* the Earth, i.e., leading in a way that allows the world (including us humans) to re-flourish. This would be a truly *environmental* form of leadership. But how can such a form of leadership be realized? Insofar as it first requires conception before implementation, then the present work attempts such a conceptualization. The author draws on his general model of leading outlined in *Following Reason* to derive and develop a specific model of properly environmental leadership. The task involves identifying and critically analyzing the two basic and incompatible positions associated with the way we construe and interact with the non-human: anthropocentrism (human supremacism) and ecocentrism (ecological egalitarianism). By rigorously exploring this polarity, the author is able to outline an innovative theory of eco-leadership together with some of its confronting-but-necessary measures, thereby delineating a truly authentic *leading for the Earth*.

ACKNOWLEDGMENTS

A book like this one takes a serendipitous mix of good luck and hard work to come to fruition. I was very lucky and very grateful to receive Research Training Program funding from the Australian Government, which was administered by Charles Darwin University. A number of staff from the University also proved to be my lucky charms. Nicolas Bullot championed my research into leadership in general, while Wayne Cristaudo provided the impetus for the realization that my general model could also generate a specific environmental one. Other CDU staff also played crucial and uplifting roles. Brian Mooney and Michael Christie have been ardent supporters and graciously gave of their time, providing wonderful guidance. What good luck to have such good souls in one's corner. Sharon Ford was also a keen supporter of the project. Finally, world-leading anthropologist Elizabeth Povinelli has been very generous with her time and feedback, which – as you can imagine – has been extremely edifying.

I am also very grateful to those directly involved with the publication process. First of all, I thank the Series Editors of *Leadership: Theory and Practice*. Georgia Sorenson – who sadly passed away during this book's production stage – and Ron Riggio have shown much faith in my work, first with *Following Reason* and now with *A Theory of Environmental Leadership*. They have obviously championed thinking that contests existing orthodoxies in leadership studies.

I also thank Routledge/Taylor & Francis for publishing my work. Once again, Editor Christina Chronister has proven to be amazing, and Editorial Assistant Danielle Dyal has likewise been exceptional. The net result has been the smoothest publication process imaginable – even during such a disruptive and disastrous year.

More good fortune comes in the form of my family and friends, who have also unconditionally encouraged me to pursue this work in environmental leadership. My wife, Paula, is my luckiest charm of all. And Keysha, my grandchild, who was born during the time of this book's writing, would often find her way into my office, and, as urgent as completing this book may have been, it took a backseat to precious time with Keysha. Also a shout-out to my nephews Cheston and Junior – they, too, have brought immeasurable joy.

Now, while acknowledgments are usually addressed to humans, in keeping with the uncompromisingly environmental character of this book – whereby the non-human is stridently acknowledged and cherished – I also hereby express appreciation for some particular non-humans. First of all, Tyga the Cat, who may be the most mischievous being I have ever encountered, is nonetheless – and perhaps because of his cheekiness – also my friend and comrade. He spent endless hours by my side, apparently completely oblivious to my endeavors, but what a wonderful companion. Then there is the humble laptop used to write this book and these words. While it has not always complied (thereby demonstrating that even "the mindless" have minds of their own), it has proven indispensable for this venture and adventure. Of course, giving thanks to cats and computers appears strange to us Westerners – but it is precisely the aim of this book to show how a deep appreciation of the non-human is not only reasonable and ethical but also necessary if we are to revitalize the Earth.

INTRODUCTION

"Leading for the Earth"?

A Story of Leading

If/to the extent that we now inhabit a meta-postmodern age, whereby the postmodern "incredulity toward metanarratives" (Lyotard 1984: xxiv) is itself being met with sufficient incredulity so that we are beginning to retell grand stories, I begin by offering one of my own. Suppose the history of humanity's relationship to the world may be described according to categories or even "stages" (not always linear, clear-cut, and so on). Perhaps the history of the relation between the human and the rest of the Earth may be described as a history of leadership, formerly *by* the Earth *over* humanity, and now the reverse, i.e., humanity's leadership *of* the Earth.

Once upon a time (and still occurring in some places), the Earth "led" the human in the rather crude sense that it dominated us, expressing its power in a number of ways (climatic forces, natural disasters, diseases, predators, and so on). Nature dictated our destiny. Radical social ecologist Murray Bookchin calls this period of human history "first nature," "whereby humans were often subject to so-called 'natural laws'" (1991: 83). We learned to live with nature's brute power and within its laws and limits. One could call this learning-to-live-with "primitivity" if not for the word's stigmatization. During this stage of human history, the Earth "led" and humankind "followed." And there was much thriving.

However, humans eventually came to master and dominate the world. Humanity became "leader" and the world "follower." How was the leader–follower dynamic reversed? Various forces came into play, though perhaps an inaugural factor was the advent of farming. A number of authoritative scholars tell the compelling story that our rise to dominance appears to have been linked to our discovery of agriculture: the cultivation of crops led to the subjugation of everything beyond them (Sahlins 1967; White 1967; Shepard 1982; Manes 1990; McLaughlin 1993; Mathews 1999a; Morton 2013, 2016). Agrarianism generated food but it likely also fomented *anthropocentrism*, which means that we humans think and act as if we are the center and apex of Creation. This human supremacism inferiorizes the non-human other and thus exploits or exhausts it (much more will be said about anthropocentrism as we proceed). With such anthropocentric arrogance, it's unsurprising that our mis/leading of the Earth has led to the multipronged ecological crisis.

But "leading by the Earth" and "mis/leading of the Earth" may not be the whole story. What if there is/might be a third stage? This stage would involve humanity "leading *for* the Earth." While humankind remains in power, remaining the leader, we could lead in a way that leads for all. Instead of leading *anthropocentrically*, we humans might lead *ecocentrically*, which is a leading for every existing thing, from the organic to the manufactured, from natural ecosystems to built environments (much more will be said about ecocentrism as we proceed). This would be a *truly environmental* kind of leadership (also substantiated as we proceed). And, as if it needs to be said, this leading would "also" be a leading *for* humanity: after all, we humans are a part of the Earth – something we anthropocentrists often forget.

We could thus say – since I'm telling a story – that the three stages roughly correspond with "what was," "what is," and "what might be" (or even "what ought to be"). The Earth led; we now lead. But what would it mean to lead for the Earth? This question and this hope take the form of a book here.

To theorize this "leading for the Earth" is an ambitious venture (if this is not already evident, it will become so). But I think the venture's ambitiousness may be managed – even harnessed – by proceeding in a very systematic and structured manner. What is constitutive of this process or pathway? In order to cultivate a certain understanding of *environmental* leadership, what must first be articulated is an understanding of *leadership*. While my meta-narrative somewhat crudely configures it as a kind of power or domination, we shall need to be more precise about this phenomenon if we are to come to a more analytical understanding.

In the first chapter, I explain in some detail how, prior to the present research, I conducted a study into the fundamental nature of leading. In *Following Reason: A Theory and Strategy for Rational Leadership* (2019), my first task was to attempt to define leading. If I were compelled to describe the way by which I came to my formulation, it might be called "quasi-Cartesian/phenomenological." As the name implies, it's inspired by the method developed by the famous philosopher René Descartes: as is well known, Descartes sought a secure foundation for human knowledge; in order to do so, he "bracketed" or "suspended" everything he knew or thought he knew; he proceeded "as if" he knew nothing, gradually building a body of knowledge "from scratch," so to speak (Descartes

1960). The philosophical school of phenomenology proceeds in a similar way: the "natural attitude" (consisting of our background assumptions, common-sensical notions, metaphysical biases, etc.) is suspended as the phenomenologist attempts to describe experiences as they show themselves as themselves (Husserl 1982, 1983, 2001). (We may also parenthetically note how leadership scholarship has been increasingly drawing on phenomenology, e.g., Jankelson 2005; Ladkin 2010; Küpers 2013; Zafft 2013; Souba 2014; McGraw 2016. While this is important work, I shall not be examining it in this monograph, given that it falls under the rubric of the phenomenology of leadership, while my work is a quasi-phenomenological theorization of environmental leadership.)

The Cartesian and phenomenological approaches informed (more roughly and implicitly than exactly and explicitly) my own method: when seeking to broach the question "what is leadership?" – or more precisely: "what does it do?" – I suspended my pre-reflective conception of it. As part of this suspension process, I did not commence my investigation by first exhaustively exploring the leadership literature, which would have colored/biased my thinking. Instead, I reobserved, as if for the first time, what we ordinarily construe as leadership phenomena, from the most mundane to the most historically significant (2019: 15–17). What I discovered/conceived was that leadership actions across time and place appear to share two basic conditions or criteria: leading involves attempts to transform given "situations" (states of affairs, from the most mundane to the most complex political–economic ones) into sufficiently different situations, or leading attempts to maintain given situations amidst competing leadership seeking to change it (2019: 17–32). Leadership thus has to do with situational transformation/maintenance. By comparing my conceptualization with existing scholarly configurations, I showed how my model seems to significantly advance our understanding of leading (some of these innovations are elaborated as I proceed). In case this extremely abbreviated summary is somewhat unclear, the first chapter systematically articulates my general model, given that it acts as a ground or foundation for the rest of the study. Indeed, as will become apparent, this introductory chapter only *begins* to clarify the book's key terms, propositions, and processes; the rest of the work seeks to more fully define, develop, and refine them.

As I explain in the first chapter, my conceptualization of leadership did not only appear to provide us with a definition of leading at its most fundamental level: it also opened up a way of analyzing and contrasting *specific* forms of leading. It involves the following process. First of all, one requires the provision of two (roughly) antithetical categories whereby given situations may be described or classified according to either one of the categories. Expressed formulaically: there are two competing categories, "X" and "anti-X"; the relation between them is basically antagonistic and irreconcilable; situations may be (roughly) classified according to either X or anti-X. This classification process allows us to then determine whether leadership occurs: it takes place if an X situation is transformed into an anti-X situation, or when an X situation is maintained in the face of situational contestation by anti-X leaders and followers.

In *Following Reason*, the two basic categories are "rational" and "anti-rational" (2019: 3). So rational leading involves transforming anti-rational situations into (more) rational ones and protecting (more) rational situations from anti-rational contestation. In the present work, the two competing situational classifications are "anthropocentrism" and "ecocentrism" (which, incidentally, is the first polarity listed in *Following Reason*). If we're able to gain a comprehensive understanding of them, then we would be able to ascertain whether given situations are basically anthropocentric or ecocentric; ecocentric leading would therefore involve changing anthropocentric situations into (more) ecocentric ones and protecting (more) ecocentric situations from anthropocentric contestation. And, as I indicated during my story and will begin to explain shortly, I posit that this is a rigorous way – perhaps even a fundamental way – of defining and enacting *genuinely environmental* leadership.

Anthropocentrism vs. Ecocentrism

How, then, do I seek to contribute to the development of our understanding of the two concepts-phenomena of "anthropocentrism" and "ecocentrism"? The second chapter is devoted to explicating the meaning of "anthropocentrism" with the assistance of scholars who have identified it, studied it, and critiqued/criticized it. A first thing to note is that I employ a constellation of words and phrases as synonyms for anthropocentrism, both to further clarify our understanding and to minimize lexical repetition: "human-centeredness," "homocentrism," "human chauvinism/racism," and so on. My favored synonym is "human supremacism" because it clearly stipulates how anthropocentrism is a prejudice rather than merely the inescapable human perspective (the distinction is discussed as we proceed).

In order to develop our understanding of human-centeredness, I then provide what might be a rather novel way of elaborating the notion: I identify five key ways in which anthropocentrism is concretely expressed or manifested in situations – what I call situational "expressions." The names I employ for these anthropocentric expressions are: "hyper-instrumentalism," "hyper-consumption," "hyper-production," "eco-colonization," and "ecocide." Going by their names, one may already begin to intuit their character, but we leave their exposition for the second chapter.

Now, the discussion of these five situational expressions not only proves useful for furthering our understanding of homocentrism. They provide the kind of specificity we require when developing our model of environmental leadership: rather than postulating in a general way whether given situations might be "anthropocentric," we may explore whether they're characterized by one or more of these expressions, and if so, then it may be reasonable to assume that the situations are predominantly human-centered. And whenever this is the case, then truly environmental leadership could target these particular expressions, and in doing so, facilitate their efforts of transforming existing situations into (more) ecocentric ones and preserving contested ecocentric situations.

Our sustained description and analysis of "ecocentrism" in the third chapter develops in a similar fashion to our investigation of human-centeredness. A key first feature of the third chapter is my emphatic differentiation of "ecocentrism" from "biocentrism" – the latter refers to "life-centeredness," whereby living things are now included in a center formerly reserved for humans. As much as biocentrism is a radical leap beyond anthropocentrism, I argue that it remains restricted. Drawing on a small handful of cutting-edge scholars – primarily prominent Australian eco-philosopher Freya Mathews, but also quasi-/proto-ecocentrists like German physicist-philosopher Klaus Michael Meyer-Abich – I contribute to the task of extending the center to include *everything*. And when everything is included, nothing is excluded, so there is technically no longer any "center" or "periphery" – only a radical egalitarianism. As I noted in my grand narrative, ecocentrism or Earth-centeredness includes both the biotic and the abiotic, both natural environments and built ones. (This is the reason I don't refer to the ecocentric or environmental as "green": my "expanded" sense of these terms also includes the "gray" that might represent the manufactured – and every "color" in-between.) No doubt, this concept-practice appears strange and even ridiculous to our homocentric sensibilities: how could a rock, a computer, or a building be construed as somehow "equal" to humans and other living beings?

In the third chapter, I explain how ecocentrism – a thoroughgoing, consistent ecocentrism – is a sophisticated egalitarianism. First of all, I employ the Maslowian (1943) schema of reasonable human "ends" (inclusive of both necessary material needs, such as food, clothing, and shelter, as well as "higher" needs, such as education, creativity, love, etc.) in contrast to unreasonable human wants (such as the gratuitous destruction of the non-human). I posit that an uncompromising eco-centeredness endorses the satisfaction of proper human ends and proscribes the satisfaction of unreasonable human wants. So while the non-human might be appropriated to meet human needs, it is not appropriated to meet unreasonable human wants. Such an imperative would allow more non-humans to freely unfold rather than be used, abused, and eradicated. One may already intuit how ecocentrism involves an ethos/ethic of letting-be. (My "preference" here is "ethos" because an ethos is a kind of habitual/habituated way-of-being, while an "ethic/s" often connotes a rigid and even "moralistic" behavioral code or system.) So we can already glean how Earth-centeredness seeks to maximize the free unfolding of all things, minimizing our intrusions for the sake of meeting our reasonable basic-higher needs and also intermittently intervening on behalf of non-human others in exceptional circumstances (e.g., when the intervention might be more beneficial for an ecosystem). In the third chapter, I also comprehensively address a range of objections against ecocentrism. As with my brief introduction to anthropocentrism above, if/to the extent that this compacted summary is somewhat unclear, the extensive third chapter aims to offer clarity and a compelling case for Earth-centeredness.

Earth-Centered Leadership

In the fourth chapter, we get to the crux of the study: unraveling and developing the very notion of "leading for the Earth," i.e., leading in a way that fosters the world rather than diminishes it. This is how I proceed: given that the third chapter focuses on a thoroughgoing explication, refinement, and defense of a consistent and thus "radical" ecocentrism, I leave it to the fourth chapter to discuss the five eco-centered expressions that are the five antithetical corollaries to the five homocentric ones: "eco-instrumentalism," "eco-consumption," "eco-production," "eco-liberation," and "eco-preservation." Just like the five anthropocentric expressions, their explication clarifies and adds further specification to the meaning and practice of Earth-centeredness. And just like the anthropocentric expressions, their foregrounding also proves methodologically useful: when I discuss the ecocentric manifestations, I then also identify and discuss leaderly measures or actions that might allow the eco-expressions to remain/become situationally dominant, for when Earth-centered expressions are the dominant ones, there is a greater likelihood that the overall situation will be (more) ecocentric.

For instance, when I explore eco-instrumentalism, which is the Earth-centered approach to utilizing the non-human (moderate use allows us to meet reasonable human ends), I then identify a number of measures that may facilitate eco-instrumentalism. A first measure is sustained, society-wide eco-education, which might allow us to change the very way we construe non-human things (i.e., that they are more than their instrumental dimension), thereby informing how we should use them. A second measure is human population stabilization (*not* reduction), as there is a correlation between the amount of humans and the amount of non-humans we utilize. Given that a number of measures are contentious, I offer sustained and sensitive arguments for their implementation. Obviously, these controversial measures are likely to be challenged by anthropocentric society – but this is/might be the very nature of truly environmental leadership: of going against the anthropocentric grain. After all, our environmental woes have not only persisted but have multiplied and intensified, so that what has thus far passed for environmental leading needs to be re-examined and likely superseded.

Other Key Words-Things

Thus far, I've commenced the task of defining the key terms of "leadership," "anthropocentrism," "ecocentrism," and "Earth-centered leadership" but these are obviously not the only major lexemes and phrases employed in this work. Another key word is "environmental," given that the research is a contribution in/for the field of *environmental* leadership studies. I've already signaled my intention to construe "environmental" and "ecocentric" *synonymously* but how is this synonymity justified? Apart from the stylistic justification (the use of synonyms reduces lexical repetition), there is a more substantive claim. First of all, I recognize that the word "environment" and its variations (environmental/ism) commonly refers to the physical contexts within which we humans are situated. We refer, for example, to "natural/built environments" (we shall briefly discuss "nature" and "the natural" shortly). And I think this is a reasonable use of the term to distinguish the non-human from the human (also discussed shortly) – after all, I'm not arguing against the distinction; I'm arguing against the supremacism that exploits it. However, while acknowledging the popular definition, this work also recognizes that "environment" means more than the non-human context: for example, each human being is an environment, housing a range of other beings (bacteria, viruses, and so on). Hence, "the environment" does not always and everywhere strictly refer to non-human contexts (cf. Meyer-Abich 1993: 2). Indeed, Meyer-Abich identifies how this narrow signification is marked by "its unfortunate anthropocentric connotation" (1997: 169), i.e., the environment is humanity's inferior exterior. And so, in this monograph, "environment" is understood in its broader, non-anthropocentric meaning of everything-that-exists – including humans. That's why this work treats "ecocentrism" and "environmentalism" synonymously. In the present context, "environmental leadership" and "ecocentric leadership" say much the same thing.

Likewise, I use the word "ecology" as a synonym for "ecocentrism." I recognize its origins in the scientific field of ecology (Schwarz and Jax 2011), but it's employed here in an expanded sense, referring to all things and their contexts, thereby bringing the word into close semantic orbit with "ecocentrism." We also note here (and elaborate in the fourth chapter) how the two terms share the same "eco" prefix, which derives from the Greek word *oikos*, meaning "home" or "household," which may be ecocentrically understood at expanding scales (from one's body-as-home, to one's dwelling, locality, the Earth, the cosmos . . .).

Another key term-phrase that requires brief articulation here is "(the) Earth": what do I mean by it? Once again, its popular meaning refers to this world we inhabit. But its ecocentric signification emphatically includes the various geophysical aspects of this world, including the Earth's surface, its interior, its atmosphere, and all the entities located in these regions, including living beings, manufactured things, and natural and built environments. Now, given our expansive configuration of the *oikos*, one could respond that "the Earth" is still too narrow a concept, excluding what lies beyond our world. This is technically true: a rigorous eco-centeredness doesn't limit its attention to the Earth but also casts its focus on the rest of the universe (or multiverse, or whatever it may be). Hence, "Earth" may also be understood in a more symbolic or figurative sense in this study, also engendering whatever lies beyond it. However, given that almost all of the anthropogenic destruction occurs on/in/around the world, it is the Earth itself that requires our most immediate attention.

Another important term employed in this book is "nature" (or "Nature") and its variations, including "natural." To begin with, I fully recognize that this constellation of terms is quite problematic. For instance, the natural is often pitted against both the "supernatural" and the "artificial," and it's often identified with the ethical, so that "the unnatural" typically denotes the unethical or "immoral" (McLaughlin 1993: 1). For these and other reasons, some authoritative ecological thinkers reject "nature" (e.g., Morton 2007). I suspect this might be an overreaction. To begin with, some words or phrases are so problematic that they should be abandoned – such as the use of gender-exclusive language in certain contexts (hence, problematic gender-exclusive terminology cited by the present work is usually flagged here with the "*sic*"). However, I think "nature" should remain in usage, provided it's utilized in a sophisticated and nuanced way. Several distinctions are required. To begin with, as environmental philosopher Andrew McLaughlin explains, we distinguish between two fundamental significations of "nature": it can include everything (save, perhaps, the supernatural), or it can more specifically refer to the non-human. So whenever McLaughlin employs the term in his excellent *Regarding Nature* (1993), he clarifies the sense in which he's using it; for example, he often refers to "non-human nature." Whenever the word is used here, the context should indicate the sense in which it's employed.

Next, the word "natural" is not used in this book with its un/ethical signification in mind. However, I do employ the term "natural" and differentiate it from what Mathews calls "artifice" but what McLaughlin and I call "artifacts" and "the artifactual" (since words like "artifice" and "artificial" perhaps intractably insinuate "the superficial"). McLaughlin explains this distinction: "We [humans] act on nature and transform it, creating artifacts – manufactured things and whole environments" (1993: 5). As lengthily discussed in the third chapter, Mathews elaborates this distinction. To begin with, she confirms that we humans are a part of nature – but then so is our "handiwork" or artifacts: "since human beings, as biological organisms, surely belong to nature, and since making things comes to us as naturally as eating and drinking do, our handiwork itself has as much claim to be considered part of nature as the handiwork of spiders, insects and marine life does" (1999a: 120; cf. Mathews 1996). (Incidentally, from this rigorous observation, the astonishing ecocentric conclusion is drawn: "cars and ships and fax machines" cannot be simplistically excluded from the ambit of nature – but, as I say, this line of thinking will be elaborated in the third chapter.)

Now, even though ultimately all things belong to nature, the following additional distinction can be identified/constructed: the natural is what is allowed to unfold in its own way, while the artifactual emerges when we humans intentionally intervene in this non-human unfolding in order to meet our ends (Mathews 1999a: 120; once again, this condensed logic – crucial to the overall argument of the study – will be unpacked in the third chapter). And so, "nature" is understood in the present work in diverging senses: on the one hand, it refers to all material things, including humankind; on the other hand, it refers to the non-human; furthermore, "the natural" is contrasted with "the artifactual," whereby directed thoughts–actions act upon the former to fashion the latter.

Another important distinction for this study is "the human" and "the non-human." The distinction itself is fairly self-evident (we distinguish here between *distinguishing* these sets of entities and *defining* them, the latter being a rather daunting task that's not attempted here). But the question remains: *do* we humans differ in some substantive sense from other creatures? While I welcome the growing throng of scholarship that undermines problematic conventional proclamations of difference (e.g., Noske 1997; Derrida 2008; Taylor and Twine 2014; Ohrem and Bartosch 2017), the question – and its answer/s – are ultimately irrelevant for ecocentrism: even if one could convincingly make the case that we humans differ from others in some fundamental sense/s, anthropocentrism exploits any purported differences as justification for its supremacism. In other words, humans may construe themselves as somehow being fundamentally different to the other-than-human, but such construals don't automatically entail supremacism; but anthropocentrism is driven by the false assumption that difference authorizes oppression.

What *is* problematic about the human/non-human distinction for ecocentric discourse is that we don't really have a thoroughly proper way of referring to the latter. Whether we use this term or similar turns of phrase like "other(wise)-than-human" or "non-human other," we note that the key/denominated term is the "human": one could perhaps claim that anthropocentrism expresses itself even at the linguistic level, given that the "non-*human*" requires the human as its reference-point and that the "*non-*" infers that the non-human is the human's opposite or negation (cf. Nimmo 2011: 60). There's some force to this argument, though one could perhaps counter that one might be reading too much into language here. Maybe there is truth to both perspectives, but whatever the case may be, as I noted with regard to "nature," I think it suffices that we're aware of the somewhat problematic nature of some of our terminology. (I parenthetically note that I shall not be employing the even more problematic phrase "more-than-human." While I recognize that it's used with good intentions, there are two basic problems. It still employs the human as the reference-point; indeed, it implies that the non-human is constituted by the human plus something else/more. Secondly, and somewhat paradoxically when considering the first problem, "more-than-human" implies a kind of reverse supremacism, whereby the non-human is now considered superior to the human.)

Situating the Study, Previewing Its Contributions

We have begun to define or clarify some of the work's key words and phrases (a process, we recall, that continues throughout the study). And by having commenced this conceptual work, we have begun to sketch the basic aim of each chapter (i.e., the first focuses on leadership; the second, on anthropocentrism; the third, on ecocentrism; and the fourth, on Earth-centered leading). We may now begin to outline the fifth chapter: I compare and contrast the study with a number of the most important works within the discipline of environmental leadership studies (ELS). Hence, the fifth chapter acts as a kind of literature review. But why does the review appear at the end of the study rather than at the beginning (which is what ordinarily occurs)? I recall the quasi-Cartesian/phenomenological method that I employed during my prior investigation into the fundamental structure of leadership: the same approach is applied to the present study, i.e., I did not first examine the ELS corpus to ensure that it did not color/bias my conceptualization of environmental leadership; instead, I carefully followed the methodological pathway opened up by my general model, which basically involved working through the anthropocentrism–ecocentrism polarity.

I think the process succeeded: after mapping the theory, I surveyed the existing literature, and I was able to locate not only commonalities but also points of difference and departure, which appear to contribute to a better understanding of environmental leadership. Given the philosophical bent of the study, a number of the innovations have to do with conceptual matters, including the critique of background assumptions and the clarification of concepts. Before proceeding with a brief perusal of some of these particular innovations, we note how the following academic remarks testify to the importance of these matters. Management scholars Pratima Bansal and Hee-Chan Song perceive that "A field's development is shaped by the clarity of its constructs and underlying assumptions" (2017: 105). Leadership theorist John P. Dugan observes how "Definitional clarity is essential to understanding a particular theory and its underpinnings as well as how we engage in leadership practice" and "A clear definition of leadership will anchor a theory and serve as the springboard from which its assumptions are derived" (2017: 3, 5). And environmental leadership theorist Rian Satterwhite notes the imperative to "surface and question the hidden assumptions and constraints of our cultural and discipline-based perspectives" (2018: 44).

With regard to background/unexamined assumptions, the study focuses on the destructive anthropocentric premise (i.e., that we humans are superior to the non-human), the better biocentric premise (that many/all living beings are equal in some sense), and the optimal ecocentric premise (all things, biotic and otherwise, are equal in some sense). Regarding the existing ELS literature, I observed how it generally remains ensconced in the biocentric assumption, which is vastly better than homocentrism but nevertheless bettered by eco-centeredness. Likely the most striking feature of the study is its insistence on the inclusion of what has been typically trivialized, ignored, or disdained by human-centered and even life-centered humanity.

As has already become apparent, the book is also heavily focused on clarifying key concepts. Eminent pioneering leadership scholars lamented the lack of definitional clarity (e.g., Pfeffer 1977: 105; Burns 1978: 2), and I think this remains the case for leadership studies, inclusive of ELS, even though – somewhat paradoxically – there's been a flood of formulations since the 1970s (Stogdill 1974; Rost 1991; Bennis and Nanus 1997). Indeed, leadership's meaning has remained so contested and unclear that some prominent leadership scholars are skeptical of the search for a general definition or model (e.g., Miner 1975: 200; Ciulla 2004: 305; Zoller and Fairhurst 2007: 1338; Ladkin 2010: 2–3; for discussions of the search and the skepticism around it, refer to Burns 1978: 3, 448; Goethals and Sorenson 2006; Manolopoulos 2019: 8–15). As the first chapter makes clear, I posit that my previous work upon which this study is grounded has led to greater conceptual clarity, with various beneficial consequences, such as being able to differentiate leadership from other (often similar) phenomena, such as management, which is the maintenance of uncontested situations (2019: 33–52; also briefly discussed in the first chapter). Obtaining more conceptual clarity regarding leadership at the fundamental level also allowed us to derive/develop a clearer definition of environmental leadership (i.e., the transformation of human-centered situations into more Earth-centered ones, and the preservation of Earth-centered situations from homocentric contestation). Hence, the theory appears to allow us to differentiate genuine Earth-centered environmental leadership from anthropocentric forms of "environmental" leadership and management.

The Study's Parameters

Despite the contributions this research has sought to make to the field of environmental leadership studies, it's certainly not a "theory of everything eco-leaderly." There are obviously parameters to the study; the work is comprehensive but not "complete." Various questions and subjects are raised throughout the study but cannot be adequately addressed. While some of the most important ones are reiterated in the Conclusion, I now turn to some of the ways in which the research has been circumscribed to ensure that it is not lengthy or sprawling but rather stays focused on the task of enumerating the meaning of "leading for the Earth."

We may commence with a general caveat: given that my specific model of ecocentric leadership is grounded in my general model of leadership, and since my general model is based on approximate formulations that are therefore inevitably marked by a certain degree of ambiguity (Manolopoulos 2019: 21–22, 29, 30–31, 32, 46, 47), this approximation and ambiguity somewhat carries over into the present study. My awareness of the incomplete character of the work is signaled from the beginning: I stated earlier that "we shall need to be more precise about this phenomenon [leading, and by extension, eco-leadership] if we are to come to a more analytical understanding" – note the crucial qualifying term "more" used twice here. What we are seeking is greater understanding – not absolute conceptual mastery. In sum: just as leading is often an "inexact art," a phenomenon that defies "precise" definition and theorization, so, too, is leadership studies an "inexact science"; by extension, ELS is an inexact subdiscipline, of which this work is an example. Hence, there appears to be scope to provide further specification and clarification wherever possible. But what I've sought to do here is provide the outline or basic architecture of a theory of environmental leading.

What, then, are some of the specific limits of this book? To begin with, the study does not seek to comprehensively verify the extent to which we're ruining the Earth. The eco-crisis is here basically "assumed" rather than painstakingly established or confirmed. I very much identify with the following sentiment provided by environmental leadership philosopher Benjamin W. Redekop and his co-contributors in a book on eco-leading: "Rather than spending time cataloging and bemoaning the myriad environmental problems that we face, the authors of this volume seek to understand the leadership dimensions of achieving sustainability" (Redekop 2010a: 1; Redekop cites Diamond 2005: 486–496 for a comprehensive catalog of eco-challenges). However, rather than taking an "either/or" approach in this regard (i.e., either providing a wealth of evidence, or not providing any), I have steered a kind of middle path: I provide *some* empirical data at certain points throughout the work to support various propositions, but I focus on how the crisis may be overcome with ecocentric leading. Empirical data are important for a number of reasons (tracking the destruction; attempting to persuade skeptics, etc.), but the nature of the present study is primarily theoretical–philosophical.

Next, I focus on what eco-leadership *does* or *might do* rather than what it *is* or *might be*. That's why I focus on identifying and discussing leaderly measures rather than engaging with questions like the particular forms the leadership might take in order to carry out these measures. I thus basically bracket the very important and expansive *political* question: under what political conditions or systems might these kinds of actions be implemented? In other words, what might be the politics of truly environmental leadership? However, given the significance of this question, I briefly discuss it in the chapter on Earth-centered leading, noting how the present study focuses on the subject of environmental *leadership* rather than environmental *politics*.

We may briefly flag another important question that is not significantly engaged by this book: why prefer "leading for the Earth"? Why insist on the shift from anthropocentric leadership to ecocentric leadership? Despite appearances, there's no easy or convincing answer to this simple fundamental question. One could respond that continued homocentric leadership will only intensify the eco-crisis. But the cynic or pessimist may reply that this is merely the nihilistic bent of humanity, the compulsion to oppress and destroy (and one could argue that cynics and pessimists have history on their side). I faced the same conundrum in *Following Reason*, where I privileged the rational over the anti-rational: "we . . . have no 'big reason' for choosing Reason over anti-rationalism. Even the proposition that 'a more rational or thoughtful world is preferable' faces the objection that it's subjective, speculative, idealistic, utopian, etc." (2019: 7). In that book, I go on to propose that we could somehow ground or reinforce the rational "preference" by relating it to the ethical (i.e., that rationality and ethicality are somehow related), but this only shifts the onus to ethics: why be good?

The same conundrum applies here. We note how, at the end of my story, I described the third (ecocentric) stage of leading as "'what might be' (or even 'what ought to be')": there is a connotation of the ethical in "what might be," which is made more explicit by the phrase "what ought to be." A key not-so-underlying premise of the book is that Earth-centered leading is an ethical mode of leading, while human-centered leading is an unethical mode – a premise that is itself based on the premise that being-doing *good* is related to thinking-acting *ecocentrically*. But, once again, there's no real way of "justifying" the ethical over the unethical. Nonetheless, the ethical dimension of the environmental leadership model presented here is not completely suppressed just because it can't be convincingly justified, and given that the ethical question is too important to completely bracket, I briefly return to it toward the end of the fifth chapter.

There are also other questions opened up by the study that cannot be comprehensively treated by it, and, as noted earlier, some of the more significant ones are recalled in the Conclusion. But, as I say, this work is not a "theory of everything eco-leaderly": it "merely" seeks to begin to conceptualize ecocentric leadership, which would be a truly genuine kind of leading for the Earth. So let's begin.

1

FROM GENERAL LEADERSHIP TO ENVIRONMENTAL LEADERSHIP

This chapter accomplishes two basic tasks: (a) it provides a summary of the general definition of leadership I develop in my book *Following Reason: A Theory and Strategy for Rational Leadership* (2019), with some additional comments relating to the present work; and (b) it reiterates how this general definition may be utilized in order to theorize more specific modes of leading, including rational and ecocentric modes. While the second task shall merely remind us of the study's method outlined in the Introduction, the first task involves quite an extensive retracing of my general model, as we proceed with the assumption that readers may be unfamiliar with it, and given that the environmental model of leadership that I outline is predicated on the general one, then a sufficient grasp of the fundamental model is required in order to comprehend the specific eco-centered one.

The review begins by re-emphasizing the difficulty of the task of conceiving a general definition. I then summarize the "obvious"-yet-innovative way in which I pursue a definition by re-observing both mundane and historically significant instantiations of leadership. I then recall the outcome of applying this approach: acts of leading appear to involve efforts by leaders and followers to transform existing situations into sufficiently different situations or preserve situations from competing leadership seeking to change them. I foreground the ambiguity and problematic nature of the definition's elements ("situation," "sufficient change/maintenance," etc.). I also briefly address the element of followership in my general formulation, and I explain that the specific question of ecocentric followership is bracketed in the present work because it exceeds the study's limits. I end the section by explaining that I offer an elementary ecocentric ethic/ethos because the focus of the project is the outline of a theory of eco-centered *leadership* "rather than" a comprehensive ecocentric *ethic/ethos*. In the subsequent section, I rehearse how the general definition allows us to differentiate leading from managing, two phenomena that have often been fused or confused in leadership and management studies. By the end of the study, we might be able to conclude that what often passes for "environmental leadership" is actually human-centered-environmental management. In the final section of the chapter, I explain how the proposed general formulation of leading appears to open up the possibility of theorizing more specific forms of leading, including ecocentric leadership.

Retracing the Pathway

Perhaps one way of differentiating "the modern" from "the (purportedly) postmodern" is the former's predilection for definition, and the latter's suspicion of it (or at least complication of it). For "the scholar," the first task is to define the terms of one's argument. This is meant to lead to clear and cogent argumentation. Philosopher Nuel Belnap insists that "[d]efinitions are crucial for every serious discipline" (1993: 115). And yet, as I emphasize time and again in *Following Reason* (2019: 3–4, 8, 53, 70), the word "leadership" belongs to a category of words and phenomena – like "love," "beauty," "Reason," and so on – that apparently defy definition: we think we know what they are, and yet we're confounded when we're pressed to conceptualize them. Perceptive leadership theorists have been aware of the difficulty of defining leadership for quite a long time (e.g., Miner 1975; Pfeffer 1977: 105; Bennis 1989: 1). While there are the optimists (e.g., Burns 1978: 3, 448; Blake and Mouton 1982: 275; Bass 1997; Robinson 2001; Goethals and Sorenson 2006; Dugan 2017: 3, 5), some of the most prominent contemporary leadership thinkers remain suspicious about the possibility of finding/conceiving a general model of leading (e.g., Ciulla 2004: 305; Zoller and Fairhurst 2007: 1338; Ladkin 2010: 2–3). In *Following Reason*, I recognize but also critically respond to these suspicions (2019: 8–17), thus paving the way for re-opening this venture in a tentative and epistemically humble manner.

   How, then, do I proceed to identify/construct a general definition or model of leadership in *Following Reason*? I commence by recalling the most famous quotation in leadership studies, written by the great James MacGregor Burns: "Leadership is one of the most observed and least understood phenomena on earth" (1978: 2). The simultaneous force and familiarity of this remark have the effect of obscuring the opening: its descriptive power continues to overwhelm us, often preventing us from "mining" it, while its familiarity also tends to foster the assumption that there is nothing to be mined (Manolopoulos 2019: 15). But the opening is there: leadership is a phenomenon that is *observed*; it is observable. Observing is not merely a passive receiving of sensory data: the process involves not only perceiving the phenomenon but paying sustained attention to it; observation therefore involves perception, analysis, and reflection, resulting in grounded speculation (Norris 1984, 1985; Daston 2008; Eberbach and Crowley 2009, 2017). Hence, by more closely observing leadership phenomena, I claim that we might be able to better understand them, especially in terms of identifying them and differentiating them from other, often apparently similar phenomena (2019: 15–16).

Following Reason therefore invites readers to participate in the act of observing "as if for the first time," attempting to carefully describe and analyze purported leadership phenomena. While observing or re-observing these events, the following kinds of questions are posited to assist in the task (2019: 16): what is occurring? What is being done? What do leaders (i.e., leadership groups or networks, often personified or epitomized by one or several agents) do when they lead? Do these leadership phenomena exhibit certain elements or features that are common across the range of leadership experiences? If so, might these be identified or construed as common or universal conditions or characteristics that may therefore be co-opted into a general formulation of leadership? And could this fundamental formulation allow us to identify leadership phenomena and differentiate them from others?

One can already discern that this "largely-phenomenon-centered" method differentiates itself from more conventional approaches, which focus on agency, character, virtue, etc. (e.g., Weber 1947; Stogdill 1948; Tucker 1968, 1977; Burns 1978; Bennis and Nanus 1985, 1997; House, Spangler and Woycke 1991; Bass and Steidlmeier 1999; Sankar 2003; Chun 2005; Sosik 2006; Crossan and others 2017), and especially *male* agency (for excellent critiques, refer to, e.g., Sinclair 1998; Gronn 2000; Ospina and Sorenson 2006; Uhl-Bien 2006; Ladkin 2010; Case and others 2015; Liu 2015; Grint, Jones and Holt 2016). The pathway developed and applied in the book focuses our attention on the act itself *more so* than the participants, their characters, motivations, etc. The focus lies *more with* "the doing" than the "doer" – on the action *more than* the actors – though the question/element of leaderly subjectivity is not completely suspended.

Why is a "more-than-agent-centered" approach laid out in *Following Reason*? First of all, the conventional pathway has not sufficiently progressed our understanding of leading, so why tread down that well-worn path again? Pursuing a relatively novel path seems to have produced new/renewed insights. And so, a fundamental part of the approach used in *Following Reason* (2019: 16–17) was to try to temporarily suspend or bracket received notions of leadership. (Once again, my approach mirrors Cartesian and phenomenological methods.) Attempting such a procedure was necessary because predominant notions were likely to obscure or distort our observations. We also reiterate that the suspension was temporary because the study recalled and compared certain landmark scholarly formulations and everyday "understandings" with the proposed theory, a process that reinforced and refined the formulation.

The Basic Conception

What, then, might be disclosed by carefully observing purported acts of leadership? In *Following Reason*, I commence with a mundane (and therefore relatively straightforward) example (2019: 17–18). Why an everyday example? Several scholars insist that leading takes place at this level. For instance, Burns rightly contends that "leadership . . . is far more pervasive, widespread – indeed, common – than we generally recognize" and that "Leadership begins earlier, operates more widely, takes more forms, pervades more sectors of society, and lasts longer in the lives of most persons than has been generally recognized" (1978: 426, 427). Another prominent leadership scholar, John Kotter, confirms the phenomenon's prevalence: "Leadership in a modest sense – i.e., leadership with a lower-case (little) 'l' – is far more prevalent and far more important than most people realize. Not flashy or dramatic, it rarely attracts much attention, and often goes unnoticed" (1990a: 83). And eminent leadership ethicist Joanne B. Ciulla prudently instructs: "scholars might be missing something about leadership when they study only exceptional types of leaders" (2004: 320). So we observe even banal cases of leadership.

The example provided in *Following Reason* is a parent taking their child on a walk (2019: 17ff). The parent leads the child; the child follows. But what is the parent doing, "exactly"? The parent leads the child from one physical location to a sufficiently different one (due to any number of reasons – which are irrelevant for our purposes of identifying any general conditions). Several remarks are required at this point. First of all, the notion that the parent classifies as a leader might appear strange or weird to us (Manolopoulos 2019: 18) because we typically identify leadership with grander acts; we normally associate leadership with "high-end" political, military, or business activity. But, as noted earlier, outstanding leadership scholars emphatically claim that mundane acts of leading are still leading. Next, we focus on what the parent is doing: the parent leads the child from one physical location or "situation" to another location or situation.

Before proceeding, we should briefly define "situation." In *Following Reason*, I predominantly employ this word – though synonyms may include "phenomenon," "act," "event," "state of affairs," etc. – to describe a set of circumstances, ranging from "simple" banal scenarios to what I call "mega-situations" (2019: 23), such as complex global systems like neoliberalism (which is traversed in the fourth and fifth chapters). As stated in the Introduction, I employ an orbit of words for key concepts in this work not only to minimize repetition but also to suggest that no one word perfectly describes or "captures" what is being signified. But the term "situation" appears to be quite useful as the keyword because it easily encompasses trivial settings (such as leading a child on a walk) and "middle-of-the-road" phenomena (such as cultural events) but it may also be "stretched" to name the most serious social formations (such as political-economic states of affairs). As will be shown, "situation" is an integral element of the definition of leadership that I develop in *Following Reason*. (In that work [2019: 17], I also register my recognition that the notion of "situation" as a conceptual lens for understanding leadership phenomena is not a new one [e.g., Stogdill 1948; Hemphill 1949; Sanford 1950; Hersey and Blanchard 1977; Bass 1990a], but the earlier research doesn't employ the concept of "situation" in the service of developing a general definition of leading in the sustained and systematic way that I do.)

Returning to our example, one observes that the parent–leader leads the child–follower from one situation to a sufficiently different one. By observing the mundane example of a parent leading a child, could it be that one discovers a condition or criterion of leadership phenomena? (Manolopoulos 2019: 17). Might the leadership act involve the attempt to guide the follower/s (in this case, the child) from one situation (in this case, one particular location) to a sufficiently different situation/location?

As stated earlier, we must also observe historic examples to determine whether they confirm the proffered condition of "sufficient situational difference." The first "historic" example I identify and discuss in *Following Reason* is that of Moses (2019: 19; it remains irrelevant for our purposes whether the Mosaic exploits actually occurred). One can straightaway confirm that the Mosaic exodus is an exemplary case of leadership: to begin with, as with the case of the parent, there is a literal leading of followers from one physical location to another; moreover, the Mosaic leadership group also leads the followers from the economic–political situation of Egyptian bondage to the radically different one of liberation and freedom (Wildavsky 1984; cf. Sinclair 2007). Moses certainly meets the condition of sufficient situational change and even "surpasses" it, i.e., the situational change is not only sufficient but radical. And so, I posit that *leading appears to involve attempting to sufficiently change the situations of followers*.

There is obviously much overlap between this criterion and mainstream definitions, which emphasize movement and direction (e.g., Burns 1978, 2003; Bass 1990b, 1997, 2007; Graham 1988, 1995). This conventional set of conceptualizations is nicely summarized by Ciulla with the formulation: "leadership is about a person or persons somehow moving other people to do something" (2004: 306). However, the crux of my definition is whether this "doing something" has led to a different situation for those involved. The concept of sufficient situational transformation somewhat "thickens" the standard definition (but not to the extent that this thicker conception no longer applies as a general formulation). We're now on the way to developing a general definition of leading: one of its conditions appears to be sufficient situational change.

So far, I've shown how some leadership phenomena, from the banal to the historic, reveal that a basic criterion is sufficient situational alteration. But attempting to precisely circumscribe what constitutes "sufficient alteration" is problematic. Consequently, in *Following Reason*, I propose that sufficient situational difference is determined by the situation itself. For mundane cases, the sufficient difference is minimal, while the difference would be more substantial as the situation becomes more expansive and complex (Manolopoulos 2019: 22). While this general rule may assist us, we recognize that the question of what constitutes sufficient situational change remains quite a vexing one. In *Following Reason*, I return to the relatively clear example of the parent-and-child (2019: 22). We recall our proposition that what suffices as situational difference is a different location, i.e., the parent will have led the child if the parent has guided the child from one location to an adequately different one. But is there any line or border that demarcates when the parent and the child have passed from one location to a sufficiently different one? At what point in space-time have they moved from one physical site to an adequately different one? A few yards from the point of origin? A mile away? These sorts of questions recall us to the fact that the task of determining whether leading has taken place is often unavoidably imprecise and ambiguous – even when we analyze everyday states of affairs. However, I would add here that we may somewhat mitigate our concerns by noting that the imprecision associated with this measure might be counteracted when engaging with specific modes of leadership, such as ecocentric leading (i.e., whether anthropocentric situations have been sufficiently transformed into eco-centered ones).

In *Following Reason*, I underline another feature of the partially complete definition: leading involves an *attempt* to guide followers from one situation to an adequately different one (2019: 24–27). The word "attempt" is explicitly included in the formulation, and necessarily so: I contend that leadership may occur even when adequate situational transformation does not take place. The intent might exist and serious material effort might be made, but the leader or leadership group fails in the task of transforming the followers' state of affairs. The task may be obstructed, for example, by competing leaders and followers who are more powerful. How do I substantiate this contentious proposition in *Following Reason*? I return to the parent-and-child example (2019: 25): the parent attempts to lead the child from one location to another but is impeded by inclement weather. It would be unreasonable to assess the parent as being "unleaderly": the parent tries to lead the child to another location but is hampered. Failed leadership is still leadership. The leaderly action occurs even though it may be ineffective in terms of outcome. I also recall some historical examples to reinforce the argument that ineffectiveness does not annul leaderly phenomena. One of the examples I provide is Napoleon at Waterloo: does Napoleon's loss imply that the Napoleonic leadership team was no longer leaderly by virtue of the fact of its loss at Waterloo? While Napoleon failed to win, he did not fail to lead (2019: 25). The fact that this leading involved losing doesn't annul it.

Of course – and once again – a certain ambiguity marks the element of "attempted situational change." What constitutes "a sufficient attempt"? But, as

I explain in the book, the difficulty of determining whether a serious, genuine effort has been made does not nullify the necessity of including this feature in our definition: otherwise, cases like Napoleon-at-Waterloo would not classify as examples of leadership (2019: 26).

There are obviously leadership theorists that would contest the proposition of "attempted change" and insist on "real change" (Burns 1978: 413–421; Zaleznik 1977/1992; Bass 1985, 1990a; Kotter 1990a, 1990b, 1996). As the present work unfolds, it becomes apparent that I, too, am very much in favor of leadership that produces real situational change (i.e., transforming anthropocentric situations into ecocentric ones and preserving ecocentric situations from anthropocentric contestation). However, any excessive privileging of transformational leadership leads to the distorted notion that actual change is the only/fundamental measure of leading (cf. Schedlitzki and Edwards 2014: 145). For if it becomes the overarching criterion, then we cannot continue to assert that phenomena like Napoleon-of-Waterloo are leaderly because they failed to create situational change. Indeed, as I'll now show, sometimes leadership involves the *exact opposite* of situational alteration. How so?

In *Following Reason*, I repeatedly note that attempted situational difference is an incomplete formulation. So what else needs to be "added" to our formulation, which, in its present form, could (somewhat unfairly) be conceived as yet the following variation of "a person or persons somehow moving other people to do something." In my book (2019: 27–28), I recall another WWII example of leadership to show the insufficiency of the formulation: Churchill (the name "Churchill" stands for the individual, the broader leadership team of which he was a part, and the group's followers). Now, according to the first criterion of leading (sufficient situational alteration), it would be questionable to describe the wartime Churchill as leaderly: Churchillean leadership did not adequately change what may be approximately described as "the British situation." What the leadership team accomplished was the defense of Britain from the competing Nazi leadership. In other words, Churchill *maintained* a state of affairs. Does Churchill's maintenance of the British situation mean that he was not leaderly? No: the Churchillean defense is one of our most vivid examples of leadership.

Hence, what presents itself is the seemingly paradoxical proposition that an additional or alternative criterion of leading is situational maintenance – but this condition, on its own, would contradict the first condition. (I return to this significant point in the next section.) Therefore, something more should be added: recalling the Churchillean example, we observe that the Nazi leadership group competed for the British situation, i.e., it sought to invade it and transform it. So we recognize that the given state of affairs is *contested*. From this observation, I drew the following conclusion: leading *also appears to involve attempting to sufficiently maintain the contested situations of followers* (2019: 28). Leading may transform a situation, but it may also preserve it in the face of competing leadership. So leaders do not always create situational change; they can also maintain contested states of affairs.

As with the measure of sufficient situational change, the conditions of "sufficient situational maintenance" and "sufficient contestation" are marked by ambiguity (Manolopoulos 2019: 29). I acknowledge that it may often be problematic to attempt to ascertain "exactly" whether/when a situation is adequately preserved or contested. Once again, this point demonstrates that our definition is certainly not clear-cut. But we should also recall the proposition that our concerns regarding such questions may be mitigated when it comes to theorizing and evaluating specific modes of leading: in the present context, measures like adequate preservation and contestation might be more discernible when considering purportedly situation-transforming/preserving actions by ecocentric leadership.

Another issue considered by *Following Reason* is whether the criterion of *attempted* leadership applies to preservational leadership (2019: 30). In other words, is an act leaderly even when it fails to adequately preserve a state of affairs? The book recalls further WWII examples to support the contention that events may be leaderly even when they fail to maintain situations. When the Nazis attacked various nations, a number of these countries valiantly resisted but failed to defend themselves; i.e., they failed to preserve their situations. The failure to preserve a state of affairs does not entail that leading does not take place; it simply means that the competing leadership succeeds in dominating and thereby changing the situation, typically because it's more powerful in some way. It's akin to the case of transformational leadership: just as leaders who fail to transform situations are still leaders, so, too, are leaders who genuinely attempt to preserve states of affairs but fail to do so. While Churchill led successfully against the Nazi onslaught, other leaders led unsuccessfully in their attempts to preserve their national situations, but they may still be identified as leaders. This nuance is registered in the definition with the word "attempting": leading happens when leadership figures or groups seek to preserve contested scenarios.

Once again, this aspect of the definition can be ambiguous: while, for example, treasonous automatic surrender by WWII leaders would appear to count as clear-cut cases where a genuine attempt to preserve a situation was not enacted, I acknowledge that there are many cases when it's much more difficult to determine whether serious preservational efforts have been undertaken (Manolopoulos 2019: 30). As with other elements of our formulation, "attempted situational maintenance" is an unavoidably problematic notion. But while there are unavoidable problems associated with this second condition of leading, *Following Reason* also foregrounds its significance for our understanding of this set of phenomena (2019: 30–31). This criterion or condition fundamentally challenges the predominant set of formulations which, in one way or another, foreground transformational leadership at the expense of preservational leadership.

By identifying contested situational maintenance as a criterion of leadership acts, we provide a fuller formulation of leading. For leading does not always involve changing situations. Recalling Ciulla's reduction – "leadership is about a person or persons somehow moving other people to do something" – this "something" that is done turns out to be two diverging acts: attempting to change situations or maintain contested ones.

But how novel is the notion of preservational leadership? In *Following Reason*, I note that I've been unable to identify research that closely approaches or overlaps with the notion of preservational leading (2019: 31). Some prior research borders this notion (e.g., Zoller and Fairhurst 2007; Fairhurst and Zoller 2008; Levay 2010), but I think my theorization most robustly brings this dimension of leading to the fore. Indeed, by making it one of the two fundamental conditions/criteria, it challenges change leadership as "the prevailing discourse in leadership studies" (Schedlitzki and Edwards 2014: 145).

Now, it will have been observed that my dyadic definition of leading includes the element of following. In *Following Reason*, two of the chapters are devoted to this element: "Foregrounding Following" (2019: 53–71) is a relatively brief exposition of following as it pertains to my general formula of leadership, and then I present a sustained description of followership as it pertains to my specific model of rational leading in the chapter "Faithfully Following Reason" (2019: 97–135). The crux of "Foregrounding Following" is to insist on the crucial part followers play in the leadership process. Following the lead of a growing number of scholars (Burns 1978; Heller and Van Til 1982; Kelley 1991; Hollander 1992; Graen and Uhl-Bien 1995; Howell and Shamir 2005; etc.), I contend that following and leading are *interdependent*: the one does not occur without the other; each element requires the other. Such an approach steers a middle course between leader-centered models, where followership is ignored or downplayed (for criticisms, refer to, e.g., Burns 1978: 3; Heller and Van Til 1982: 406; Wortman 1982: 373; Hollander 1992: 71), and any hyper-Hegelian perspective that might risk framing followers as the leaders of leaders (e.g., Litzinger and Shaefer 1982: 78; refer to my critique: 2019: 57–58). Now, unlike my presentation of a sustained exposition of followership in the context of rational leadership in *Following Reason*, the present book does not undertake an investigation of ecocentric followership, as an engagement with this question exceeds the already-large scope of the study. Scholars are beginning to broach the question of eco-followership (e.g., McManus 2018; Brown and McManus 2018; Western 2018).

You may have also observed that the postulated general definition does not include any elements or criteria that would allow us to ascertain whether leadership phenomena are ethical or unethical. Why didn't I seek to articulate a fundamental formulation that incorporates this dimension in *Following Reason*? First of all, akin to the way in which leadership occurs irrespective of its success or failure, leadership at the fundamental level occurs irrespective of its ethicality or unethicality. The ethical question is a "second-order" one: the "first order" has to do with whether leading occurs, while the un/ethical order is located at another level (2019: 21, 39, 50). What counts at the fundamental level is whether attempted situational transformation or maintenance is occurring. Fusing the two orders leads to conceptual confusion. For example, Burns claims that leadership has the "connotation" of being ethical: "leadership has – quite rightly, in my view – the connotation of leading people upward, to some higher values or purpose" (1978: 452). But Burns also concedes that "Presumably one can lead others *downward* – down the primrose path or down the road to barbarism" (1978: 452), so Burns acknowledges that leading may be unethical. Ciulla confirms this point: "great leaders in history include everyone from Gandhi to Hitler" (2004: 310). Even though Nazi leadership was evil, its unethicality does not annul its status as leaderly, precisely because the ethical dimension is a "second-order" one. And so, as strange as it may seem according to the common misunderstanding that leadership at the basic level is intimately bound with the ethical, a fundamental conception of leading does not require its incorporation.

But does the question of the ethical become more relevant when we seek to understand specific forms of leading, such as rational leadership and ecocentric leadership? I think it does: I posit that these two forms of leading are ethical forms of leading. (I also posit that these two modes of leading might amount to the same thing – but that hypothesis would constitute a whole other story and study.) But the question of their ethicality is complicated in the sense that it's difficult to substantiate what counts as "ethical" and even how we may justify our "preference" of the ethical over the unethical. In *Following Reason*, I was compelled to suspend the question of whether rational leading is ethical, for two basic reasons. First of all, the ethical question ("what is good/better?") was suspended because it is a daunting, expansive one, and would have exceeded the already-ambitious scope of the study. I point out (2019: 7) that there are so many competing schools of ethics (e.g., Aquinas 1947–1948; Nietzsche 1966, 1967; Kierkegaard 1987; etc.). As I ask in the book: "Which theory is right, or more right?" (2019: 7). So I bracketed the ethical question and instead progressed with the not-so-implicit assumption that readers might concur that rational leadership is (more) ethical while anti-rational leadership is (more) unethical – even though the nature of the ethical and unethical is unspecified. Now, in this monograph, I *do* sketch outlines of the beliefs and practices of anthropocentrism and ecocentrism, whereby I propose that the latter is more ethical than the former – or in "even stronger" terms: eco-centeredness is ethical while human supremacism is unethical. During my relatively detailed descriptions of these mindsets-systems in the subsequent chapters, this proposition should be borne out in certain ways. However, we must constantly keep in mind that the core aim of the treatise is an explication of "ecocentric *leadership*" rather than an explication of an "ecocentric *ethic*" (though the two cannot be neatly divided). Of course, an implication of "ecocentric leading" is that it is an ethical leading.

How the Definition Differentiates Leading From Managing

The earlier summary of my general model of leadership articulates my proposition in *Following Reason* that an understanding of leadership would not only allow us to identify leaderly phenomena but that it might also allow us to differentiate it from other phenomena, especially similar or seemingly similar ones. I show in that work how the general formulation appears to accomplish the first task (identifying leaderly phenomena), but how does it accomplish the second? Can it differentiate acts of leadership from other acts? The task of differentiation is extremely pertinent, given that leadership is often confused with *management*, by both leadership–management theorists and laypersons (Bennis 1975; Zaleznik 1977/1992; Kotter 1990a, 1990b, 2013; Kotterman 2006; Lunenberg 2011) – and, as I show in the concluding chapter, also by environmental leadership scholars. But why are these two phenomena often confused?

First of all, we acknowledge that the fusion or confusion is completely understandable: recalling here Ciulla's reduction ("leadership is about a person or persons somehow moving other people to do something"), I explain in *Following Reason* that this reductive formulation may just as readily apply to management (2019: 34). One could even propose that this might be a common definition of managing. But, as is the case with leading, this formulation is simultaneously so thin and expansive that it can apply to any number of phenomena. Hence, we require a more specific definition of "management" – or at least a formulation that allows us to differentiate managing from leading.

Interestingly, our suggested conception of leading appears to provide a way of progressing, in terms of both explaining this confusion and providing a basic concept of management. In *Following Reason*, I turn to each condition of leadership in my search for clarity (2019: 34). First, management does not involve adequate situational alteration, for if it did, then it would be leadership. So we may straightaway reject the first criterion of leading as somehow relating to the phenomenon of managing. Next, there is the criterion of situational maintenance (2019: 34–35). To recall: leaderly maintenance occurs where the situation is contested. This element is a crucial component of the criterion. Now, what occurs when the element of contestation is removed from the formula? We are left with situational maintenance. I contend that *managing attempts to maintain existing uncontested situations*. Management is the process of preservation-without-opposition. Hence, managers (agents and groups of agents) work toward maintaining situations that are adequately free of contestation. My definition echoes the formulation of managing proposed by Abraham Zaleznik, a pioneering scholar engaged in the task of differentiating leadership from management: "Managers see themselves as conservators and regulators of an existing order of affairs" (1977/1992: 9). This "existing order of affairs" is expressed in the terminology of the present study in terms of existing (uncontested) situations.

Given that we appear to have a proposed formulation of managing "derived" from our proposed formulation of leading, *Following Reason* is able to identify and critique moments in the work of great leadership theorists who exhibit confusion over the two phenomena. For example, Burns recognizes that they are different (1978: 451; he cites Bennis 1975: 11) but he bases the difference in ethics: "Divorced from ethics, leadership is reduced to management" [1978: 389]. But, as already explained, leadership at a fundamental, "first-order" level is divorced from ethics; expressed otherwise: leadership may be ethical or unethical, but it's still leadership – so long as it seeks to sufficiently transform situations or maintain contested ones. The difference between leading and managing at the basic level does not involve the question of the ethical but rather whether given situations are contested or uncontested (Manolopoulos 2019: 39). As noted earlier and discussed in due course, the confusion is not limited to eminent leadership thinkers but throughout the discipline, including scholars working in environmental leadership studies.

From the General Theory to Specific Ones

I stated at the beginning of this chapter that it seeks to accomplish two tasks: (a) to provide a detailed summary of my general conception of leading as articulated in *Following Reason*, with some additional remarks relating to the present study; and (b) to remind ourselves how specific forms of leadership may be derived/generated from the general model. In the preceding pages, I completed the first task; I now turn to the second. First of all, we recall that one requires the provision of two more-or-less antithetical categories whereby given situations may be classified according to either one of the categories, "X" and "anti-X." This classification process is crucial, for it allows us to then determine whether leadership occurs: leading takes place if an X-type situation is transformed into an anti-X-type situation, or when an X-type situation is maintained in the face of situational contestation by anti-X-type leaders and followers. Now, in *Following Reason*, the two basic categories are "rational" and "anti-rational." I very briefly describe these two categories in that work (2019: 3) in terms of two columns of binaries, with the anti-rational being listed in the first column and its rational opponent being listed in the second (mirroring, to some degree, the status quo and the progressive alternative). Some of the polarities include anthropocentrism vs. ecocentrism, sexism vs. gender equality, and classism vs. egalitarianism.

We straightaway register our recognition that given situations do not always follow such a neat schema – hence, my use of qualifying terms like "roughly," "more," and "more-or-less." Nonetheless, the basic point seems reasonable:

while situations may not always be classified as strictly one or the other, they can be broadly classified according to these categories, even though, as situational complexity increases, so does the ambiguity.

Now, the procedure deployed in this study differs somewhat from the approach in *Following Reason*. The 2019 book doesn't undertake the daunting task of an exhaustive description and analysis of the two categories of "rational" and "anti-rational" (it confers that role to a kind of collective reasoning process, which is described in the book but doesn't need to be recounted here), whereas this study *does* attempt to extensively describe and analyze the two categories of anthropocentrism and ecocentrism. Sufficiently accomplishing this task is crucial, for eco-leadership involves determining whether situations are more anthropocentric or more ecocentric, thereby allowing us to identify measures that might assist with transforming anthropocentric situations into more eco-centered ones, and maintaining ecocentric situations against anthropocentric opposition. Hence, the next two chapters are devoted to transmitting a thorough understanding of these two competing situational categories. We first turn to anthropocentrism: what is it, and how does it permeate situations?

2

THE NATURE OF ANTHROPOCENTRISM (HUMAN SUPREMACISM)

Introductory Remarks

In the previous chapter, I provided a detailed summary of the general formulation of leadership I developed in *Following Reason*, as well as an outline of the way in which the general formulation appears to open up a pathway for theorizing more specific modes of leading, such as rational leadership and environmental leadership. Now, in order for the theory to do its work, we require a thorough understanding of the two antithetical positions. Hence, this chapter is devoted to a thorough delineation of anthropocentrism, and the subsequent chapter attempts the same task regarding ecocentrism. By thoroughly understanding the two competing worldviews-practices, we shall then be able to determine whether given situations are more human-centered or more Earth-centered and then be able to identify the kinds of measures that might enable ecocentrically oriented situational change and preservation (some of these measures are discussed in the fourth chapter).

The term "anthropocentrism" brings together the concepts of *anthropos* (human) and *kendros* (the center). Before we investigate this relation, we first note that the word *anthropos* has a dual meaning, referring to the species and the individual person. How do we negotiate this dual signification when it comes to the meaning of "anthropocentrism"? The *anthropos* of anthropocentrism refers to humanity as a group, for we have other terms at our disposal that signify the "centrism" expressed by the individual for whom the self is the center or apex of existence, such as "egocentrism," "self-centeredness," and so on. Of course, it's not unreasonable to claim that the two centrisms – anthropocentrism and egocentrism – are related (refer to, e.g., Bateson 1972: 485; Merchant 1992; Plumwood 1993; Purser, Park and Montuori 1995: 1062), but an analysis of their correlation exceeds the contours of this study. Returning to the obvious point that the word-concept "anthropocentrism" is comprised of two elements (the *anthropos* claimed to be the *kendros*), we repeat the aforementioned point that it does not simply have to do with distinguishing between humanity and its others but exploiting the distinction. The human lies at the center; the non-human is vanquished to the periphery.

When and how does the word "anthropocentrism" enter discourse? This particular term – and its synonyms (discussed shortly) – appears to be a relatively recent one, likely emerging in the nineteenth century (OED; Wolloch 2009: 46). It remains a relatively obscure term; nevertheless, the force it names powerfully pervades our lives and societies, fundamentally constituting our reality (Boddice 2009: 5; Moore 2017: 5). Indeed, as I aim to show, anthropocentrism is so ubiquitous and embedded that its familiarity conceals its nature (McLaughlin 1993: 153; on how the familiar obscures itself by virtue of its familiarity, refer to, e.g., Hegel 2003: 17–18; Wittgenstein 2009: 104). Our proximity to anthropocentrism undermines our awareness of it. Hence, the requirement to vigilantly identify it, critically analyze it, and seek to dislodge it.

When does the word "anthropocentrism" enter academic discourse? A pioneering short paper by historian Robert Livingston Schuyler, titled "Man's Greatest Illusion" (1948), is a short discourse on anthropocentrism. The author succinctly defines this "greatest illusion" in terms of humanity's purported occupation of "a central position in the universe" and that "we are at the apex of creation" (1948: 46–47). We may note here – as a kind of entry into our exploration of the meaning of anthropocentrism – that the terms "central/center" and "apex" are exactly the way I define the concept, i.e., anthropocentrism involves the set of attitudes and practices whereby humanity considers itself the center and apex of existence. Now, we further note that Schuyler also describes our anthropocentrism as "subconscious vanity": we vainly (arrogantly) assume this position of superiority but it's largely "subconscious" in the sense that (as noted earlier) it's so pervasive and apparent that we are typically unaware of it. It should also be noted that Schuyler's paper does not approach the problem from an ecological perspective (Moore 2017): the author's aim is to critique anthropocentrism in terms of its epistemic arrogance; Schuyler attempts to show how a more modest understanding of our place in the cosmos will allow us to advance epistemically.

In the 1970s, synonymous terms for "anthropocentrism" were invented/recollected. The pioneering animal-rights activist Richard Ryder coined the word "speciesism" (1974) (though, as will become clearer as we proceed, speciesism remains within the confines of biocentric thinking). Prominent Australian eco-philosophers Richard Routley (later, Richard Sylvan) and Val Routley (later, Val Plumwood) foregrounded the phrase "human chauvinism" in a series of cutting-edge papers (1973, 1979, 1980). Given that "chauvinism" refers to a posture of superiority (whether in terms of one's nationality, gender, etc.), then "human chauvinism" powerfully describes anthropocentrism. And by construing the other as inferior, we are able to abuse it and annihilate it (five key manifestations or expressions of human-centeredness are discussed in the next five sections). The Routleyan phrase has not subsequently gained much traction (either academically or publicly), perhaps at least partly because the word "chauvinism" (like the word "sexism") might be considered a lexical relic of the 1970s. But given the phrase's succinct and dynamic encapsulation of anthropocentrism's meaning, I intermittently employ it here.

Other synonyms for "anthropocentrism" that I utilize here include "human-centeredness" (e.g., Eckersley 1992; Plumwood 1999) and "homocentrism" (e.g., Rodman 1980; Rolston 1986; Gladwin, Kennelly and Krause 1995). But perhaps my favored synonym is "human supremacism": it nimbly sums up the truest or "strongest" meaning of "anthropocentrism" (I'll shortly discuss the ways in which it has been diluted or softened). Pioneering ecological thinker, Lynn White Jr., who wrote the seminal 1967 article "The Historical Roots of Our Ecologic Crisis" (referenced throughout this treatise) powerfully describes anthropocentrism according to this kind of terminology: "We are superior to nature, contemptuous of it, willing to use it for our slightest whim" (1967: 1206). Years later, Meyer-Abich will express the same/similar sentiment – albeit in a more diluted way: "Modern people tend to consider themselves as something better than nature" (1993: 66). Note, too, eco-law philosopher Ben Mylius' excellent definition: "This worldview understands humans as independent from, and superior to, all else in the world" (2013: 106). Anthropocentrism can thus be construed as "superiority complex writ large."

The present work thus construes this concept-practice in its profoundest sense, for certain scholars render the term in much "weaker" senses, e.g., as the unavoidable human perspective (Beckerman and Pasek 2010: 86); as "an acknowledgement of human ontological boundaries" (Boddice 2011: 1); that it is still consistent with environmentalism (Passmore 1974; Burchett 2014); that there is an "enlightened" form of it, so to speak (e.g., Thompson 1990; Hayward 1996; Wood 2019). This semantic dilution and splintering are perfectly epitomized by the *Oxford English Dictionary* (OED), where the first rendering reflects the "soft" signification, and the subsequent one reflects the fullest meaning: "Primary or exclusive focus on humanity; the view or belief that humanity is the central or most important element of existence, esp. as opposed to God [*sic*] or the natural world" (2016: n.p.). As far as this book is concerned, the strong sense is the truest one, since the soft renderings may be more clearly expressed by other established terms or propositions, such as "perspective," "focus," etc.

We also note that the second OED formulation is still insufficiently strong, given that it specifies anthropocentrism as a "view or belief" rather than stipulating that it also includes actions, institutions, and systems. Anthropocentrism expresses itself in attitudes, behaviors, practices, organizations, and social structures. It's not just an idea or ideology but a way of life – or more accurately: a way of destruction. Of course, the concept-phenomenon's complexities and minutiae cannot be encapsulated in brief general definitions: the process of qualification and refinement unfolds as we proceed.

We may end this introductory section by very quickly noting some of the drivers of anthropocentrism's emergence and intensification. Sufficient scholarly attention has been paid to the following forces: Hellenistic philosophy and modern philosophy and science (White 1967; Renehan 1981; Harrison 1999; Wolloch 2009; Steiner 2010; Kureethadam 2017); mainstream Christianity (Bible 1993, e.g., Genesis 1: 26, 28; White 1967; Santmire 1985; Harrison 1999; Marangudakis 2001); and modern democracy (White 1967; Riley 2014). This last factor is often forgotten or ignored but White could not be any clearer in this regard: "Our ecologic crisis is the product of an emerging, entirely novel, democratic culture" (1967: 1204). Another overlooked backgrounded factor is perhaps the most crucial (and certainly the most controversial): homocentrism appears to have emerged with the rise of agriculture (Sahlins 1967; Shepard 1982; Manes 1990: 225–234; McLaughlin 1993: 10; Purser, Park and Montuori 1995: 1057, n. 1; Mathews 1999a: 122; Ruddiman 2005; Morton 2013, 2016: esp. 38–52, 66–76; cf. White 1940, 1962, 1967; Passmore 1974: 1, 12). Unfortunately, due to the limits of the study, we cannot discuss this hypothesis here, but it appears to be quite a compelling one, and if/to the extent that it is true, then it confirms the antiquity, rootedness, ubiquity, and magnitude of human supremacism.

We now turn to the task of identifying and expounding some of the most significant and powerful ways in which homocentrism expresses itself in terms of contemporary social attitudes, practices, institutions, and structures. These "expressions" of anthropocentrism are mutually or dialectically related: they facilitate and are facilitated by each other; human-centeredness fosters these manifestations and is in turn strengthened by them. As we aim to show, they thrive as vicious circles/spirals. Now, one could propose that anthropocentrism pervades just about every aspect of our (especially Western) lives and societies, exhibiting itself in a multitude of ways – too many to be enumerated and treated in a relatively short treatise. Hence, I "limit" the exposition to the following five sets of attitudes-actions: hyper-instrumentalism, hyper-consumption, hyper-production, eco-colonization (the colonization of nature), and ecocide (mass ecological destruction). I will proceed in the following manner: first, each phenomenon is defined and described, and then I show how human-centeredness is a fundamental condition for its realization. We shall advance by proceeding from the more apparently innocuous attitudes-actions to the most blatantly disastrous ones. The discussion of each expression shall show how existing (especially Western) situations tend to be overwhelmingly anthropocentric. Finally, and perhaps most importantly, a delineation of each of these five expressions will allow us to then line them up against their corresponding Earth-centered opposites (Chapter 4); the comparison will allow us to identify and discuss leaderly measures that would replace the anthropocentric expressions with the ecocentric ones, thereby leading to situational transformation, and the comparison will also allow us to identify and discuss leaderly measures that would preserve eco-centered situations from anthropocentric contestation – this dual action is the very process of the kind of Earth-centered leadership advanced in this study.

So I now turn to the task of identifying and analyzing various key ways human chauvinism exhibits or expresses itself, given that the logic of human supremacism manifests itself in/as various attitudes, behaviors, institutions, and systems. (The way human-centeredness manifests itself in these various logics and practices is akin to the way ideas or feelings express themselves in acts; for example, happiness may be expressed by the act of smiling or dancing: the feeling discloses itself via these materializations.)

Hyper-Instrumentalism

A first set of cognitions, practices, and social systems that express anthropocentrism is "strong instrumentalism." Before describing that particular experience, we must first define the root phenomenon: "instrumentalism." As the word suggests, instrumentalism refers to those acts where an entity (e.g., a creature, object, environment) is used by another entity (human or otherwise – I return to this point shortly) as an instrument or means to achieve an end. We humans use various entities in order to realize our needs and wants. For instance, fruit is instrumentalized as food; oil is employed to fuel cars and other machinery; beaches are utilized for sun-tanning; and so on. It should also be noted that instrumentalism is not a strictly human experience: other creatures also instrumentalize various objects. For instance, capuchin monkeys use stones to crack open nuts in order to eat the contents (Ottoni and Izar 2008): the monkeys utilize the stones as shell-breaking tools so that they can access the food inside the nuts. Hence, instrumentalism is a normal aspect of existence: entities are required to instrumentalize other things in order to survive and thrive. There's therefore nothing abnormal about the practice of instrumentalizing as such (Leopold 1989: viii; Worster 1980: 46; McLaughlin 1993: 97; Manolopoulos 2009: 170–171).

However, as the prefix "hyper-" makes clear, hyper-instrumentalism refers to the set of phenomena where there is *excessive* instrumentalization (Worster 1980: 46). This occurs when objects are constantly, exclusively and/or overwhelmingly used as mere means for our ends. Entities are strictly or fundamentally reduced to their instrumental dimension. Things are construed as instruments – and nothing/not much else. Hyper-instrumentalism is either ignorant or intentionally dismissive of their being ends-in-themselves; it completely/fundamentally disregards the noninstrumental dimensions of enti-ties (the question of the ways in which entities may be construed beyond their instrumentality is broached in the next chapter). What results is an intensive, unrestricted, eco-destructive instrumentalism, i.e., hyper-instrumentalism.

As part of our investigation into this attitude-practice, we draw on Plum-wood's pioneering work in this regard, given that it's an abiding concern for her (e.g., 1991, 1993, 2002). First of all, we note how Plumwood rightly insists on the distinction between moderate instrumentalism and what she calls "intensified" or "strong instrumentalism" (which are synonymous with "hyper-instrumentalism") (1993: 141, 142): "We must distinguish instru-mentalism in this strong sense from the sort of use of the other which does not reduce that other to an instrument for use" (1993: 142). We note how Plumwood could be more nuanced here by inserting a qualifying term like "totally" or "completely" after the 'not' as confirmation that *some* use is com-pletely acceptable.

Furthermore, while Plumwood distinguishes between stronger and weaker forms of instrumentalism, she doesn't consistently stick to the distinction (at least not explicitly): whenever she refers to "instrumentalism," it almost always refers to the totalizing variety. In the present work, I constantly signify the distinction. In order to avoid excessive repetition, I use the terms "hyper-instrumentalism" and "strong instrumentalism," and I also occasionally employ the well-known analogue "objectification," which is also employed as a synonym by several authors (e.g., Plumwood 1993: 53; Nhanenge 2011: 113; Soppelsa 2011: 45). Accordingly, when citing Plumwood's work, I insert the prefix "hyper-" when-ever she refers to instrumentalism in the strong sense, in order to clarify that the term is being used in this sense.

How, then, do we treat the non-human hyper-instrumentally? Let's con-sider the way we tend to treat "inanimate" manufactured objects like utensils for eating: in our everydayness, we typically reduce forks and knives as mere utensils and use them in this capacity. Our strong instrumentalism disallows us from considering them in any other way; we rarely (if ever) consider their non-instrumental dimensions (this point is elaborated in the next chapter). And this thoroughgoing or complete reduction of a thing to its instrumental dimension is correlated with our anthropocentrism: when we consider ourselves different, separate, and superior to the non-human other, the "inferior" object is denied any noninstrumental aspects; it is objectified, a mere object of use, and thus often misused and abused. One could respond that it's very difficult to consider kitchen utensils as anything other than cutlery, as mere instruments to be used as means to human ends (eating) – but this difficulty arises precisely because our human-centered hyper-instrumentalism thoroughly/completely reduces these things to the status of utensils; there is little/no remainder.

Of course, our hyper-instrumentalism is not only merely reserved for "inan-imate" everyday artifacts but also applies to other creatures. (Humans also strongly instrumentalize other humans – the extreme case is slavery – but our focus here is on the totalizing objectification of the non-human other.) Once again, we draw an example associated with eating: note how we typically tend to construe non-human animals when it comes to sustenance. In strongly anthropocentric societies, certain animals we consume are thoroughly/completely instrumentalized as food. Cows, chicken, fish, etc., are often basically reduced to the status of the edible. We pay little attention to the fact that these beings are not strictly food-for-humans but are also – and *first of all* – things-in-themselves. Their reduction to the level of the edible authorizes all kinds of animal abuse, from factory farming (Harrison 1964; Johnson 1991) to cruel live export practices (Coghlan 2014).

The following remark by Plumwood also reminds us that we do not just hyper-instrumentalize individual objects but also groups of entities, including whole environments and indeed the Earth itself: "The natural world and the biosphere have been treated as a dump, as forming the unconsidered, [hyper-]instrumentalised and unimportant *background* to 'civilised' human life" (1993: 69). Elsewhere, Plumwood observes how nature is "a mere thing for human use" (1993: 110). Our hyper-instrumental attunement to the natural world testifies to our collective status as "master": "The treatment of nature as no more than a resource for human ends . . . presents the class of humans as master" (1993: 147). Plumwood also cites the words of feminist philosopher Marilyn Frye in this regard, whereby we survey "everything that is as a resource for man's exploitation. With this world-view, men see with arrogant eyes which organise everything seen with reference to themselves and their own interests" (Frye 1983: 67 cited in Plumwood 1993: 145; one could rightly note here that Frye uses gender-exclusive language – referring only to males – though one would also need to take into account the degree to which males have misled the Earth). Plumwood's conclusion is hyperbolic but basically true: "the world is not only conceived instrumentally, but completely [or almost completely] instrumentalised" (1993: 193).

Furthermore, Plumwood draws our attention to the fact that hyper-instrumentalism is not just practiced by human individuals and groups but also by our systems of organization and power. Plumwood notes how capitalism was to "turn nature into a market commodity and resource without significant moral or social constraint" (1993: 111). While we would obviously qualify this statement by noting that capitalism neither created hyper-instrumentalism nor solely facilitates it, we confirm with the likes of White and Plumwood that key social structures or "mega-situations" like our dominant economic and political systems foster and intensify the hyper-instrumentalization of the non-human other (a point further articulated as we proceed). The fact that objectification occurs at personal and communal levels is unsurprising: where human chauvinism reigns, it pervades the individual, the collective, and the social.

Hyper-Consumption

Another prominent expression of human chauvinism is "hyper-consumption" (Manolopoulos 2009; Lipovetsky 2011). As with hyper-instrumentalism, we are required to first define "consumption" as such. To consume things is to "appropriate" them in various ways, from the most literal and elementary (e.g., we literally consume air, water, food, energy) to the more complex and technological (e.g., we appropriate timber for housing or firewood; we "consume" cultural products such as art and cinema). Consumption/appropriation is a normal aspect of creaturely life: corporeal beings (human and otherwise) are required to consume other things in order to survive and thrive. There is therefore nothing anomalous about this practice as such.

For example, moderate consumption would involve eating a sufficient amount of food to sustain a body or society (this point is developed in subsequent chapters). But we (more affluent) consumers have increasingly hyper-consumed food (refer to, e.g., DeSilver 2016; AIHW 2017). Another example of hyper-consumption is our appropriation of oil: world oil consumption is approximately one hundred million barrels per day (IEA 2018). Our levels of appropriation are so excessive that researchers have been speculating whether/ to what extent we've already passed "peak oil," the point at which oil production will begin declining (Hubbert 1962; Campbell 1991; Campbell and Laherrère 1998; Deffeyes 2005; Owen, Inderwildi and King 2010; Nashawi, Malallah and Al-Bisharah 2010). Whatever the accuracy of scholarly estimates, the *mere thought* that oil levels might be already declining startlingly reveals the extent to which we hyper-consume oil.

What is the relation between hyper-consumption and hyper-instrumentalism? First of all, let's note the relation between appropriation and instrumental-ization. When a thing is construed as an instrument to be used, then one of its uses might involve being appropriated. For instance, I may use a piece of fruit as a source of sustenance and satisfaction; its utilization involves the act of consumption. However, instrumentalism will not always lead to consumption. For example, a hammer may be routinely used but it is not "consumed"; the entity remains. The same principle applies with the excessive forms of these practices: hyper-instrumentalization will often but not always involve hyper-consumption; it depends on whether the utilization involves "incorporating" the object. The link between hyper-instrumentalism and hyper-consumption is confirmed by the following statement from Plumwood: "The other is rein-vested with agency and purpose only through being brought captive as means within the master's sphere of ends, through assimilation to the sphere of self via [hyper-]use, in commodification or [hyper-]consumption" (1993: 192). There's an explicit link here between "use" and "consumption" – I previously noted how Plumwood doesn't always nuance her terms, so we may rightly infer that these words in this context should be understood in the strong sense. (We also quickly note that consumption and commodification are overlapping but not equivalent terms.)

Now, given that strong instrumentalism leads to "runaway consumption" (WWF 2018: 30), and given that anthropocentrism gives rise to strong instrumentalism, then it follows that anthropocentrism also gives rise to hyper-consumption: when we humans consider ourselves the center-apex of Creation, then we tend to ignore, deny, or be unaware that entities are more than their consumptive dimension; we narrowly consider them as things to be appropriated. Our enduring and intensifying homocentrism has therefore paved the way for hyper-consumption. To be sure, I don't claim that human-centeredness alone is to blame for our hyper-consumption: there are also other, "more obvious" drivers (hunger, greed, etc.), but this is precisely my point: human supremacism provides the largely undetected framework by which such problematic behavioral patterns are allowed to arise and thrive.

Hyper-Production

"Hyper-production" is another fundamental contemporary expression of human chauvinism. Like instrumentalism and consumption, we are first obliged to understand production as such. "Production" is here used in a very broad sense: it not only signifies the manufacture of goods and services (together with processes such as packaging, marketing, and distribution) but also the processes of agriculture, hunting, and so on (subjects that are further explored in subsequent chapters). And, like instrumentalism and consumption, we must emphasize that making is not an exclusively human practice (e.g., via photosynthesis, plants produce glucose). So production occurs across species. Hence, as is the case with instrumentalism and appropriation, moderate production (which is explored in the fourth chapter) is not a problematic practice.

By contrast, hyper-production is extremely problematic. But what is it? The term "hyper-production" as it is used here signifies a number of phenomena, including the manufacture of too many goods and services, the speedy manufacture of these products, and the type of items produced, which often have eco-negative effects. First of all, "hyper-production" is meant in the sense of overproduction: more goods and services are made than are required or desired; there's an "over-abundance" of commodities; the world is flooded with them. Overproduction appears to be a particular hallmark of capitalist society (Marx and Engels 1888/1910: 20; Clark 1999). Overproduction means excessive waste (I employ the qualifier "excessive" because, as material beings, we humans inevitably expend at the individual and collective levels). According to the U.N. Food and Agriculture Organization (FAO): "Roughly one third of the food produced in the world for human consumption every year – approximately 1.3 billion tonnes – gets lost or wasted" (FAO n.d.). *One third* is a massive amount by any measure.

The term "hyper-production" as it's conceived and employed here also encapsulates the radical *speed* with which commodities are manufactured by us humans, especially "bio-products" (i.e., other creatures). We make (and consume) so rapidly that any opportunity for replenishment is exceeded by production (and appropriation) rates (Guha and Martinez-Alier 1997: 40). A dramatic example in this regard is the fishing industry's effects on biomass depletion. By the beginning of the twenty-first century, already 75% of major fisheries were either exploited or depleted (FAO 2002: 23), and 90% of large predatory fish have been wiped out (Myers and Worm 2003). Given these kinds of statistics, it is little wonder that environmental sociologists Rebecca Clausen and Brett Clark introduce their study by foregrounding the rapidity with which ocean fish loss is occurring: "The world's oceans are experiencing a crisis of rapid biomass depletion" (2005: 422).

"Hyper-production" also denotes here the mass manufacture of goods and services that harm the ecosphere and its inhabitants in radically effective ways. The most confronting example is military hardware: while we humans are often aware of weaponry's devastating effects on human lives, we typically – that is, *anthropocentrically* – fail to acknowledge the ways in which war machinery decimates the Earth and its non-human inhabitants. Warfare between nations is also warfare on the environment. (The term "*World* War" now reveals or acquires a more-than-anthropocentric signification: warring nations also wage war on the world; one of the biggest-yet-unrecognized casualties of war is the environment.) And akin to the aforementioned pollution-creating consequence of overproduction, the manufacture and utilization of high-tech weapons lead to radical pollution, especially in terms of radiation and other harmful pollutants. As ecological theologian Rosemary Radford Ruether powerfully expresses it, militarism has become "the ultimate polluter of the earth" (1992: 109; Manolopoulos 2009: 124).

We should also add here that hyper-production does not exclusively refer to the manufacture of devastating goods and services: it includes a whole gamut of mass-produced items, including those that radically differ from military hardware. These commodities are typically cheaply made and cheaply sold, mass-produced, manufactured from synthetic materials, and often lack practical and aesthetic value. Now, I must straightaway insist that I'm not denigrating such objects: as I aim to show as I proceed, an eco-centered perspective values all entities – including cheap mass-produced things. After all, "even" cheap mass-produced commodities remain valuable to us ecocentrists; a thoroughgoing, consistent Earth-centeredness cuts across all entities; it is all-inclusive. In *If Creation is a Gift*, I state: "Does mass production prevent the possibility that its products and reproductions bear no trace of excess?. . . . [E]very thing bears such a mark, be it a raging river or a plastic bag. . . . – at least in terms of the elusive, mysterious *phusis* [the pre-existing materiality] from which the product is manufactured" (2009: 121; incidentally, I ecocentrically ponder the much-derided plastic bag in the third chapter).

Now, while we confirm a commodity-thing's irreducible excess, we eco-centrists are nonetheless aware of the environmentally problematic nature of such entities. For example, mass-produced items are typically created from synthetic materials that have been proven to be toxic to humans, other creatures, and the environment (Andrady 2003; Halden 2010; *Dark Waters* 2019). Furthermore, owing to the fact that the mass-produced is often considered "junk" that is "made to break" (Slade 2006), become obsolete, and is therefore readily disposable (Pye 2010) – a point further developed in subsequent chapters – it further contributes to the waste/pollution crisis (Desai 2001; Derraik 2002; Leonard 2010; Pye 2010). Taking these kinds of factors into account, we ask with Meyer-Abich: "What will be the real costs of products which are apparently cheap?" (1993: 100). And so, it is not inconsistent to simultaneously propose that we ecocentrists cognize the excess in mass-produced goods and recognize their utility (Thompson and others 2009), but we also oppose their *ongoing* hyper-production (a point extrapolated in the fifth chapter).

But how is hyper-production an expression of anthropocentrism? The various dimensions of hyper-production identified earlier disclose in their own ways the human supremacism that drives it. To begin with, overproduction occurs due to a radical disregard for the produced objects: we over-producers are only concerned about making as many commodities as possible (for as much profit as possible), with no regard for captured entities or "raw materials" (elaborated shortly). The fact that hyper-production involves the delivery of both cheap and harmful mass-produced products also testifies to our human chauvinism. First of all, destructive commodities are intentionally made in order to harm other humans but there is also an absolute disregard for non-human "collateral damage" – the non-human creatures and environments who are caught up in our conflicts. Another disclosive aspect of environmentally "unfriendly" products is that they exemplify the degree to which we consider just about every non-human thing as a mere resource for us humans: entities are considered "raw materials" to be used in the making of the most useless products – their only value is to contribute to the making of a valueless or minimally valuable item; entities are appropriated and reduced to the level of a useful ingredient for a useless product. In such a pervasively anthropocentric environment, we're unable to construe or perceive the other beyond its dimension of "productness."

We also observe how hyper-production is intertwined with hyper-consumption: producers create consumer demand, and consumers drive further manufacturing (McCarthy 1960; Mandel 1986; Falk 1994; Edgell, Hetherington and Warde 1996; Nava and others 1997; Sulkunen and others 1997; WWF 2018: 35). (We elaborate this point in the fourth chapter.) But this is not just a vicious capitalistic circle but also an anthropocentric one: the circle quickens and intensifies precisely because entities are radically reduced to products for appropriation. Within the frenzied loop of production-consumption, there's no time or space to recall the other as something that is more than and otherwise than a component of a production process resulting in a commodity to be consumed.

Eco-Colonization

While the practices of hyper-instrumentalism, hyper-consumption, and hyper-production are deeply disturbing, we have not yet addressed the most extreme and alarming expressions of human supremacism: eco-colonization and ecocide. We commence with the phenomenon of eco-colonization. "Colonization" is here meant in the same way that it's ordinarily applied to human-to-human affairs: it refers to the invasion, domination, and appropriation of others for one's own interests – but in the case of *eco*-colonization, the colonized is the non-human other. In this context, "the non-human other" includes creatures, their environments, human-built environments (buildings, streets, etc.), and non-human-built environments (termite nests, spider webs, etc.). Expressed in a nutshell: eco-colonization is the overpowering of the other-than-human. While one could claim that human colonization presupposes or at least takes place in conjunction with eco-colonization (in order for colonizers to successfully colonize other humans, they simultaneously conquer their environments), eco-colonization hones in on these various non-human others (Leiss 1972; Collard and Contrucci 1988; Purser, Park and Montuori 1995: 1071; Smalley 2017).

Some of the environmental thinkers retrieved in the present work refer to the process of the colonization of the non-human. Aldo Leopold, a pioneering biocentric thinker who's referenced throughout this work, refers to humankind as a "conqueror" (1989: 204). And, in her characteristically pith way, Mathews describes our eco-colonization of the other: "We comport ourselves as invaders, conquerors, buying up the matter which means nothing to us, and trashing it when we are tired of it" (1999a: 129). Meyer-Abich invents/employs the synonymous term "eco-colonialism" (1993: 56). Plumwood is another thinker who reconceives colonialism in environmental terms: "The master's logic of colonisation is the dominant logic of our time" (1993: 190) – though I would also add that it was also dominant before our time: if/to the extent that we accept the thesis that anthropocentrism arose with agriculture, then the "master's logic of colonisation" of the land arises and begins to dominate with the onset of agrarianism. So we may posit that the colonization of the non-human began in earnest with civilization itself.

The empire of humanity has since continued to expand exponentially across *terra firma*, above the ground and below it, such as agrarian expansion and underground mining. Consider Western-style agriculture: the FAO estimates that approximately 25% of the Earth's land mass is now used to maintain livestock, and a further 11% is used for crop production (2003). So approximately one-third of the Earth's land surface is given over to agriculture. To be sure, eco-colonization is not limited to the agrarian: we witness it everywhere in all kinds of ways, such as our usurpation of oil (Boesch, Hershner and Milgram 1974; Marland and Rotty 1984; Cotton 1986; Schmalemsee, Stoker and Judson 1998; Alcraft 2000; Casper 2010; Shriver 2017).

Of course, our colonization is not restricted to the land: humanity has been steadily colonizing bodies of water and the skies and beyond. Turning first to the colonization of waterways, a particularly violent form is the dam. Its construction causes massive disruptions to existing ecosystems (Baxter 1977); it wreaks ecological destruction whenever it fails or breaks (Babb and Mermel 1968; Goldsmith and Hildyard 1984–1992); it causes "natural disasters" like flooding (McCully 2001); it ferments water-associated diseases (Jobin 1999) – and let's not forget its disruption/destruction of existing human settlements. This is not to say that dams should be dogmatically rejected in every case; however, the negative consequences of dam-building are dismissed or downplayed by us colonizers, precisely because we anthropocentrically construe our objectives as the only/primarily important ones. The various waterways are reduced to sources of drinking water, parts of irrigation systems for our farms, etc. – but they're rarely considered beyond these instrumentalized dimensions.

We humans also seek to colonize sky and space. This form of conquering is obviously more recent than land and sea colonization, and more "subtle" and less palpable, so our mastery over the air might not be construed as "colonization" in any strong sense. But when we consider the exponential growth in air traffic (ICAO 2017; Addepalli and others 2018) and its staggering environmental impacts – for example, our planes guzzle five million gallons of fuel per day and contribute 2.5% of total carbon emissions, set to rise to 22% by 2050 (Tyers 2017; cf. Gössling and Upham 2009) – then the notion that we humans are usurping the skies appears more feasible. And as we dream of interstellar conquest, our narrative remains distinctly colonialist (e.g., Schmidt and Zubrin 1996; Levine and Schild 2010). "Space is the final frontier" – indeed, anthropocentrism's final frontier. We could even suggest that, given our attempts to colonize both outer space and "inner space" – by employing, for example, nanotechnology (Drexler 1986; Allhoff, Lin and Moore 2010) – our astronautical and nanotechnological homocentrism knows no bounds, seeking to expand infinitely in both directions.

Now, even though I have focused here on the domination of various domains of the ecosphere (lands, seas, and skies/space), I reiterate that, from an eco-centric perspective, "eco-colonization" refers to the domination of anything non-human, including manufactured things and built environments. Anthropocentric oppression expands in all directions.

Eco-colonization is also interconnected with the previous three expressions of human-centeredness. For instance, it's intimately bound with strong instrumentalism: what is used can also be possessed. Plumwood confirms this correlation in terms of anthropocentric subjectivity: "The structures of self involved in human domination and colonisation are reflected, repeated and confirmed in the [strong/total] reduction of non-human nature to an instrument" (1993: 142). She goes so far as to propose that colonization involves a very strong form of instrumentalism: "In this stage [i.e., colonization] there is a more intense and totalising form of instrumentalisation" (Plumwood 1993: 192). While we agree with this summation, we also emphasize that the relation between eco-colonization and hyper-instrumentalism (and the other anthropocentric expressions) is not simply linear (i.e., we first strongly instrumentalize the world and then we colonize it) but rather ceaselessly circular: we hyper-instrumentalize the Earth, which allows us to colonize it, which allows us to hyper-instrumentalize it, and so on.

So one could posit that hyper-instrumentalism and eco-colonization often appear to be conditions of possibility for each other. Eco-colonization and hyper-consumption and hyper-production are also fundamentally correlated: these latter excesses are possible because the entities are subjugated: when a thing is dominated, the master is able to dominate it in whatever way the master desires. When we humans subjugate the other, they may be subjugated in these various reduced ways (i.e., as instruments, as consumed products, as materials, etc.). We humans colonize what we consider different and inferior to us; we do not subjugate who we typically consider to be our equals (e.g., other humans) or superior to us (e.g., deities). Of course, the colonized thing is "valuable" to us, but it is not considered "equal" in any sense – the mere notion is/ would be met with anthropocentric mockery.

Ecocide

The fifth and most radical, devastating expression of anthropocentrism is "ecocide": the term is used here to denote acts involving the widespread elimination of the non-human. Leading environmental philosopher J. Baird Callicott refers to "biocide" – "abrupt, massive, wholesale anthropogenic species extinction" (1989: 40) but "ecocide" encompasses everything non-human.

Obviously, there are parallels here with genocide (on their comparison, refer to, e.g., Crook, Short and South 2018); while genocide may be more decidedly an intentional act, ecocide is real – indeed, it's expanding and intensifying. The Earth is said to be experiencing a geological period where human activity is impacting the world to such an extent that it is now being classified as "the Anthropocene" (Crutzen and Stoermer 2000; Zalasiewicz and others 2010; Ferrando 2016; cf. Marsh 1864; Lankester 1913). So we already have geological authorization that we are significantly impacting the ecosphere. Likewise, scientists and theorists are also claiming that we're entering/have entered a "Sixth Mass Extinction," akin to the five previous mass extinctions in the past half-a-billion years which are attributed to events such as volcanic eruptions and meteorites, but this time the driving factor for the mass extinction is purported to be human action (Diamond 1989; Broswimmer 2002; Higgins 2010; Kolbert 2014; Ceballos and others 2015; Brannen 2017).

Now, after reviewing a representative body of the relevant literature (e.g., Wilson 2002; Monastersky 2014; de Vos and others 2015; Pearce 2015; WWF n.d.), one could surmise the following: while it appears that the rate of extinction of species has risen due to human activity over the past few centuries, it might be problematic at this stage to dogmatically describe it as a period of *mass* species extinction, especially when comparing it with the previous mass extinctions. This is not to suggest that we aren't entering such a phase, but – and this is the point we should be focusing on – we *are* annihilating species. We humans *are* committing ecocide in its most literal biocentric sense (the annihilation of species).

What is significantly easier to confirm at this point in time is that ecocide is also occurring in terms of the anthropogenically induced decline in the *numbers* of creatures. For instance, the World Wildlife Fund (WWF) estimates that vertebrate animal populations have decreased by an astonishing 60% since 1970 (2018: 4, 7). We have purportedly killed off 83% of freshwater species (WWF 2018: 7), and the same staggering 83% rate also appears to apply to wild mammals (Bar-On, Phillips and Milo 2018). In the USA alone, nine billion chickens, over one hundred million pigs, and around forty million cattle are slaughtered per year (Keim 2018). According to the data, there's no doubt that anthropogenic ecocide is occurring in terms of the eradication of vast numbers of organisms. So, in many cases, the whole species might not be wiped out by human activity but large numbers of the species are being annihilated. In the same way that we describe acts as "genocidal" even when the whole ethnic group is not eliminated (not all Jews, Romani/Gypsies, Rwanda's Tutsis, etc., were killed during sustained genocidal activity), the perpetrator's intention is to eradicate the ethnic group or at least as large a portion as possible. Similarly, we humans are ecocidally killing off large portions of species.

What is also undisputed is that we humans are committing ecocide in terms of eradicating massive numbers of fauna. The most striking and well-known example in this regard is what is euphemistically known as "deforestation," a term that obscures the severity and expansiveness of this practice. Roughly half the world's trees have been lost since we humans started felling them in concert with the rise of agriculture, and an estimated fifteen billion trees are cut down each year (Crowther and others 2015). Almost twenty million acres of forest are eradicated each year. According to terms that simultaneously visualize and downplay the horror of deforestation, one football/soccer pitch per second is being destroyed (Carrington and others 2017), and, since the 1990s, we've apparently razed forest areas equaling the size of India (Watson and others 2016). As strange as the terminology may be used that is to describe it, what we have here is a clear case of the "ecocide of forests." (We parenthetically note how some researchers also refer to forest ecocide in the context of war, e.g., Weisberg 1970; Zierler 2011.) We also observe how the ecocide of forests has disastrous flow-on effects for other entities living in nourishing forest ecosystems (Barlow and others 2016), given that forests house more than 80% of terrestrial species of plants and animals (WWF 2018: 50). One form of ecocide compounds another; ecocide begets ecocide.

Another group of entities included in our ecocentrically expanded sense of ecocide are the built environments constructed by non-humans and humans alike. In other words, "ecocide" here also signifies the destruction of things such as termite mounds, bird nests, and spider webs, but also humanly constructed things, such as buildings, bridges, and roads. As explained in the next chapter, while we typically construe human-built environments as "artificial" or artifactual, they (also) count as part of the *oikos*. Hence, since human and non-human artifacts should be ultimately considered "natural" or at least a part of the *oikos*, then the human destruction of these things ecocentrically counts here as one of the meanings of "ecocide." Accordingly, we recognize the ecocidal dimension of a human activity like "redevelopment": existing built environments are incessantly demolished to make way for shiny, new, and profitable environments (housing estates, shopping centers, etc.). Thus, ecocide does not just include phenomena like species extinction and deforestation but also the demolition of existing human and non-human structures. The same site may therefore endure several ecocides: first, the erasure of the original habitat and inhabitants to make way for human developments (farms, ski resorts, etc.), and then continual cycles of "redevelopmental ecocide." The relatively scant research addressing issues related to this form of eco-destruction (e.g., Lélé 1991; Alvares 1992; Linkenbach 1994; Shrivastava 2012; Sayan 2016) reflects the fact that we rarely construe development and redevelopment in ecocidal terms – precisely because we think and act anthropocentrically.

Having considered ecocide here according to its various dimensions, how is it related to the other homocentric phenomena described earlier? While one may identify various relations, what is perhaps most noteworthy is the asymmetry between, on the one hand, the first four anthropocentric expressions, and ecocide, on the other hand: while we humans might find some non-human things valuable insofar as they might be utilizable, consumable, parts of the production process, or exploitable, ecocide finds no worth in the thing whatsoever. The non-human thing is considered more valuable dead/non-existing than alive/existing. To be sure, various "logics" might be at play – such as the profit motive – but these logics can ultimately only be justified according to the illogic of human supremacism. While human genocide is both relatively uncommon and almost universally decried, the annihilation of the non-human is far more common and even vindicated – precisely because we are anthropocentrists.

On Our Way to Ecocentrism

What I've sought to achieve in this chapter is to provide an outline of human chauvinism and its various key expressions so that we familiarize ourselves with this force and the ways in which it constitutes or marks so many (especially Western) situations. Anthropocentrism is deeply entrenched, pervasive, and expanding (both within and beyond the West). We can already intuit that Earth-centered leadership would constitute a radically decisive break from the status quo, given that it challenges the very essence of agrarian-civilizational society – but we are getting ahead of ourselves here: before extrapolating the nature and actions of ecocentric leadership, we must first comprehensively understand eco-centeredness as such, which is the subject of the next chapter.

3

THE NATURE OF ECOCENTRISM
(ECOLOGICAL EQUALITY)

Having provided a re-articulation of my general theory of leadership (Chapter 1) and an elucidation of the meaning and manifestations of anthropocentrism (Chapter 2), I now turn to an exposition of the profoundest sense of Earth-centeredness. A thorough exposition (but not an exhaustive one, which would exceed the study's scope) is required not only to reclaim the radical signification of ecocentrism but also to be able to begin to enunciate/build an environmental leadership model. Now, in order to complete the exposition, several tasks will need to be undertaken. I commence by acknowledging ancient and modern biocentric discourses out of which eco-centeredness emerges, as well as those modern texts that are quasi/proto-ecocentric. Next, I define eco-centeredness as a radical egalitarianism that is inclusive of all entities, including organic and manufactured things, and both natural and built environments. I elaborate this conception by drawing heavily on the work of Freya Mathews, and a few other thinkers; in doing so, the definition is refined and ecocentrism's ethos/ethic is articulated. Next, I briefly discuss emotions or affective states associated with Earth-centeredness. I then ground and defend the position. I survey various possible justifications, favoring the fundamental right to existence extended to all things. I then address six objections to ecocentrism – five identified by the eminent Australian eco-political theorist Robyn Eckersley, and one raised by McLaughlin. The chapter ends with a short concluding section. Unlike the previous chapter on human-centeredness, which includes summaries of anthropocentric "expressions" (hyper-instrumentalism, hyper-consumption, etc.), the present chapter does not discuss the "corresponding" antithetical ecocentric expressions: for the sake of structural cohesiveness and the avoidance of repetition, these are identified and discussed in the subsequent chapter, as part of the sketch of ecocentric leadership.

From Biocentrism to the Edge of Earth-Centeredness

One could reasonably propose that ecocentric thinking emerges from biocentric discourse-practice; some familiarity with the latter will therefore lead to a better understanding of the former. To begin with, what is meant by "biocentrism"? The Greek word *bios* means "life," so "biocentrism" signifies "life-centeredness." We therefore straightaway recognize how it radically surpasses anthropocentrism: the center is now expanded to include other living things. Biocentric thinking can be traced back to a number of discourses, e.g., ancient Eastern (Callicott 1987a; Hall 1987; Rolston 1987; Jamieson 1996; Callicott and McRae 2014); premodern Western, exemplified by figures like Francis of Assisi (White 1967; Coates 1998; Nothwehr 2002; Delio 2003; Mizzoni 2004, 2008; Moore 2008; Warner 2011; Egerton 2012); and Native American (Nash 1988; Greenberg and Greenberg 2013; Chang 2016; Woodhouse 2018). Modern Western biocentric thinking coalesces in the second half of the nineteenth century. Some of the pioneers are female, such as Mary Hunter Austin and Mabel Wright (Ranney 1992: 115–123) – and, of course, later on, there is the epochal work of the likes of Rachel Carson (1962) – but most of the foregrounded figures are male, including Henry David Thoreau (1854, 1962; cf. Cavell 1972; McGregor 1988), John Muir (1901, 1911, 1997), and Gifford Pinchot (1910, 1998) (on the Muir-Pinchot relation, refer to, e.g., Meyer 1997; Smith 1998). We therefore agree with – but also crucially qualify-modify-extend – Eckersley's claim that "ecocentrism [the author's term for biocentrism; this point is shortly discussed] may be seen as representing the cumulative wisdom of the various currents of modern [*and ancient*] environmental thought" (1992: 179).

Then there are key figures who have contributed to later-twentieth-century biocentrism. They could perhaps be categorized according to the key ways they seek to justify or defend life-centeredness. For instance, there's the biocentrism associated with the extension of rights. They're extended to sentient animals (Singer 1975; Regan 1975, 1980, 1982, 1983; Regan and Singer 1976); to all animals (Ehrenfeld 1978); to other organic entities like trees (Stone 1972; Hartshorne 1979; Attfield 1981; Hall 2011; Grear 2012); to subatomic particles and cosmic entities (White 1978), and to ecosystems (Leopold 1989; Naess 1973; Povilitis 1980; Nash 1989). There's also the associated theme of intrinsic value (e.g., Worster 1980; Taylor 1981, 1986; Callicott 1984, 1986, 1987b, 1989, 1992; Rolston 1986, 1988; Zimmerman 1988; Vilkka 1997). Several points must be made at this stage. To begin with, a number of these cited thinkers allude to ecocentrism or can be appropriated to clarify our understanding of it, so they'll be recalled as we proceed with our exposition. We also note that, while the themes of rights and intrinsic value traverse this work in certain ways, they will not be investigated for the somewhat paradoxical reasons that, on the one hand, an investigation would require wading through complex debates, and, on the other hand, as Plumwood rightly observes, non-human rights is basically a sensible notion that has been over-debated (1993: 212, n. 4) – an assessment that I think could/should also apply to intrinsic value.

Now, a number of notable books, book chapters, and articles began to be published during the 1980s and 1990s that employed the word "ecocentrism" in the title and/or featured it throughout the work (e.g., Callicott 1989; Eckersley 1992; Senseman 1993; McLaughlin 1993; Fieser 1993; Rowe 1994; DiZegera 1996; Hettinger and Throop 1999). However, the texts do not clearly or emphatically advance a full-blown Earth-centeredness because "ecocentrism" is still basically used in a biocentric sense, referring to natural entities and their contexts. Hence, these writings may be more accurately described as life-centered or only nominally ecocentric. (We also parenthetically note with some enthusiasm that some leadership scholars also began employing the term "ecocentrism" from the 1990s onwards, e.g., Shrivastava 1994b; Purser, Park and Montuori 1995; Swann 2001; Hoffman and Sandelands 2005. However, in the concluding chapter, where I review some of the key environmental leadership texts and compare them with my model, I show how these works likewise use the word in its life-centered sense.) We may briefly examine some of the writings to confirm this point.

To begin with, Callicott comes tantalizingly close to espousing a proper eco-centeredness. Callicott – who is an ardent Leopoldian and self-described ecocentrist (1989: 3) – refers to "inanimate entities," which seems to signal an Earth-centeredness that exceeds the biotic; however, he goes on to cite "oceans and lakes, mountains, forest, and wetlands" (1989: 37) as examples. On the one hand, Callicott distinguishes ecocentrism from biocentrism ("A biocentric – not ecocentric – ethic") but goes on to describe his "ecocentrism" as "an ethic with a broad biological concern or orientation" (1989: 11). While the author expands in a Leopoldian way the circle of care/concern from individuals to "terrestrial nature – the ecosystem – as a whole" (1989: 3–4), this is more of a movement *within* biocentrism than a move *beyond* it. McLaughlin also employs the term "ecocentrism" in his excellent book *Regarding Nature* (1993); indeed, he admirably titles the concluding chapter "For a Radical Ecocentrism." But his writing appears to express a rather confused understanding of the word: on the one hand, he correctly notes that ecocentrism is inclusive of "inanimate objects" (1993: 158); on the other hand, his version of eco-centeredness "calls for the flourishing of all life" (1993: 204): this is a biocentric call ("all life") rather than an ecocentric one (all things).

We turn to two more examples where scholars have employed the term "ecocentrism" in a life-centered sense. First of all, we refer to Robyn Eckersley's *Environmental and Political Theory* (1992), where the sub-title reads *Toward an Ecocentric Approach*. One could immediately counter by asking whether the "Toward" refers to ecocentrism as well as the approach. However, in the body of the work, it becomes clear that the author defines and refers to ecocentrism in a biocentric sense: "ecocentric theorists adopt an ethical position that regards *all* of the various multilayered parts of the biotic community as valuable for their own sake" (1992: 28; also refer to, e.g., 1992: 128, 131–132, 181, 185). Another example of a text which employs the word "ecocentrism" and its variants in its biotic sense is eco-historian Keith Mako Woodhouse's *The Ecocentrists* (2018). It's an excellent work, but like Eckersley, the author employs the word "ecocentrists" as a synonym for biocentrists. Now, while the likes of Callicott, McLaughlin, and Eckersley employ "ecocentrism" in a biocentric manner, they – like some of the decisive biocentric pioneers cited previously – prove indispensable for the present study and are therefore repeatedly summoned.

To be sure, some of the above-cited thinkers come tantalizingly close to a full-blown ecocentrism. For instance, one could propose that Leopold alludes to radical ecocentric egalitarianism when he states that "a land ethic changes the role of *Homo sapiens* from conqueror of the land-community to plain member and citizen of it" (1989: 204). That we *Homo sapiens* would be "plain members and citizens" of the Earth community – *plain* and not privileged or superior members: such a claim could only come from an unequivocal antianthropocentrist – indeed, by someone who signals the way forward to Earthcenteredness (cf. Purser, Park and Montuori 1995: 1072).

Meyer-Abich also appears to reach the very precipice of – or perhaps even crosses over to – a truly inclusive ecocentrism. He advocates what he calls "physiocentrism" (1993, 1997; cf. Meyer-Abich 1984), a term that appears to be indicative of all-encompassing inclusiveness of everything physical. Meyer-Abich calls for supplanting human-centeredness with physiocentrism, and we note that his inclusion of the word "inanimate" in the following statement confirms the notion that his work pushes biocentrism beyond itself: "The physiocentric world picture which should replace the anthropocentric allows everything, living or inanimate, its own dignity within nature's whole" (1993: 83). Nevertheless, it seems that Meyer-Abich doesn't fully develop the radical inclusivity of his philosophy. For example, at one point in *Revolution for Nature* he refers to objects like "rubbish dumps, motor vehicles and high-voltage cables," but he claims that "to consider the whole of the physical world as natural" would be "extreme" and "a little odd" (1993: 44). But we've already explained (and will continue to clarify the proposition) that every thing is ultimately natural. The fact that Meyer-Abich finds rubbish dumps, cars, and cables notnatural might indicate that he's not a thoroughgoing ecocentrist. He thus seems to remain on the threshold of a truly radical physiocentrism.

Full-Blown Ecocentrism

There's no doubt that biocentrism is radical, given that it dislodges the human from the center. With life-centeredness, all living and life-giving things are now included in the center. Humankind is no longer assumed to be superior to everything non-human, for now other living things are considered co-equal with the human. The human now shares its privileged status with other living things and the life-giving systems that sustain them. Despite the radical departure, the living or organic is still considered superior to everything inorganic or manufactured. In order for there to be thoroughgoing equality, the non-living or other-than-living also needs to be incorporated into the center (incorporated in a qualified way, as we shall demonstrate), which ultimately entails the dissolution of both the center and periphery, for if everything occupies the center, nothing occupies the periphery, and the hierarchy collapses. Of course, without the biocentric move, one wonders whether the radical–logical leap to Earth-centeredness could have been conceived and theorized. But ecocentrism – not nominal ecocentrism but true, radical ecocentrism – is yet another seismic conceptual–experiential shift even beyond biocentrism, and thus even more antithetical to human-centeredness. Earth-centeredness – as I understand and advance it – is something other than biocentrism, or perhaps more accurately, something *more* than it. But how on Earth could we conceptualize, endorse, and defend a centeredness that includes *everything* – even the common, trivial, disposable, and repulsive?

This is known as the "demarcation problem" (Hunt 1980; Frey 1980; Thompson 1990): whatever justification is advanced (whether rights, intrinsic value, ethical consideration, etc.), we enter a *reductio ad absurdum*, whereby "even" manufactured objects will need to be considered or included. As environmental ethicist Lars Samuelsson explains: "we will be forced to hold that some nonnatural things – such as cars, computers, or guided missiles – have morally significant interests as well, but that view is absurd" (2010: 248, n. 4). The rest of this chapter is aimed at showing how eco-centeredness is not only *not* absurd but positively logical and compelling – even when it comes to questions like guided missiles and other appalling objects (which are discussed later). Disclosing ecocentrism's cogency and robustness is a worthy task in itself, but it is imperative here because Earth-centeredness is a key building block for our eco-leadership model. Once the task of confirming ecocentrism's rigor is accomplished, we can then superimpose it onto our formulation of leading, thus drawing closer to articulating (even if somewhat introductorily) our model of ecocentric leadership.

In order to define "ecocentrism" in its fullest, profoundest sense, let's first etymologically examine the word itself. Like "anthropocentrism" and "biocentrism," "ecocentrism" is composed of two words. The *kendros* is "the center," with its echoes of separation and superiority. Now, the "eco" in ecocentrism derives from *oikos*. The original Greek word *oikos* refers to "house" or "dwelling" (OED; Rolston 1986: 53; Bate 2005: 75), but "not only of *built houses*, but of *any dwelling-place*," according to the authoritative *Liddell-Scott-Jones Greek-English Lexicon*. The word also signifies "household" and "family" (Schwarz and Jax 2011: 145). The expansiveness and pliability of *oikos* have been reflected in the word's translations and appropriations. Max Weber, for example, employed the word to denote social groups (1978: 348). As a prefix, the *oikos* or "eco-" signifies a number of things: for instance, "economy" means the (financial) management (*nemein*) of the house (*oikos*). "Ecology" was coined by German scientist Ernst Haeckel in 1866, whereby "any dwelling-place" hereby signifies biological environments and systems (Haeckel 1866); synonymous terms for ecology have included "natural history," "biology," "bionomics," and "ethology" (Jax and Schwarz 2011: 155). "Ecology" has since been borrowed and widened by the environmental movement (Jamison 2011) and its discourses (Sessions 1987).

The "eco" in "ecocentrism" therefore typically refers to "ecology-centered," which is how Eckersley casts it (1992: 3). However, as I explained in the introductory chapter, "ecological" (and "environmental") is understood as being synonymous (and perhaps equivalent to) "ecocentric," so there's no need here to specify whether the "eco-" in "eco-centered" refers to the ecological or ecocentric, for they're ultimately the same (or at least very similar). Furthermore, the *oikos* in ecocentrism has also come to mean not just particular places and ecosystems but also the Earth itself (Mylius 2013: 106). This re-casting is warranted because our world *is* a "dwelling-place": it's the dwelling-place housing all earthly dwelling-places; it's the ecology of all ecologies. It's an ultimate dwelling – a dwelling at a massive, geophysical scale. This scaling does not end with our world – hence the use of the word "an" rather than "the" in the previous sentence: the Earth's *oikos* is the universe, which itself might dwell in a multiverse or among other universes. Hence, eco-centeredness is ultimately about a cosmic egalitarianism, though the focus here is on the Earth itself.

Now, what would it mean if the ecosphere (or the whole cosmos) were considered "the center"? If everything is the center, if there is no ontological hierarchy, if there is no superior and inferior, then *no one thing or set of things* (like "humanity," "the biotic community," etc.) constitutes the center. In effect, both the center and periphery dissolve. Mylius states: "Ecocentrism has no apex at which humans, or any entity, can be placed. Rather, it is a system of ecologies, networks and relationships, in which each entity relies upon and influences those around it" (2013: 106). Since Earth-centeredness includes every entity, it's a truly radical egalitarian. It's the concept-practice whereby we humans do not regard ourselves as superior to non-humans but co-equal with them.

The radical ecocentrism I'm endorsing (and seeking to develop and refine) is indifferent to the question regarding any qualitative differences between humans and other material entities. As noted in the previous chapter, strong distinctions between humans and non-humans have become increasingly problematized; whether there's any difference makes no difference to Earth-centeredness: unlike human supremacism, which justifies itself according to various purported grounds (i.e., divine likeness, sentience, consciousness, rationality, ethicality, language, etc.), ecocentrism disregards such "justifications" and instead considers all things equal. ("All things being equal" thus takes on a radically new literal signification – perhaps a catchcry for Earth-centeredness.)

Ecocentrism is thus radically antithetical to anthropocentrism but not – as Meyer-Abich brilliantly points out (1993: 113) – in the crude simplistic sense of its "exact opposite" or the mere reversal of the hierarchical binary, whereby the non-human replaces the human at the center/apex and is now considered superior to the human. Mere reversal would merely maintain supremacism – just in an inverted form – whereas Earth-centeredness rejects any and all forms of superiority, including any centrisms that privilege the non-human. As Meyer-Abich concisely explains, the interests of *both* humanity *and* the non-human are taken into account by ecocentrism/physiocentrism (1993: 113). Mylius also brilliantly argues against mere reversal: "ecocentrism does not involve 'turning the tables,' effacing the human from its privileged position only in order to replace it with nature or some other entity" (2013: 107). I myself independently came to the same conclusion regarding the refusal to simply "turn the tables" or merely invert the human/non-human hierarchy, primarily via my decades-long engagement with deconstructive philosophy, which aims to undo problematic and oppressive hierarchical binaries rather than merely reverse them (Derrida 1976, 1995; Manolopoulos 2013: 26–27, 2018: 105–106). And so, just to reiterate: the human is no longer the center – and neither is anything else – so everything is included, including the human.

Another general point regarding our definition of a thoroughgoing Earth-centeredness refers to the question of whether it privileges the whole over the individual. The foregrounding of notions such as "the land," "community," and "ecosystems" suggests a certain privileging of the whole. One could say that the privileging of the whole counters the contemporary privileging of the individual (epitomized by existential and postmodern philosophies, whose refocus on the individual are themselves responses to epistemic currents like Hegelian holism). However – and once again – we should resist any mere reversal: eco-centeredness seeks to incorporate individuals and their contexts. The character and challenges of this negotiation will be elaborated as we proceed.

Now, before further fleshing out the concept-practice of ecocentrism, we briefly remind ourselves at this juncture why we are required to offer a comprehensive description and defense: the adoption or application of the fundamental theory of leadership I outlined in the leadership chapter is dependent on clearly distinguishing and pitting ecocentrism against human chauvinism. To recall: my general theory of leading requires two (roughly) antithetical categories that describe situations ("X" and "counter-X"): in this case, ecocentrism is the "counter-X" to the "X" of anthropocentrism; ecocentric leadership involves identifying measures that transform homocentric situations into Earth-centered ones and measures that maintain Earth-centered situations from anthropocentric contestation.

Refining the Definition, Developing the Ethos

In order to further develop our definition of ecocentrism and its accompanying ethos/ethic, we critically appropriate and extend the thought of Freya Mathews. Now, while Mathews doesn't employ the word "ecocentrism" or its synonyms in any recurring or thematized way, she pioneers its theorization in a relatively sustained and methodical (and beautiful) manner, thus providing a framework allowing me to more fully develop it, refine it, and defend it. We may quickly add here that the twenty-first century has witnessed more Earth-centered environmental theory (e.g., Washington and others 2017) and, more broadly, the emergence of a set of thing-focused philosophical currents with ecocentric echoes and potentialities, such as actor–network theory (e.g., Latour 2005), new materialism (e.g., Bennett 2004, 2010; Morrison 2015, 2019), eco-phenomenology (e.g., Wood 2001; Brown and Toadvine 2003), and speculative realism and object-oriented ontology (e.g., Harman 2002, 2018a, 2018b; Meillasoux 2008; Brassier 2009; Bryant 2011; Bryant, Srnicek and Harman 2011; Bogost 2012; Morton 2017). These exciting epistemic currents provide fertile ground for developing the thinking and practice of thoroughgoing Earth-centeredness and Earth-centered leadership. I occasionally reference some thinkers from this set of engaging discourses (e.g., Jane Bennett, Graham Harman, Timothy Morton), but I set aside the task of critically appropriating contemporary thing-centered philosophies for the study of ecocentrism (and eco-centered leadership). Instead, as I say, I focus on Mathews' pioneering thinking.

While a number of Mathews' texts might be relevant here (e.g., 1996, 1999b, 2003b), I hone in on "Letting the Earth Grow Old: An Ethos of Countermodernity" (1999a), which I think is the richest and most relevant document for our purposes. In the Abstract to the article, she provides the following re-definition of environmentalism, which can also be employed as a formulation for all-encompassing ecocentrism: "the affirmation of the given" (1999a: 119). I articulate the nature, scope, and consequences of ecocentric affirmation as our exposition of the article proceeds. Mathews commences the essay proper by noting that her thinking is informed by a reconception of panpsychism (the belief that *psyche* or soul/spirit/mind permeates all things): for Mathews, material things are marked by what is variously described as "an internal principle, or subjectival dimension," "immanent telos," "laws," or "conatus" (1999a: 119–121; cf. Mathews 1996, 2003a, 2005). Straightaway, we emphasize that one needn't unconditionally accept panpsychism as a premise of Earth-centeredness, even though the notion of an internal principle proves to be, at minimum, heuristically useful, and also quite possibly true: left to their own devices, things tend to unfold according to their own internal logic. Mathews ecocentrically emphasizes how this process applies to all entities, biotic and otherwise: "All things, whether conscious or unconscious, living or non-living, have laws of their own unfolding" (1999a: 120). While these "laws" may be more obscurely inscribed in the "physical and chemical dispositions" of the inorganic, they are more perceptible in complex biotic entities like humans, who possess "instincts, reflexes, and other spontaneous responses" (1999a: 121).

We'll shortly return to this crucial point of unfolding. Before we do so, we note how Mathews seeks to identify the most suitable definition of "nature" – an enterprise that proves to be eminently useful for developing the concept-practice of radical ecocentrism. To begin with, she questions conventional definitions (from the cosmological one, which is too broad, to the biological one, which is too narrow), as well as the standard environmental formulation, i.e., "parts or aspects of the world which have not been created or unduly modified by human agency" (1999a: 120). Mathews responds: "since human beings, as biological organisms, surely belong to nature, and since making things comes to us as naturally as eating and drinking do, our handiwork itself has as much claim to be considered part of nature as the handiwork of spiders, insects and marine life does" (1996: 120). The philosopher therefore questions the classification of "trees and rocks and animals, not to mention webs, hives, termite mounds, and coral reefs, as falling within nature, and cars and ships and fax machines as falling outside it" (1999a: 120).

Mathews therefore introduces here the startling proposition that things like "cars and ships and fax machines" might fall under the remit of "nature." However, Mathews immediately identifies a crucial distinction between "nature" and its contrary, "artifice" (we recall that I'm replacing this relatively confusing word with "artifact/ual") – and here we return to the thematic of unfolding: "This is the distinction between what happens when things are allowed to unfold in their own way, or run their own course, and what happens when, under the direction of abstract thought, agents intentionally intervene to change that course of events for the sake of abstractly conceived ends of their own" (1999a: 120). Mathews is thus able to define "nature" as "whatever happens when we, or other agents under the direction of abstract thought, let things be" and "artifice"/the artifactual is "what happens when such agents redirect events towards their own ends" (1999a: 120).

This set of conceptions–distinctions is rich and decisive, requiring much unpacking and expanding. First of all, we already briefly discussed "unfolding" in the sense that entities appear to have a certain internal logic of becoming, but here Mathews introduces a further dichotomy: we *either* intentionally allow things to unfold "in their own way" *or* we intentionally interfere with them for our own ends. The natural is what occurs when the former takes place, while the artifactual is what occurs when the latter takes place. Mathews judiciously qualifies this distinction by stating that it is "not absolute" (1999a: 121). We may also emphasize here that abstract thinking-practice is not an exclusively human enterprise, a point that is implied by Mathews when she states that "we [humans], or other agents" intentionally allow or intervene. We may recall here the case of capuchin monkeys: when they use suitably sharp stones to crack nuts open, it seems plausible to speculate that the monkeys are displaying abstract thinking-practice rather than simply being guided by their instincts; using Mathews' lingo: the monkeys artifactually intervene in the natural unfolding of the nuts. These qualifications (i.e., the distinction's non-absoluteness; its application to non-humans) signal how one shouldn't rush to the rash conclusion that abstract thinking-practice is an automatically and exclusively problematic or unethical human phenomenon – a point that will be elaborated as we proceed.

Note, too, the word "allowing" and the precept "let things be" in the above quotation: letting-be is fundamental to Mathews' ecophilosophy and likewise pivotal for the present work. No doubt, "letting-be" initially appears somewhat enigmatic, esoteric, and even "impractical," so it will be elucidated as we proceed. However, it shall be elucidated in terms of its significance in the context of radical ecocentrism rather than a thoroughgoing retracing, given its long and venerable history in the East and West (Heidegger 1966b, 1971; Schürmann 1973; Liu 1991; Slingerland 2000; Pezze 2006; Haugeland 2007; Introna 2013; Dallmayr 2014). Deep ecologist Warwick Fox provides the following formulation, prefacing it with the provision that it occurs "within obvious kinds of practical limits," which shall also be enumerated as we proceed: letting-be "allows all entities (including humans) *the freedom to unfold in their own way unhindered by the various forms of human domination*" (1989: 6). Eckersley explains how "An ecocentric orientation is . . . concerned with 'letting things be,' that is, allowing all beings (human and nonhuman) to unfold in their own way" (1992: 155–156). Meyer-Abich aptly qualifies his formulation in the following way: "When there is no sufficient cause for change, things should be left to their own processes of transformation" (1993: 105). As we proceed, we shall enunciate these "sufficient causes." The other important point to make from the outset is that, given that letting-be appears to be an "easy" practice – what could be easier than passively allowing things to unfold? – we emphasize its utter difficulty, especially in an increasingly frenetic world (Heidegger 1971: 31; Schürmann 1973: 104).

Now, we observe how letting-be plays out in Mathews' differentiation of the natural and artifactual. She contrasts what occurs when abstract thinking deliberately allows things to either naturally unfold or when it intervenes in their unfolding for one's own ends. The former typically entails flourishing for individuals and ecosystems, while interference is often destructive (more on this point very shortly). Mathews provides some "colorful" examples of the latter case, where humans "kill off a particular species for the sake of its coloured feathers, for instance, or pollute a lake with manufacturing dye for the sake of people who have decided they want purple hair" (1999a: 122).

Given that Mathews focuses on negative examples, one could be forgiven for thinking that intentional intervention – and especially intentional intervention for our own ends – is automatically problematic or unethical. However, we must emphasize that interference can be a positive process according to two basic categories. First of all, there's the category of intentionally intervening *for others*, human and otherwise (which is perhaps implied by omission in the passage given earlier). This interventionism tends to occur on behalf of some non-human others during their interactions with other non-human others, typically for the sake of greater ecological integrity, stability, variety, beauty, etc. (one could therefore argue that intervening-for-others is often also in our interests). Examples of this kind of positive interference include human action to prevent noxious weeds from over-running a healthy ecosystem; efforts to halt desertification; breeding programs for endangered species, etc. We intervene in order to halt harmful intervention, so that our intervention aims to allow the intervened to be liberated from the destructive interference and thus allowed to resume with their natural unfolding. Eckersley rightly notes that an ecocentric orientation does not exclude human interference (1992: 57). Hence, even though this other-oriented interference or "other-defense" is "artifice" in Mathews' sense of the word, it may be regarded as ethical or ethically neutral.

The second category of intervention relates to those interferences designed to meet our individual and collective human ends – but, once again, a further division is required (another distinction that is not absolutely watertight), a division that is not articulated in Mathews' text. First of all, ethical intervention relates to intentional interference in the unfolding of non-human others in order to meet reasonable human *needs-wants*, in terms of both material necessities, such as food, clothing, shelter, and so on, and requirements that may be variously called "higher," "enlightened," "psycho-spiritual," etc., such as love, education, and freedom, so that we may individually and collectively survive–flourish (Maslow 1943; cf. Mandel 1986: 15, 25; McLaughlin 1993: 213; Sterba 2010: 184–188; Stober, Brown and Cullen 2013: 12). Fulfilling these basic-higher ends often requires intervention in the unfolding of non-human others, e.g., killing creatures or consuming plants for food; cutting down trees to build homes; killing an animal in self-defense, etc.

Several eco-thinkers recognize the inevitability and necessity of harmful intervention (indeed, even sometimes its *benefits* for harmed species). I cite several eco-thinkers to demonstrate how rigorous environmental thought is realistic and practical rather than idealistic and impractical (which is one of the objections to ecocentrism, further discussed later). To begin with, Albert Schweitzer, famous for his investigations into the historical Jesus but also a pioneering biocentrist, observes: "The necessity to damage and destroy life is imposed upon me" (1974: 387 cited/translated by Meyer-Abich 1993: 71). We also note how deep-ecology founder Arne Naess cites the notion of biological egalitarianism and immediately adds an "in principle" caveat: "The 'in principle' clause is inserted because any realistic praxis necessitates some killing, exploitation, and suppression" (1973: 95). With remarkable nuance and profundity, eminent eco-theorist Kenneth E. Goodpaster states: "We must eat. . . . We must have knowledge. . . . We must protect ourselves from predation and disease, and sometimes this involves killing (though not always). The regulative character of the moral consideration . . . asks . . . for sensitivity and awareness, not for suicide" (1978: 324). White nicely references human and non-human requirements in the following remark: "A man [*sic*] has a right to build a house, and a right to kill living things – vegetable or animal – to eat, just as a coyote has a right to dig a den and to kill to eat" but this right should not be "impinging on the ability of our [non-human] companions to satisfy their needs" (1978: 107). Prominent eco-philosopher Holmes Rolston III powerfully reminds us that "violent death of the hunted means life to the hunter. . . . [N]utrient materials and energy flow from one life stream to another. . . . The pains of the prey are matched by the pleasures of the predator" (1992: 253). Rolston goes on to identify advantages of predation *even for the eaten*, in terms of population regulation, gaining skills in avoiding predation, and so on; hence, as counter-intuitive as it may appear, "Being eaten is not always a bad thing, even from the perspective of the prey species" (1992: 253).

And so, the principle of letting-be is not absolutistic, instead allowing for the attainment of requirements such as eating, defending, and so on. Indeed, Mathews herself makes this point: "as beings with a constitutive interest in our own self-preservation and the preservation of our nearest and dearest, we are on occasion called upon to intervene in these unfoldings, just as hunter–gatherers do in the course of their daily lives" (1999a: 123).

Then there are the interventions that are questionable or unethical: they're connected to the satisfaction of gratuitous human desires, i.e., those ends that are not directly related to human survival–flourishing, from the extremely ambitious (such as obtaining obscene wealth or power) to the apparently trivial (such as the examples provided by Mathews). However, as noted earlier, in "Letting the Earth Grow Old," Mathews does not explicitly posit the crucial distinction between reasonable needs–wants and unreasonable ones – a distinction that clarifies the fact that some human ends and their attainment via abstract thought–action are ethical or ethically neutral, while others are unethical and destructive.

This discussion of allowing and intervening leads logically to the gist or essence of a radically Earth-centered ethic/ethos. Its basic framework has already been provided by Eckersley, but we insert a necessary clause, given that we are here advancing an expansive ecocentrism: "When faced with a choice . . . those who adopt an ecocentric perspective will seek to choose the course that will minimize such harm and maximize the opportunity of the widest range of organisms [and non-organisms] and communities – *including ourselves* – to flourish in their/our own way" (1992: 57).

So far, we have discussed *intentional* kinds of interventions, but we should also register a further category: *unintentional* interference. This category is not discussed by Mathews in her article, but it's another important distinction, and it further qualifies the principle and practice of letting-be. Unintentional intrusion is the set of interferences caused by the fact that we are material beings co-existing and competing with other material beings (organic and otherwise). To begin with, we concur with environmental law scholar, Douglas M. Johnston, in recognizing that "human 'interaction' with nature, by any definition, is unavoidable" (2006: 395). Meyer-Abich also states the obvious (being so obvious that it remains obfuscated) when he remarks that "other living beings in the world are not only *around* us, but *with* us" (1993: 1) – and, I would add, *within* us. So when we humans go about living (working, washing, traveling, etc.) we unavoidably violate and destroy countless other entities. Once again, we reference some eco-thinkers in this regard. Schweitzer refers to the act of walking along a path and killing countless figures underfoot (1974: 387 cited/translated by Meyer-Abich 1993: 71). Ecotheologian Jay McDaniel explains: "life inevitably involves the taking of other life. Every time we wash our faces we kill billions of bacteria" (1990: 66; cf. Manolopoulos 2009: 119). Unintentional, unavoidable destruction is intimately bound up with corporeal existence; it is thus ethically neutral rather than unethical. Of course, as we humans become more ecocentrically attuned, recognizing how our materiality affects the world, we become more aware of our intentional and unintentional impacts on other entities, so we attempt to live less destructively – to "walk gently [or at least *more* gently] through this world," as the Buddha is said to have uttered.

As preliminary as it may be, the aforementioned discussion of unfolding, allowing, and interfering goes some way toward demonstrating how letting-be is not totalizing in the hyper-literalistic sense of the absolute cessation of intervention: not only is this physically impossible due to our corporeality, but some intentional interference is positively good, both for ourselves and for non-human others.

We now turn to Mathews' brilliant articulation of one of the implications and imperatives of an ecocentric ethos of letting-be: she urges us to *intentionally allow the artificial to unfold naturally* – a process she calls "returning to nature" but could just as well be dubbed "turning to ecocentrism." Rigorously and poetically, Mathews states: "'returning to nature' in an urbanised world means allowing this world to go its own way. It means letting the apartment blocks and warehouses and roads grow old" (1999a: 124). She adds: "Things which initially seemed discordant and out of place gradually fall into step with the rest of Creation. Old cars take their place beside old dogs and old trees; antiquity naturalises even the most jarring of trash" (1999a: 124). Letting-*be* means letting-*grow-old*.

Moving way beyond the biocentrists and nominal ecocentrists, Mathews passionately includes built environments and manufactured objects in her schema. Earth-centeredness not only protects ecosystems "but *all* material things, from undue human disturbance, including things that do not usually arouse the concern of environmentalists, even non-anthropocentric environmentalists, such as deep ecologists" (1999a: 132; cf. Eckersley 1992: 40). So Mathews' inclusion of buildings and fax machines and cars is a crucial advancement, surpassing life-centeredness, which, by comparison, now appears rather restricted and restricting. Mathews expands "the boundaries of the community" (Leopold) to such an extent that there is no longer any hierarchical division between "community" and "non-community."

At this point in "Letting the Earth Grow Old," Mathews admirably acknowledges that our inhabitation of the urbanized world often requires certain interventions (maintenance, aesthetic enhancement, etc.), emphasizing that such inhabitational intervention "is compatible with a fundamental attitude of letting be, of acquiescence in the given, and of working within its terms of reference, rather than insisting upon further cycles of demolition and 'redevelopment'" (1999a: 124). This is another important, rich, and nuanced statement. For instance, I read/interpret "fundamental" as "crucial" but not "absolute" or "total"; I read/interpret "working within [the given's] terms of reference" in terms of precepts like intervening for the sake of non-human others and for our own needs (but not destructive wants).

In this regard, while Mathews rightly criticizes "redevelopment" with vigor, we should not fall into the trap of completely demonizing it. Some construction and reconstruction are permitted and even ethical. First of all, sometimes demolition of the old is an ethical imperative, such as when a building's structural integrity is compromised or when it's been constructed with dangerous materials like asbestos. "Old roads" that have become unsafe due to deterioration will require repair or replacement. Furthermore, construction is a particularly noble endeavor whenever what is constructed is socially necessary (housing, schools, hospitals, and so on). Then there's the process of the renovation of "old warehouses" and the restoration of "old cars": this practice contributes to their structural integrity and ongoing unfolding, as well as their re-beautification – though we ecocentrists also adore the rundown and weather-beaten. There's even the contemporary trend of simultaneously letting-grow-old *and* restoring: old rust-covered vehicles lovingly receive protective coats to ensure that they endure over time in their existing, weathered states (Bolig 2016). And so, there are certainly cases when development and redevelopment in their various forms are necessary, ethical, and beautifying.

We should also insert at this point how letting-be applies – should also apply – to ourselves, individually, and collectively. Mathews' words have proven eerily prophetic: "Instead of letting ourselves be, we compulsively make ourselves over to match external ideals, where this can result in all kinds of aberrations, from neurotic individualism to fanatical collectivism or patriotism" (1999a: 122–123). Mathews also notes how we humans "treat ourselves, our own bodies, in the same way, truculently professing to own them and reluctant to allow them to be reclaimed by the world, reluctant to see the world tenderly revealing itself to us through them" (1999a: 129–130).

And so, Earth-centered praxis involves a variety of diverging but ultimately non-contradictory – indeed, *complementary* – actions, from allowing to intervening; Eckersley sums up these actions well: "Humans are just as entitled to live and blossom as any other species, and this inevitably necessitates some killing of, suffering by, and interference with, the lives and habitats of other species. . . . [T]hose who adopt an ecocentric perspective . . . will minimize such harm and maximize the opportunity of the widest range of organisms and communities" (1992: 57). Earth-centeredness is a skillful interplay between this maximizing and minimizing.

Earth-Centered Affects

Given that this monograph is philosophically oriented, the risk presents itself that Earth-centeredness is a purely/basically cognitive position-stance devoid of any affective states that co-inform it. However, many biocentric and ecocentric writers have foregrounded a variety of eco-feelings that drive this anti-anthropocentric worldview-practice. After all, eco-centeredness does not only call on us to *consider* the non-human but also inspires us to *feel* certain ways toward it. Given the parameters of the study, I only briefly retrace some of the most decisive affects associated with ecocentrism. To begin with, we note the wide array of foregrounded affective dispositions, ranging, for example, from "affirmation" (Mathews), "regard" (Leopold, McLaughlin), "respect" (Leopold, Taylor, Plumwood, Mathews, Schmidtz [2011]), "reverence" (Muir), "care" (Callicott, Warner, White) and "love" (Leopold, Rolston, Mathews). Now, due to a variety of factors (personal dispositions, the way our lives unfold, opportunities or lack of opportunities for learning and development, etc.), different people will respond differently to the non-human. So, in a sense, all of these responses are "valid." However, I think we should first of all cultivate the minimal, "bassline" response of an abiding *recognition* of the non-human other. Acknowledgment of the other is a/the pre-condition for meaningful interaction with the other. This is not to say that we should always and everywhere be actively acknowledging the range of non-human objects around us – this would leave little time for us to do anything else; it's more of an abiding attitude or disposition than a constant activity: an ethos of awareness. Indeed, we could posit that all of the other affective responses cited earlier – affirmation, respect, love, etc. – flow on from this basic disposition of deep recognition.

Of course, the most exemplary eco-affective state is love. To love the non-human, even the abject and vile (discussed as we proceed) – would be the ultimate ecocentric comportment. We recall here the words of the "Canticle of the Sun" by Francis of Assisi, whose love for the non-human rivals that of familial love: "sister moon," "brother sun." Leopold also heavily foregrounds the affect of love, which is refreshing in the context of mainstream academic discourse, which often tends to be dry and detached. For instance, Peter Singer – the eminent Australian animal-rights philosopher – strenuously declares at the start of his *Animal Liberation* that he "didn't 'love' animals" (1975: ix; for powerful critiques, refer to, e.g., Callicott 1989: 53; Donovan 1990: 351). Singer's rejection of emotion-informed argumentation is both understandable and regrettable, given that modern philosophical discourse typically excludes love from its exchanges, simultaneously forgetting/ignoring the fact that *philo-sophia* is itself *a loving of wisdom*.

In any case, Earth-centeredness does not demand that we love the world: I think that what is required is a basic but profound recognition of the equality of the non-human, an acknowledging that propels humankind to maximize non-human unfolding and minimize our interventions.

Justifications

But how do we ecocentrists justify the "preposterous" proposition that all non-human entities and natural and built environments are neither inferior nor superior to us humans and should therefore be treated in an egalitarian way? After all, anthropocentrists could argue with some force that the "truth" of human supremacism is evidenced by the fact that humankind is now so decisively imposing its mark on the ecosphere that we're living in the Anthropocene. One could therefore claim that we humans *are* "superior" in the sense of overpowering much of the rest of the world, most vividly expressed by eco-colonization and ecocide. However, natural catastrophes and pandemics exemplify how we humans *are not* superior, often remaining at the whim of nature. But the debate over who/what is more superior ultimately obscures the falsehood that just because we humans are more powerful in some respects justifies our oppression of the non-human. This point also relates to other forms of supremacism, e.g., patriarchy is premised on fallacies like "greater physical strength warrants the suppression of females." Likewise, while humanity has the capacity to "subdue" the Earth, it does not mean we are superior to it – just that we're in some cases "stronger" than it. Physical strength should not be confused with ontological superiority.

We may flag here another "negative" argument for ecocentrism (i.e., an argument against human chauvinism): given that the predominance of anthropocentric expressions (hyper-instrumentalism, hyper-consumption, etc.) are wreaking major havoc on the Earth, then it's likely that eco-centeredness will halt this devastation and commence the tasks of biospheric rejuvenation and flourishing. In other words, another argument for ecocentrism is that its antithesis – anthropocentrism – perpetually exploits, oppresses, and annihilates non-human others. Eco-centeredness, on the other hand, would not perpetuate such destructive practices, and instead more gently interact with the world, liberate entities and ecosystems, and foster eco-prosperity for all. It would maximize natural unfolding and restrict interference to necessary levels. This leads to a kind of teleological argument: an ecocentric world of tomorrow would be in much better shape than the anthropocentric world of today.

There are further "stand-alone" arguments in favor of eco-centeredness (i.e., arguments that do not necessarily rely on comparing it to homocentrism). We commence with some of the more conventional pathways. First of all, we could emphasize the fact that reality is constituted by an awesome and mysterious energy materiality. In this regard, one could draw upon impressive figures like the seventeenth-century French polymath, Blaise Pascal, who brought our attention to the fact that not only does there appear to be an outward infinity to the cosmos but there's also an inner infinity to things (1958: 18). Entities and their contexts are ultimately abyssal; an awareness of this kind of depth to things and environments has the ability to foster ecocentric awareness and affects like wonder and love. Of course, this pathway has widened with modern scientific disciplines like quantum physics and cosmology, which are entertaining all sorts of wonderfully weird discourses regarding materiality, from quantum physics to relativity theory, e.g., string theory and blackholes (e.g., Zukav 1979; Sagan 1980; Hawking 1988; Calder 2005; Kaku 2008). Another justificatory pathway – though certainly more tentative and speculative – would be via theological routes. For instance, in *If Creation is a Gift* (2009), I explored the rather conventional monotheistic doctrine of the divine creation/co-creation of the cosmos: if what-is is somehow a gift from the divine, then it follows that *all* things should be considered gifts, and received and treated accordingly. Such a line of thinking thus leads to Earth-centeredness (or at least a "theo-eco-centeredness").

Another justificatory approach would be to contend that all entities are imbued with certain various properties that we humans cherish. Our very brief retracing of biocentrism flagged the two most foregrounded ones: intrinsic value and non-human rights. As noted earlier, the parameters of the present work permit me to offer only a few provisional observations and propositions that are directly relevant to the study. First of all, I reiterate that I think they are basically cogent notions (Plumwood 1993: 212, n. 4), but their rigor is perhaps fortified when they are employed as part of a broader, multipronged argument. A second point is that these concepts appear to be interrelated: for an object to possess intrinsic value, it would be assumed to have rights, and vice versa. Rolston seems to make a move in this direction when he refers to "intrinsic goodness, and accompanying rights" (1986: 20). Meyer-Abich explicitly makes the connection: "legal rights for the connatural world [non-human nature] are . . . one way to recognize its intrinsic value" (1993: 138). Eco-philosopher Bruce Morito (who is a critic of inherent worth) makes the same point when summing up eco-ethicist Nicholas Agar's position in *Life's Intrinsic Value* (2001): "Since intrinsically valuable, they [other species] are also possessors of an inherent right to life" (2003: 319). One could also cite here the strange case of a 1980 article by eco-historian Donald Worster (who is also the author of the excellent 1977 book, *Nature's Economy: The Roots of Ecology*): the paper is titled "The Intrinsic Value of Nature" but it is actually a short historical retracing of the emergence of human-rights discourse and the extension of these rights to the non-human. In the article, Worster never refers to intrinsic value. On the one hand, it appears that the author has committed a gross error, given that intrinsic value and rights are clearly distinguishable; on the other hand, the "error" perhaps unintentionally discloses the truth of their interrelatedness.

Another point I wish to reinforce regarding non-human rights and intrinsic worth is that, whether we construe these properties as inherent or imposed, it is perhaps more prudent to consider them in relative, context-dependent terms rather than absolute terms. Worster recognizes this characteristic with regard to non-human rights: "The rights of nature, like the rights of groups within society, cannot be defined in a vacuum, as though they were absolutes" (1980: 46). He adds: "The value of 'rights approach' to nature is not that it establishes categorical imperatives, such as 'never kill a whale' or 'never plow the soil.' Rather, it is a means of including all the moral issues that bear on a situation, thereby complicating our behavioral choices by a fuller awareness of their impact" (Worster 1980: 47).

We may illustrate Worster's point most compellingly with some examples regarding humans, for if it can be shown that they apply in relative terms to us, then we can infer that they also apply in relative terms to non-humans. A first example is when an unborn child's birth threatens the life of the mother: in this clear-cut case, the mother's life is considered more valuable than the child's. A second example is the criminal whose right to freedom of movement is annulled when convicted and imprisoned. The criminal's right to freedom is annulled by society's right to justice and safety.

While purported attributes like intrinsic value and non-human rights appear to have some force, I contend that there is another more fundamental, compelling, and less problematic "property" that justifies or grounds our radical eco-centeredness: existence itself. When a thing exists, it should ordinarily be allowed to unfold by virtue of its existence. In a sense, this is a "mundane" proposition, precisely because we are so immersed in being that we often forget it (cf. Heidegger 1966a). Whether we have rights or intrinsic value might be open questions, but there is no doubting we "have" being. So how, exactly, can existence be employed as a kind of justification for ecocentrism?

Various ecological thinkers have alluded to existence in their arguments. There is the famous story recounted by Pinchot in his autobiography about a trek to the Grand Canyon with Muir (the two adversaries spent time together, especially during the earlier, friendlier years of their association): "when we came across a tarantula he [Muir] wouldn't let me kill it. He said it had as much right there as we did" (1998: 103). The tarantula had the right *to be there*, i.e., to exist. Muir prevented Pinchot from killing it (whether Pinchot considered it a threat or was motivated by some other factor is irrelevant here) on account of its existence and its right to continue being. Leopold also alludes to the property of existence; he remarks: "A land ethic of course cannot prevent the alteration, management, and use of these 'resources,' but it does affirm their right to continued existence, and, at least in spots, their continued existence in a natural state" (1989: 204). We note that Leopold identifies/confers upon non-human biota and ecologies their *right* to exist. (We also note Leopold's differentiation between entities that unfold naturally and those whose unfolding is modulated by interference.)

Naess also refers to the notion of existence when he states that biota possess "*the equal right to live and blossom*" (1973: 96). Significantly, Naess asserts that this right's "restriction to humans is an anthropocentrism" (1973: 96). Unfortunately, Naess doesn't develop either ideas (i.e., that living-blossoming is a right and that this right is homocentrically restricted to humans). Like Naess, acclaimed biologist David Ehrenfeld also refers to existence in *The Arrogance of Humanism* (1978). Drawing on anti-anthropocentric texts by pioneering ecologist Charles S. Elton (1958) and science journalist Bernard Dixon (1976), Ehrenfeld emphasizes (in italics) the factor of existence as justification for saving animals: "*they* [all animals] *should be conserved because they exist*" (1978: 207). Even though Ehrenfeld is limited by his zoocentrism, we nevertheless have here the codification of the idea that animals should be allowed to continue existing because they exist. We also echo and radicalize the following words from Goodpaster in this regard: "Nothing short of the condition of *being alive* seems to me to be a plausible and nonarbitrary criterion [for allowing beings to exist]" (1978: 310) – translated ecocentrically: nothing short of the condition of *being* seems to be a plausible and nonarbitrary criterion for allowing entities to exist. Worster makes the following point with regard to America's "Founding Fathers" and their participation in the development of human rights: "It was argued that every man [*sic*], by virtue simply of his being alive, could claim certain rights, such as Jefferson's familiar 'life, liberty, and the pursuit of happiness'" (1980: 43). The key phrase here is as follows: "By virtue simply of being alive." We also note how wildlife biologist Anthony Povilitis refers to existence as a "primary right" (1980).

McLaughlin likewise foregrounds existence. Indeed, he comes tantalizingly close to expanding his biocentric ecocentrism to a fully formed formulation when he refers to "existence" several times toward the end of the book, particularly concentrated in three pages (1993: 186–188) but also regularly referenced in subsequent pages. Perhaps environmental activist–author Christopher Manes has something similar in mind when he refers in his brilliant essay "Nature and Silence" to the "ontological egalitarianism of Native American and other primal cultures," which explains why there is no hierarchy of beings or "*scala naturae*" for these societies (1996: 25, 20–23). Although it remains biocentrically confined, the following citation from Earth First! perfectly expresses the existence justification: "All natural things have intrinsic worth, inherent worth. . . . They are. They exist. For their own sake. Without consideration for any real or imagined value to human civilization" (cited in Manson 2000: 170).

So, as soon as a thing comes to be, it should be allowed to be, barring various exceptions outlined earlier (the attainment of reasonable requirements; self-defense; the protection of some things on grounds like ecosystemic flourishing; etc.). And given that every being carries this property of being, then every being should be allowed to unfold. The famous Cartesian "I think, therefore I am" can be refigured and expanded as an eco-ethical maxim: "We are, therefore we (all of us, everything) should be allowed to be." One of the advantages of this ontological justification is that we might avert some of the challenges purportedly associated with the notions of inherent worth and rights. We might needn't depend on them – or depend on them as heavily as conventional environmental discourse has depended on them. This is not to say that we should simply abort these fundamental concepts. In fact, as I noted earlier, the best strategy for us defenders of consistent eco-centeredness is to employ them in concert. Indeed, when we also draw on other justificatory sources – from scientific discourses to theological contemplations – our ecocentric foundations are further augmented. But I nevertheless contend that the "property" of existence underpins every other argument for eco-centeredness, e.g., for a thing to have intrinsic worth, it first has being; for a thing to have rights, it first possesses existence, etc. I therefore propose that this attribute – existence itself – is our main foundation for radical egalitarianism.

Addressing Objections

Given that ecocentrism appears strange, controversial, and indeed threatening to an anthropocentric world, it is unsurprising that it is/would be heavily resisted and rejected. Pioneering deep ecologist George Sessions observes how "pervasive metaphysical and ethical anthropocentrism . . . has dominated Western culture with classical Greek humanism and the Judeo-Christian tradition since its inception" (1987: 105). Radical ecocentrism challenges these dominant and domineering discourses-practices. Ronald E. Purser, Changkil Park and Alfonso Montuori – who are pioneering scholars in environmental leadership studies (and thus discussed in the next chapter) – rightly observe that "a questioning of [anthropocentric] values . . . is viewed as in and of itself 'irrational' or 'unrealistic,' because there is almost no way of addressing those values without seeming to challenge 'reality' itself" (1995: 1061).

So we shouldn't be surprised when homocentric philosophers like William Grey appear to simply shrug off the very possibility of anti-anthropocentrism (be it biocentric or ecocentric): "I am not persuaded . . . that it is intelligible to abandon our anthropocentric perspective in favour of one which is more inclusive or expansive" (1993: 466). Grey's opinion is rather representative of mainstream academic and public discourse. One of the aims of the present work (and specifically this chapter) is to demonstrate that Earth-centeredness is intelligible – indeed, *wise* – while human chauvinism is ultimately unintelligible and destructive. As part of this aim, the present section addresses five objections that are identified and discussed by Eckersley in *Environmentalism and Political Theory* (1992: 55–60), and a further criticism advanced by McLaughlin (1993: 17).

The first objection is the fundamental one rehearsed in our chapter on homo-centrism: anthropocentrists would allege that we cannot escape our human perspective. But anthropocentrism conflates the human perspective(s) with the ability to critique this perspective. Eckersley nicely sums up the distinction; she clarifies how human-centeredness "conflates the trivial and tautological sense of the term anthropocentrism (i.e., that we can only ever perceive the world as human subjects – who can argue against this?) and the substantive and informative sense of the term (the unwarranted, differential treatment of other beings on the basis that they do not belong to our species)" (1992: 55).

The second common misconception is that ecocentrism is considered misanthropic. Fox calls this "the fallacy of misplaced misanthropy" (1990: 19; cf. Naess 1989: 141; McLaughlin 1993: 202). To begin with, we recall our refusal to "turn the tables" (i.e., simply replacing the human center with the non-human center): displacing the human from the center is not an act of replacing the human with the non-human but rather *re-placing* the non-human back into a genuine community of equals. Given that eco-egalitarianism is radically inclusive, it categorically includes the human and the non-human, but it insists on *vastly greater consideration* of non-humans, be they other creatures, natural and built environments, and manufactured products. As Eckersley explains, eco-centrism is "against the ideology of human chauvinism" – "not against humans per se or the celebration of humanity's special forms of excellence" (1992: 56). Eckersley notes that ecocentrism is not misanthropic but nonanthropocentric – or we could go further: ecocentrism is *misanthropocentric*, i.e., it opposes and seeks to eradicate human-centeredness and its various devastating expressions/ consequences – which harm people just as much as they harm other entities and the Earth. Eco-centeredness opposes human-centeredness precisely because the former is *proanthropic* – indeed, *philanthropic*. Earth-centeredness is *for* the human, just as it is *for* everything else. It turns out that anthropocentrism is the misanthrope.

Related to the charge of misanthropy is the charge that humankind is subordinated to something else. For example, in their noteworthy 1995 article, sustainability scholars Thomas N. Gladwin, James I. Kennelly, and Tara-Shelomith Krause rehash the naïve claim that "Ecocentrism subordinates humans to the biosphere" (1995: 888). A misunderstanding like this *might* be fostered by superficially focusing on something like Leopold's land ethic, which appears to privilege the biotic community over the individual (1989: 224–225). However, as noted earlier, there's no hierarchical reversal with a thoroughgoing eco-centeredness: nothing is subordinated to nothing else. (Incidentally, Gladwin, Kennelly, and Krause advance "sustaincentrism," which they consider superior/favorable to ecocentrism, but this is a false dichotomy: true Earth-centeredness involves an interplay or dialectic between elements of "sustaincentrism" and the genuinely ecocentric elements of their straw-man "ecocentrism.")

The third objection that Eckersley identifies is that Earth-centeredness purportedly regards humans as no more valuable than "say, ants or the AIDS virus" (1992: 57) – and of course today's microbiological counterpart is the COVID-19 virus; the question of how a thoroughgoing ecocentrism construes such things is broached as we proceed. We discern here something of the "demarcation problem" discussed earlier; if everything is considered, then doesn't ecocentrism lead to a kind of "ethical indiscriminateness," purportedly paralyzing our ability to choose between competing entities, given that they are basically inscribed with the same kind of value? "Paralyze" is precisely the term used by Gladwin, Kennelly, and Krause: "Ecocentrism may completely paralyze pragmatic action of any sort" (1995: 889). Grey likewise complains: "An austerely ecocentric or biospheric perspective delivers no determinate answer as to which of the abundant and wonderfully various unfolding planetary biotas should be preferred" (1993: 470). Even Agar – who defends the notion of intrinsic value – argues against what he calls "an everything ethic": "We need to draw and defend the moral significance of a boundary between living and nonliving things to prevent our life ethic to degenerate into an everything ethic. If absolutely everything is special, then gone will be any moral incentive to look out for nature" (2001: 68).

Not only do anthropocentrists and biocentrists oppose ecocentrism's everything ethic; even nominal ecocentrists err in this direction. Callicott states: "An ethic that embraces everything in effect embraces nothing" (1989: 10). Even physiocentrist Meyer-Abich opposes an everything ethic: "It seems like a tall order to recognize everything's intrinsic value. . . . If everything which exists must be respected and guarded as it is, do we not have to hold ourselves back from making any change in the world? How could we feed ourselves?" (1993: 83). He goes on: "In the end even a sculptor would not be able to transform a stone into sculpture, for then the stone would not remain what it was. And would that not deny its intrinsic value, or dignity?" Meyer-Abich's solution? "The intrinsic dignity of things and beings within nature's whole is revealed as what they can *become*" (1993: 84).

So how can we defend ecocentrism's "everything ethic/ethos"? We recall from our critical appropriation of Mathews' work how we humans are allowed to pursue the procurement of basic-higher ends, and this pursuit will inevitably involve interrupting the unfolding of non-human entities. So while these entities are indeed special (and special, at the most basic level, because they exist), they may be used or destroyed in order to meet our reasonable requirements.

However, precisely because these non-humans are special, they should not be used or destroyed to meet unreasonable wants. Ecocentric recognition of the specialness or value of something will not prevent us from appropriating it for our legitimate use, but it should prevent us from appropriating it for unjustifiable use. By living according to this ethos/ethic, humanity would be able to maximize the free unfolding of non-human things and minimize our interference with this unfolding.

This is the basic defense/clarification for our advancement of ecocentrism's "everything ethic/ethos" but we can also address some of the specific charges related to this objection. First of all, Agar's logic can be dislodged: if absolutely everything is special, then why would our "moral incentive" to care for "nature" be eradicated? Ethical concern is expanded to the artifactual; widening the circle of ethical deliberation does not mean *caring less* about nature – it just means *caring or caring more* about what has been even more ignored than nature (the built, the manufactured). With regard to Callicott's remarks, first of all, we insist that ecocentrism's everything ethic does indeed *embrace everything*, from humans to capuchin monkeys to fax machines and old roads. Next, even though Callicott rejects this everything ethic, the irony is that, a few pages after these comments are made, he criticizes the animal-rights/-liberationists for their selective ethics: "there is something jarring about such a graduated progression in the exfoliation of a more inclusive environmental ethic" (1989: 16). So Callicott is simultaneously against an everything ethic and a graduated one – but he can't have it both ways: one's ethic will either be selective (with its accompanying problems and contradictions) *or* "indiscriminate." And what about Meyer-Abich's argument? Setting aside the abyssal first question of who/what decides whether a sculptor's work reveals a thing's "becoming" *and/ or* imposes the artist's own abstract thinking on the stone, there's a relatively simple ecocentric solution: we straightaway point out that artistic expression-appreciation is a higher human need-want, so activities like sculpting are certainly acceptable; however, one would need to address additional concerns in order to determine whether the sculpting of a particular stone should be permitted, e.g., what are the ecological impacts of excavating the stone? Might the stone be put to some other basic-higher use? etc.

Hence, even the objections of a number of exemplary environmental thinkers are readily countered from an Earth-centered perspective. But how can we defend the position that everything – even the vilest things, the most destructive things – should receive greater consideration? How do we respond to the accusation that humans are no more valuable than "say, ants or the AIDS [or the COVID-19] virus"?

First of all, how does Eckersley herself respond to this objection? Interestingly, she does not respond very directly or specifically, instead offering general remarks. She explains that ecocentrism "seeks to cultivate a prima facie orientation of nonfavoritism" (1992: 57). "Nonfavoritism" is a superb word to describe Earth-centeredness. Eckersley adds that such an orientation does not exclude human activities like eating or self-defense. In sum: ecocentrism favors nonfavoritism and only practices favoritism under certain conditions. However, Eckersley's nonfavoritism risks being undermined by her own biocentric favoring of criteria like sentience, self-consciousness, and "richness of experience" for negotiating ethical dilemmas. Such criteria would automatically exclude viruses and possibly entities like ants from our consideration.

A thoroughgoing ecocentrism, on the other hand, is inclusive of microbes and insects – and everything besides. But how? How can this inclusivity be construed as somehow "ethical"? First of all, having developed our eco-ethos according to the distinction between reasonable ends and unreasonable wants, we can readily accommodate such entities into our schema. This kind of schema is indicated (but not elaborated) by Eckersley when she states: "A nonanthropocentric perspective is one that ensures that the interests of nonhuman species and ecological communities . . . are not ignored in human decision making *simply* because they are not human or because they are not of instrumental value to humans" (1992: 57).

Let's enumerate our position by turning to Eckersley's specific examples of ants and viruses. First, the ants. According to eco-centeredness, they should be allowed to unfold as freely as possible. And they often do. However, there will be circumstances whereby we humans are allowed to intervene in their unfolding. There's the classic example of ants over-running a picnic: given that we humans are allowed to eat and to eat hygienic food, we are certainly allowed to rid the picnic area of ants in order to meet these reasonable ends. So, ordinarily, ants are affirmed or valued in the sense that they should be allowed to freely unfold, but there will be circumstances when justified human and/or non-human needs override their free unfolding.

Of course, the question of viruses like AIDS and COVID-19 is more complex – and more emotive – so we need to proceed both sensitively and logically. However, basically, the same schema applies. "In principle," viruses – like any other entities on Earth – should be allowed to unfold freely excepting those times that this unfolding threatens human/other lives. That's why ecocentrism understands the human endeavor to annihilate particularly destructive viruses like AIDS and various coronaviruses. We are allowed – indeed, compelled – to fight these entities with all the astounding medical technologies and social strategies (such as frequent cleaning and physical distancing) we can muster. Letting-be is not radical impassivity: as I have continually insisted, it allows us humans to defend ourselves and non-human others under certain circumstances. But while ecocentrism doesn't deny the destructiveness of viruses, neither does it demonize them. First of all, Earth-centeredness reminds us of the commonalities between viruses and us, like the shared feature of being, and the drive to survive and multiply. (We note that viruses exist, but it's difficult to categorize them as "living" or "non-living" entities – they unsettle any clear-cut living/non-living distinction; refer to, e.g., Villarreal 2004; Koonin and Starokadomskyy 2016.) Next, we ecocentrists also value these still-mysterious things epistemically: by studying them, we learn more about them, ourselves, and the world; we discover that there are beneficial ecological dimensions to viruses (Falkowski 2015; Roossinck 2016; Dolgin 2019). We may also recall here Rolston's provocative but bio-scientifically brilliant 1992 article "Disvalues in Nature," which discusses challenging natural processes like predation and parasitism in a realistic-affirmative light. Finally, in an effort to provide a more objective perspective, ecocentrism even dares to ask the confronting question: which entity, the virus or the human, has been the more ecospherically destructive?

We may very briefly address here two further groups of things that we humans find vile and dangerous: waste and weaponry. How could such substances be ecocentrically "affirmed?" We first turn to human waste, both at the individual-biological and domestic-industrial levels. To begin with, Earth-centeredness recognizes that corporeal waste is a necessary, inevitable part of material existence, a by-product of bodily functioning; in a similar way, garbage created by human societies is also inevitable, a by-product of household and industrial processes. While ecocentrism admonishes the creation of unnecessary, wasteful domestic-industrial rubbish (Thompson 2015), it nevertheless acknowledges its reality. If we are to affirm creaturely life and artifactual activity, we must also affirm their by-products. Rather than ignoring or reviling rubbish, we should acknowledge it and accept it. Of course, there's a repugnant dimension to it, but, as Mathews wonderfully puts it, "antiquity naturalises even the most jarring of trash" (1999a: 124). Thankfully, there is a mounting body of work rethinking and revaluing refuse (e.g., Bennett 2004, 2010; Yaeger 2008; Hawkins 2009; Morrison 2015, 2019; White 2019). For instance, prominent eco-political philosopher Jane Bennett recounts an experience of an encounter with some rubbish (a plastic work glove, tree pollen pods, a dead rat, a white plastic bottle cap, a stick of wood): while we ordinarily anthropocentrically ignore or revile such a pile, Bennett discovers how it "commands attention as vital and alive in its own right, as an existant in excess of its reference to human flaws or projects. . . . has thing-power . . . exudes a kind of dignity, provokes poetry, or inspires fear" (2004: 350).

The final problematic object briefly analyzed here is weaponry. How on Earth can Earth-centeredness affirm it? Where's the ethics in such an affirmation? First of all, we note that weapons are made from "raw materials" (metals, chemicals, etc.). These "materials" are "natural," having unfolded rather freely; they are then collected, modified, and combined to create weapons: they are therefore constituted by a combination of natural entities and abstract thinking-manufacture; then there's also the human use of weapons. So we have three basic aspects to weaponry: the "raw materials"; the design-construction process; and use. How are we to ethically examine these aspects? First of all, with regard to the materials used to build weapons, obviously, we cannot assess them as "unethical": these things have been extracted, altered, and comingled by humans. So we already note that weapons cannot be automatically assessed in a completely negative way: there's a dimension to them that should be affirmed. Of course, the design-manufacture-use dimensions of weapons are more ethically complicated – but still not simplistically unethical: while they are designed to harm/kill, their use requires contextualization; they may be utilized in more ethical situations (such as self-/other-defense) or more unethical situations (e.g., committing crimes). And so, even weapons – which are often construed in purely unethical terms – are at least partially affirmed by Earth-centeredness, especially in terms of the elements that are coerced into forming them (cf. Manolopoulos 2009: 122).

We now turn to the fourth charge identified by Eckersley: the objection that ecocentrism is "untranslatable," i.e., inapplicable or impractical. In itself, the ethos of maximal allowing and minimal interference is clear and reasonable – and thus eminently practicable. However, its practice is obstructed because we live in an anthropocentric world as anthropocentric selves. In other words: it is not a question of some kind of "untranslatability" of the eco-ethos but rather the obstructions it faces from human supremacism and its multiple expressions.

The fifth objection against Earth-centeredness identified by Eckersley is that ecocentrists construe nature as "something that is essentially harmonious, kindly, and benign" (1992: 59; cf. Gladwin, Kennelly and Krause 1995: 888). The charge of idealization or romanticization has some traction when it comes to much environmental discourse. For example, the works of cabin-philosophers like Thoreau, Muir, and Leopold tend to foreground nature's harmony and beauty at the expense of its discord and disfigurations. Notions such as "Mother Nature" and "Gaia" – while insightful in some ways – often contribute to environmentalism's tendency to idealize the world. But radical Earth-centeredness does not subscribe to an idealistic-romanticized construal. Our discussion – and "affirmation" – of things like predation, viruses, and weapons certainly confirms ecocentrism's profound realism. My favorite ecological work in this regard is Rolston's "Disvalues in Nature" (cited earlier): as noted earlier, the essay not only foregrounds predation and parasitism but also randomness and turbulence – phenomena that destabilize the notion of a stable, harmonious biosphere (Rolston 1992; cf. Hettinger and Throop 1999). But ecocentric realism isn't one-sided, focusing exclusively on the challenging/dark dimension of the world: nature *is also somewhat* "harmonious, kindly, and benign" – demonstrated by the astonishing array of biodiversity, as well as the continued existence of humanity. And so, Earth-centeredness deeply perceives how the world is a composite of the harmonious *and* the chaotic, the kindly *and* the cruel, and the benign *and* the malignant. The trick, then, is to insist on both the lighter and darker dimensions of the world.

The sixth criticism discussed here is advanced by McLaughlin. He describes environmental thought as "typically involving discussions of ethical questions concerning the foundations of an environmental ethic or the presence or absence of intrinsic value in nonhuman nature" (1993: 17). One could say that the present study somewhat belongs to this tradition. Now, McLaughlin – who admirably focuses on the relations between economic systems and our treatment of the non-human – asks the following compelling questions: "What value do such abstract questions have when humanity faces a wide array of serious environmental threats? What is the importance, for example, of discerning that anthropocentrism, which assumes that humanity is the central or only value, is a nearly universal presumption underlying most discussions of environmental issues?" (1993: 17).

On the one hand, we understand and even partially accept McLaughlin's concerns: much attention has been paid to questions of values and ethics, while relatively little attention has been paid to structures and forces such as economic and political systems. However, we critically respond in the following ways. First of all, note how the author downplays the issues of values and ethics by framing them as "abstract questions": while there is an "abstract" – theoretical, conceptual, reflective, etc. – dimension to these topics, they are *also* extremely concrete: things like ethics and values shape our individual and collective attitudes, behaviors, actions, institutions, and systems. The abstract imposes itself on the actual – or better still: reality is constituted by both elements; attitudes and values form part of the very fabric of lived experience. One can't completely separate the abstract from the "real" – indeed, isn't the very division between the abstract and its other an abstraction itself? McLaughlin also makes light of anthropocentrism when he frames it as a "presumption": we ordinarily think of presumptions as mere thoughts/prejudices, but they also inform our actions – indeed, can there even be intended actions without presumptions?

So questions like value, ethics, and human supremacism remain crucial and still require our attention. McLaughlin himself proves this point by devoting a whole chapter to the concept-practice of anthropocentrism (1993: 143–168), asserting that "What is now most urgently needed from ethical reflection is the dethroning of anthropocentrism" (1993: 153). By examining human-centeredness, McLaughlin appears to have accomplished the very thing that he had earlier criticized. Whatever the case may be, the present work contributes to this "dethroning of anthropocentrism," replacing it with ecocentrism (which, by the way, seeks no crown or throne). Of course, McLaughlin's argument isn't without merit: ultimately, what's required is a multipronged critique (and concomitant praxis), whereby environmental theorists re-analyze and re-think (and help to change some of) the most significant aspects of human existence, including our attitudes, values, ethics, faiths, educational systems, politics, and economics.

Heading Toward Earth-Centered Leadership

Having defined, described, refined, and defended a thoroughgoing Earth-centeredness, we're at the threshold of outlining a theory of ecocentric leadership. Readers will note that the chapter on anthropocentrism includes the identification and discussion of five of its "expressions" – the main word I use to describe attitudes-actions that manifest human-centeredness (and therefore heavily constitute or color "situations," i.e., scenarios or phenomena, from the common to the complex). The "corresponding"-antithetical ecocentric expressions are not discussed in this chapter but in the subsequent one for two basic reasons. First, the practical-formal reason: their inclusion would have significantly expanded this already-lengthy chapter. Then there's the more important structural reason: by exploring the five eco-centered expressions in the next chapter, they can be contrasted with the homocentric ones, with the aim of identifying and discussing leaderly measures that would foster the transformation of anthropocentric situations into more ecocentric ones and maintain Earth-centered situations in the face of anthropocentric contestation.

4

THE NATURE OF EARTH-CENTERED LEADERSHIP

On the Precipice of the Theory

Now that I've outlined my conceptions of leadership, anthropocentrism, and ecocentrism (Chapters 1 to 3, respectively), we're on the verge of bringing leadership and ecocentrism together, a synthesis that discloses/conceptualizes a truly environmental mode of leading. The synthesis is guided by the general definition of leading I developed in *Following Reason* and rearticulated in this study's Introduction and first chapter. I'll very quickly rehearse it here, also introducing the specific tasks of the chapter as we proceed. First of all, we're reminded that the general definition's two basic conditions involve the transformation and preservation of situations (whether these "situations" are everyday scenarios or complex economic–political states of affairs); leaderly efforts are made to sufficiently transform a given situation into a sufficiently different one or to keep a given situation sufficiently unchanged in the face of competing leadership seeking to change it. In *Following Reason*, the aim was to outline a form of rational leading, which would involve transforming anti-rational situations into rational ones and maintaining rational situations from anti-rational alteration. The same methodological procedure is applied in the present study: Earth-centered or truly environmental leadership involves transforming predominantly homocentric situations into eco-centered ones, and maintaining ecocentric states of affairs from anthropocentric leadership seeking to change them into human-centered ones.

Hence, a first step for authentic eco-leading is the competent classification of given situations as being either basically homocentric or ecocentric, thus determining whether situational change or preservation is required for the given situations. The previous two chapters have considerably assisted us in terms of the task of classifying situations as being either homocentric or Earth-centered, but more detail or specificity relating to the nature of ecocentrism and eco-centered situations would prove useful – especially in terms of the ways Earth-centeredness expresses itself in concrete forms. We recall how the ways in which human supremacism manifests itself concretely was a major feature of the second chapter, whereby we explored five of its key expressions, i.e., hyper-instrumentalism, hyper-consumption, hyper-production, eco-colonization, and ecocide. Situations can be classified as being basically anthropocentric whenever these manifestations are prevalent, since they're fundamental charac-teristics or constituents of given situations.

Now, just as there are homocentric expressions, there are also eco-centered ones. But how can they be identified and theorized? Given that Earth-centeredness is essentially antithetical to human-centeredness, then it follows that they would be the diametrical opposites of anthropocentric expressions. So the five human-centered expressions described in Chapter 2 have five "cor-responding" – but in the sense of diametrically opposed – Earth-centered ones: eco-instrumentalism (vs. hyper-instrumentalism), eco-consumption (vs. hyper-consumption), eco-production (vs. hyper-production), eco-liberation (vs. eco-colonization), and eco-preservation (vs. ecocide). (We recall that the prefix "eco" can stand for both "ecological" and "ecocentric," given that the two terms are treated synonymously by this treatise.) Much of the present chap-ter is devoted to extrapolating in *some* depth these five key ecocentric mani-festations (comprehensive accounts would exceed the contours of the work). When exploring each manifestation, we shall *briefly* compare and contrast it with its anthropocentric counterpart, and then the most decisive work of this study may *begin* to be undertaken: identifying and discussing *some* key leaderly measures that would allow the five dominant homocentric expressions to be replaced by the eco-centered ones or would allow the ecocentric expressions to remain dominant. We quickly but emphatically note that the italicized qualify-ing terms given earlier ("some," "briefly," "begin") signal the crucial point that the present chapter does not exhaustively delineate eco-centered expressions and leaderly measures, which are key constituents of the theory. This book *outlines* – rather than fully develops – a theory of environmental leadership.

Now, as you'll note, the delineation of the leaderly measures does not include a discussion of *how* these policies might be implemented. Related to the ques-tion of the *how* is the massive subject of the kinds of political contexts that might be conducive for genuine environmental leadership, or even how this leadership mode might manifest itself politically. However, as I stated in the Introduction, the present book focuses on what environmental leadership *does* or *might do*; it suspends the question of what it *is* or *might be*. However, given its weight and relevance (McLaughlin 1993: 12), the political question is not totally suspended but rather briefly discussed after we examine the ecocentric expressions and some leaderly measures. We also briefly attend/return to the lingering question of the ethical preference of Earth-centered leading over anthropocentric (mis) leading. The final section acts as a bridge to the fifth chapter, which involves situating my proposed model within the burgeoning field of environmental leadership studies.

Eco-Instrumentalism

Before we articulate eco-instrumentalism, we first briefly recall its antithesis – what Plumwood calls "strong instrumentalism" and I'm calling here "hyper-instrumentalism": the constant and often-complete reduction of non-human things to the level of the instrument or utensil. This phenomenon is easily confirmed by posing the following question: how often do we anthropocentrists pick up "mundane" objects like a pen or a sandwich and conceive them strictly/mostly as a writing utensil or a piece of food? Almost always; automatically, unreflectively. The noninstrumental dimensions of these entities (e.g., the original matter or objects from which they are constituted) are either completely unrecognized, forgotten, or ignored. Now, in contrast to our anthropocentric hyper-reduction of things to implements, ecocentrism recognizes how non-human entities are *more than* their instrumental dimensions – a recognition or awareness with accompanying practices, which are discussed as we proceed.

Various environmental thinkers refer/allude to this kind of ecological instrumentalization. The following remark, which appears at the beginning of *A Sand County Almanac*, testifies to Leopold's endorsement of a measured instrumentalism: "When we see land as a community to which we belong, we may begin to use it with love and respect" (1989: viii) – we observe that Leopold explicitly refers to the "use" of land ("land" in Leopold's expanded ecosystemic sense) but with the important caveat that we use it with a certain affective disposition (we recall our discussion of eco-emotions in the previous chapter). Next, we recall how Plumwood differentiates between "strong/intensive instrumentalism" (1993: 141–142) with a moderate variant. In a long important footnote comparing the two modes of use, she explains how "[Strong] Instrumentalism implies that there are no constraints imposed by the *telos* of the instrumentalised class, which is subject to 'arbitrary use,' that in moral decision-making, the good, welfare, or *telos* of those outside the respect boundary does not have to be considered except as it contributes to that of those inside it" (1993: 211, n. 4). Plumwood describes the moderate variant in the following way: "even where the other's agency is overridden by the user's own in the process of bringing it into use, it is acknowledged as more than a means to these ends, as an independent centre of striving which places limits on the self and on the kinds of use which may be made of it" (1993: 142). As already noted, we shall elaborate how this "acknowledgment" – which, we recall, I identified/constructed in the previous chapter as ecocentrism's basic/"bassline" orientation-affect – may be concretely manifested.

We may also now be able to nuance/correct the following statement from Plumwood: "We must distinguish instrumentalism in this strong sense from the sort of use of the other which does not reduce that other to an instrument for use" (1993: 142). Whenever we ecocentrically "use" the other, the other is somewhat (not drastically/wholly) reduced to an instrument; as we humans strive to survive–flourish, this reduction is necessary – the same way that capuchin monkeys reduce stones to nut-cracking implements that allow the monkeys to eat the contents. Instrumentalization is a necessary part of creaturely survival-living. So there's nothing wrong with the reduction of the other to an instrument for use – as long as this is not a *total* reduction, with its attendant behaviors (such as simply discarding used objects). Hyper-instrumentalism is a totalizing reduction; moderate ecocentric instrumentalism is completely consistent with ecological philosophy and practice.

Let's also briefly turn to one other important remark from Plumwood regarding instrumentalization: "In practical terms, respect requires careful or respectful use, where there is use, and sometimes no use" (1993: 212, n. 4). By briefly unpacking this statement, we shall be on the way to articulating how eco-instrumentality is realizable. To begin with, Plumwood recognizes that there will be some use, but that it should be "careful or respectful" (once again, certain environmental affects accompany/inform the use). But then she adds that there should also be "sometimes no use." This "no use" is precisely the "letting-be" that was discussed in the previous chapter. Whenever possible, we should not use things. I'll recall and elaborate this point as we proceed.

We may also briefly turn here to some remarks by prominent eco-phenomenologist Bruce V. Foltz (1995), who is a brilliant expositor of the thought of towering twentieth-century philosopher Martin Heidegger (a key exponent of letting-be, and referenced in the previous chapter). Foltz expounds Heidegger's understanding of *schonen* or use, explaining that it "does not mean to refrain from using something or to set it aside, but to use it in such a way that harm is not inflicted upon it; used reflexively or with regard to things, it means 'to look after,'" and "to use it while nevertheless keeping it sound and intact"; hence, "using must be sharply distinguished from mere utilizing, exploiting, and using up – all of which represent degenerate kinds of using" (1995: 161; cf. Manolopoulos 2009: 125–127). This exposition nicely captures the meaning and practice of eco-instrumentalism.

In order to provide more specificity to this concept-practice, we may briefly address three questions: *what, how,* and *how much* to instrumentalize? (These three questions also guide our expositions of eco-consumption and eco-production). First of all, what entities are we required/allowed to utilize? We may use those things that facilitate the satisfaction of reasonable ends (from basic material needs to "higher" ones). And when we're required to use things for reasonable ends, *how* should we use them? At this point, the pertinence of the various affective states described in the previous chapter comes to the fore: what we use is accompanied by any number of feelings – care, respect, love, etc.; the non-human other is utilized carefully, respectfully, lovingly. Recalling Heidegger and Foltz's emphasis on care, we note certain effects of these kinds of affects: the used thing lasts longer, allowing it to perdure, thus also minimizing the number of other entities required for utilization. In "Letting the Earth Grow Old," Mathews eloquently foregrounds the ecocentric fondness for the familiar and long-standing: "From the viewpoint of letting things be, we would be most pleased, not with our brightest and newest things, but with those that were our oldest and most well-worn, things which had long figured in our lives, and mingled their identity and destiny with ours" (1999a: 127). An eco-ethos therefore rules out the utilization of most cheap mass-produced items that quickly end up in landfills or waterways (there might be some use for some of these items). The questions of endurance and obsolescence are elaborated as we proceed, and I'll have more to say about these affective states when we consider the subject of ecocentric consumption below.

Next, *how much* may we utilize the non-human other? In the first place, we should utilize the *minimum* amount of things to obtain our reasonable ends. This ensures that the maximum amount of entities are left alone and allowed to unfold naturally. Eco-instrumentalism therefore entails minimal production, consumption, etc., as will be elucidated in the ensuing sections. We also note that a kind of paradoxical imperative implies: on the one hand, each item that's used to accomplish our reasonable goals should be used as minimally as possible so that it can endure for as long as possible, given that instruments wear out due to use; on the other hand, rather than hastily replacing one instrument with another, we should use the original implement for as long as possible to minimize the process of replacement. In other words, the original tool or appliance should simultaneously be used as little as possible and for as long as possible. The aim, here, as Mathews puts it, is that "the ways in which we utilise matter must not conflict with, but enhance, our intersubjective engagement with it" (1999a: 130).

But what should be done with instruments once they're no longer useful? There's a variety of options. For those that survive our use (after all, some of them will be destroyed during the process of utilization), they should be allowed "to grow old" and decease: the expended instrument should be allowed to unfold without further human intervention, defiantly existing or eroding away. Natural/unplanned obsolescence is ecocentrically positively reconceived as the time when tools "retire" from their human utilization. But this is not to say that there's absolutely no room here for recycling and re-fashioning (these themes are developed as the chapter unfolds).

Some Leaderly Measures for Eco-Instrumentalism

In anthropocentric societies, hyper-instrumental expressions dominate situations, and anthropocentric expansion is contesting eco-instrumentalism in societies where it dominates. What kinds of leaderly measures may be identified that would transform hyper-instrumental situations into eco-instrumental ones and maintain eco-instrumental expressions from human-centered contestation? I focus here on broad policies (which, as we'll show, also apply for fostering/maintaining the other ecocentric expressions). The most important measure would be an intensive, sustained mass education campaign – perhaps we may also employ the word "re-education" here, for, even though it harbors negative connotations associated with authoritarian regimes, I think its power captures the profoundly sweeping nature of the proposed program. Before proceeding to describe this measure, we quickly note the dynamic between education and behavior. McLaughlin succinctly highlights how we "live within a cognitive world and act on the basis of our ideas" (1993: 5), so, to the extent that education generates or shapes ideas, then we may begin to perceive the crucial correlation between pedagogy and praxis. Now, all members of society – across every age, class, ethnicity, etc. – would receive ongoing ecocentric instruction. All major social institutions – from the education sector (kindergartens, schools, technical colleges, universities, etc.) to the mass media (television, the Internet, newspapers, etc.) – would be mobilized to teach citizens about Earth-centeredness. Eco-pedagogy would be a crucial action, especially in anthropocentric societies: human supremacism is even more ingrained and pervasive than other forms of supremacism (racism, sexism, homophobia, etc.), so we require sustained "re-conditioning" in order to become environmental egalitarians.

One of the major subjects, of course, would be instrumentalization and its two fundamental and fundamentally conflicting modes. Pedagogy would evolve around the following basic themes: utilization is necessary for meeting reasonable human ends; anthropocentrism profoundly reduces things to their instrumental dimension, thus driving hyper-instrumental practices; Earth-centered eco-instrumentalism recognizes the various dimensions of entities, so what is required is minimizing our utilization of the non-human, in terms of both number and frequency. The education campaign would need to be bold and brave, for its very goal would be to contribute to the radical transformation of our mindsets and, by extension, our practices. (What becomes apparent as the chapter unfolds is that bold policies are characteristic of genuine environmental leadership.)

The notion of radical eco-education and related topics is a major theme in some of the thinkers recalled in the present work. This is especially the case with Meyer-Abich. From the very beginning of *Revolution for Nature*, he foregrounds pedagogy as a/the way to raise and inform ecological awareness. He specifically refers to the idea of mass eco-education: "Working against the degeneration of the senses by returning to forgotten realms of life also requires teaching and information, environmental education in the widest sense" (1993: 14). Meyer-Abich incisively notes that this does not mean a focus on children, for "change cannot begin with children, because they are educated by adults. The new consciousness must have its roots in these adults, so that they can pass it on to the children" (1993: 14–15). Many other scholars have also begun exploring the question of eco-education (e.g., Evans 2012; Hovardas 2011, 2012; Cocks and Simpson 2015; Kopnina 2013; Kopnina and Gjerris 2015; Smith and Gough 2015; Smith 2017).

Another way that ecocentric leadership may minimize the instrumental-ization of non-humans is to implement/intensify mechanisms that stabilize human population levels because there is a correlation between the number of humans and the number of non-humans we instrumentalize, i.e., more humans equals more utilization. Straightaway, I recognize that the subject of demographic stabilization may/will appear to be profoundly controversial for some readers. I'm deeply aware that the notions of "over-population" and "population control" are highly provocative and even "taboo" (Singer and Kissling 2017; Kissling, Musinguzi and Singer 2018; Lawton 2019; Thornett 2019), though thankfully the population question is gaining more attention, even/especially in the public domain (e.g., Attenborough 2011, 2018). In any case, we shall proceed here with even greater caution and tentativeness than usual. Ideally, I would have preferred offering a lengthy discussion in order to proffer a stronger argument, but the study's limits dictate a more abbreviated exposition.

We may first quickly recount the brute fact of unbridled population growth. The most dramatic index is the global one. Since the advent of agriculture, the world's population has grown 1,860 times, from approximately four million people to almost eight billion (Roser, Ritchie and Ortiz-Ospina 2013/2019). World population growth accelerated during the twentieth century, increas-ing from 1.6 billion in 1900 to over 6 billion by the end of the century, with its greatest acceleration occurring in the second half of the century (Roser, Ritchie and Ortiz-Ospina 2013/2019; UN DESA 2019: 2). While the growth rate has slowed down since the peak period, we are still experiencing signifi-cant increases: the UN forecasts almost 10 billion people by 2050, and over 11 billion by 2100 (UN DESA 2019: 2–3). At the national level, China and India are approaching the 1.5 billion mark (UN DESA 2019: 26).

The eco-problematic nature of these alarming figures is most vividly observed at the level of over-crowded mega-cities, which often experience severe air pollution. Of course, the environmental impacts of population growth are numerous, continually multiplying and intensifying. In 1994, fifty-eight of the world's scientific academies united to craft a "Statement on Population Growth," which asserts that "there is no doubt that the threat to the ecosystem is linked to population size and resource use" (IAP 1994). The Statement goes on to list some of the ecological issues associated with human population pressures: "increasing greenhouse gas emissions, ozone depletion and acid rain, loss of biodiversity, deforestation and loss of topsoil, shortage of water, food and fuel," with the effect that "the natural systems are being pushed ever closer to their limits" (IAP 1994).

Now, the way I approach the population question likely differs in some respects from more conventional approaches. First of all, as I very briefly noted at the beginning of this discussion on population, the ecocentric argument is tied to the equation that more humans means more instrumentalization of non-humans; the present argument relies on the self-evident fact that we humans utilize non-human entities for the satisfaction of ends, so greater population stabilization means lower levels and intensities of utilization. The argument here does not depend on empirically calculating what might constitute "over-population" or the amount of people the Earth can sustain, which are more complex questions than might initially appear to us environmentalists (Dryzek 1987; McLaughlin 1993; Angus and Butler 2011). After all, apart from patently over-crowded cities, it is difficult to quantify such purported phenomena: when does the Earth reach a human population "limit"? I think some of the earlier overpopulation literature was well-intentioned but is quite rightly exposed to charges of alarmism (e.g., Malthus 1798; Ehrlich 1968; Hardin 1968; Meadows and others 1972; Ophuls 1977; Cohen 1995; Wilson 2002; this tendency to alarmism is sometimes displayed by some of the key thinkers cited in this study, e.g., White 1978: 108; Worster 1980: 47; Callicott 1989: 27). Now, I'm certainly not dismissing the possibility of overpopulation at the global scale. But, as I say, my argument is based on simple "arithmetical" grounds, i.e., utilization is linked to population, so less human beings means less non-human utilization. Because this argument is rather "obvious," I think it's prone to being missed by the population debate.

How, then, would ecocentric leadership pursue the goal of population stabilization? What specific measures would be implemented to obtain stable demographic levels? Obviously, I am not implying mass murder, genocide, eugenics, or any other kind of evil program: the Earth-centered goal is the prevention of sky-rocketing population growth – not the eradication of human beings. A number of options avail themselves to ecocentric leadership in this regard, ranging from the more indirect to the more radical. Eckersley admirably discusses this range of options: she refers to "ecological education campaigns" that would "explain, inter alia, the impact of human population growth on ecosystems and the need to reduce the size of families to one or two children" (1992: 131), and she also cites the population-curbing effects of the feminist and contraceptive movements (1992: 131). Let's first briefly turn to the more indirect measures before discussing the radical smaller-families set of policies.

To begin with, not only would eco-leadership support and galvanize gender equality because it is good and true (Wollstonecraft 1845; de Beauvoir 1989; Greer 1970; Daly 1978; etc.) but also because it positively influences population levels in terms of stabilizing them. Much research has shown how more educated and financially independent females tend to be less procreative (Caldwell 1980;

Weinberger 1987; Martin 1995; McCrary and Royer 2011; Roser 2014/2017), thereby contributing to population stabilization. The feminist cause may thus be leveraged toward this aim (Gladwin, Kennelly and Krause 1995: 891). Next, the contraceptive revolution is another phenomenon that appears to contribute to demographic stability: the pill, prophylactics, legalized abortion, and other birth control mechanisms became increasingly normalized in the second half of the twentieth century (Hill, Stycos and Back 1959; Westoff and Ryder 1977; Benagiano, Bastianelli and Farris 2007). There appears to be relatively little research on the relation between these progressive movements and population regulation (an unsurprising situation, given the stigma associated with both these subjects-practices), so it's edifying to note that brave scholars occasionally raise this issue (e.g., Anderson 2019). As with the feminist movement, ecocentric leadership would sustain and intensify the contraceptive revolution (via comprehensive education campaigns, legislative methods, etc.), not only because it's basically good and true (some aspects to it require refinement) but also because it may be used as another lever for addressing population growth.

Obviously, the most controversial mechanism for population stabilization involves restricting the number of children that individuals/couples are allowed to beget, historically typically limited to one child or two. The most "infamous" example is the Chinese implementation of this measure (Scharping 2003), although it also operates in Vietnam (Goodkind 1995). China initially launched the program as a two-child policy in the late 1960s, then shifted to the one-child policy in 1979, and switched back in 2016 (Vietnam also has a two-child policy). While various aspects of the Chinese policy may be problematized and criticized (Whyte, Wang and Cai 2015), it has certainly stabilized demographic growth (Myers, Wu and Fu 2019). China remains grossly populated, so we shudder to think how worse it would have been ecologically and socially if a population policy was not instigated.

Of course, serious social problems have arisen due to the one-child measure. Tragically, females were aborted or abandoned due to traditional sexism favoring males (Greenhalgh 2008). This has led to disproportionate gender numbers. One also notes how the practice deprives children of siblings (Hatton 2013). While I do not downplay these tragic consequences, I propose that this particular policy has also been excessively stigmatized in the West due to its origins in communist countries, where the ruling political ideology is very offensive to many Westerners. Given the deeply biased climate, it is impressive to note that brave philosophers like Sarah Conly (2016) have revisited the one-child question, rigorously advocating it, together with a reasonable set of regulations and incentives (cf. Cripps 2015, 2017). This rethinking rebalances the question. Ecocentric leadership would calmly and objectively assess both sides of the argument, unswayed by ideological biases. My speculation is that Earth-centered leadership would advance something like a nuanced two-/ three-child policy, taking account of factors such as geographical variations and child mortality. Once again, education would be key. In this regard, we note how countries like Iran and Singapore launched campaigns urging their citizens to voluntarily have smaller families (Youngblood 1987; Larsen 2003).

Now, despite the fairness of an Earth-centered family-planning policy, I anticipate that it would still be rejected by many Westerners. How come? Likely the most decisive reason why we Westerners tend to find enforced birth regulation offensive is that it undermines our cherished right to freely procreate. After all, shouldn't individuals and couples be allowed to produce as many offspring as they desire? We're forced to address this question in some length, not only because the particular issue of procreation is quite a complex one but also because it will become increasingly evident (if not already) that the kind of ecocentric leading developed here might be misconstrued as something that opposes freedom, given its rather "intrusive" measures.

We commence our response with the following point: the freedom to procreate is part of a suite of inalienable liberties (sexual, religious, etc.) that I strongly endorse and advance. This endorsement and advancement are abundantly evident in the present work, both in terms of privileging the maxim-practice of letting-be – which essentially means letting-be-*free* – and the shortly discussed expression of eco-liberation (i.e., freedom for colonized non-human things), which is the radical contrary of homocentric eco-colonization (the large-scale oppression of non-humans). (My high estimation of freedom is also evidenced in *Following Reason*, where I cite it as one of the fundamental rational attitudes-acts [2019: 3].) So how do I reconcile my love for freedom with population regulation measures? Quite easily: I'm not presenting a choice between procreation and its abolition but rather a choice between unlimited procreation and a restricted procreation generating all kinds of benefits, including ecological ones, such as lowering the levels of instrumentalization.

Another broader argument may be offered here regarding tempering the unthought demand for total procreational – or any other kind of – freedom, such that it dogmatically blocks even the possibility of considering population control measures. I recall here leadership theorist James MacGregor Burns, who explains in *Leadership* how two of our greatest values – liberty and equality – sometimes conflict, so there may be occasions when we're required to choose between them (1978: 389, 426, 431–432). In the West, freedom is often privileged. (Burns inclines himself toward that direction.) Which value does ecocentrism value more – freedom or equality? We've already noted how its ethos of letting-be is somewhat commensurate with freedom; however, it is not fundamentally a question of crudely choosing one over the other. In the case of family planning, eco-centeredness does not deny the freedom to have children; it would merely limit it to a reasonable, environmentally sustainable number. But given the global population pressures, there's a certain compulsion to choose in this regard: given that ecocentrism is a radical egalitarianism (i.e., there's a certain commensurability between the human and non-human, which may be based on the common denominator of existence), then equality might be said to be the "more equal" of the two. When our respect and responsibility are expanded to include the non-human and the human then some of our cherished freedoms – such as the liberty to procreate endlessly – will be modified or limited. Some liberties may even be suspended. (The suspension of certain "liberties" may be considered "extreme," but it applies to a number of practices, such as "recreational hunting," which is discussed later.) If/whenever Earth-centered leadership would be required to choose between freedom and equality, then eco-equality outweighs individualistic freedoms like having bigger families.

One could protest that our consideration of the smaller-family policy testifies to ecocentrism's "misanthropy," as it appears to want less humans on the Earth. But it's not a policy of *reduction* but of *prevention* (i.e., preventing numbers from increasing), which is beneficial for both humanity and the world. Lest it needs to be stated again: Earth-centeredness is the most philanthropic of all philosophies; it's the worldview that recognizes how humankind's flourishing is dependent on the world's flourishing, both its natural and artifactual dimensions. While one certainly has the right to question past motives for contentious measures like restricted procreation (e.g., economic pressures rather than environmental concerns), I have aimed to show how ecocentrism offers sound arguments for reconsidering this radical measure: begetting less children means less people using non-human implements for achieving reasonable ends, so working out ways to prevent unbridled population growth makes sense from an eco-instrumental perspective.

A further indicator of ecocentrism's anti-misanthropism is its ardent recognition that the imperative for demographic regulation does not exclusively apply to humans. Leopold astutely recognizes that some animals, when their number are left unchecked, do untold damage to the land: he provides the example of the eradication of wolf numbers due to human hunting led to increased numbers of deer decimating the mountain ecology, so deer numbers would also need to be controlled (1989: 130–132). White makes a similar eco-nuanced point regarding excessive non-human populations: "When locusts breed so prolifically that they swarm by the millions, devastating not only the farmers' planted fields but also green areas essential to other kinds of being, people have a right to kill locusts, but not to try to exterminate locusts [as a species]" (1978: 107; incisively, White immediately reminds us that we humans are the greater swarmers). A properly ecocentric ethic/ethos does not promote unrestricted letting-be: as emphasized in the previous chapter, there are times when we humans should/must intervene in various ways for the sake of the broader environment. Hence, consistent Earth-centered leadership would attempt to address problematic population growth across species, human, and otherwise. With characteristic style (albeit with a lingering discursive gender-exclusiveness that's not altogether inaccurate), White perfectly captures the imperative for sustainable populations, human and otherwise: "men must not crowd coyotes, or coyotes men" (1978: 107).

Eco-Consumption

Like instrumentalization, the practice of consumption is a necessary aspect of existence for humans and a variety of other beings; it's a means for meeting our basic-higher ends. As Meyer-Abich bluntly puts it with the consumptive process of eating: "we are so much a part of nature that we inevitably even share in the process of eating and being eaten" (1993: 71; cf. Plumwood 2012). Now, according to the present work, there are two basic ways humanity carries out the process of consumption or appropriation: homocentrically and ecocentrically. We recall from the anthropocentrism chapter the fact that hyper-consumption occurs when we excessively reduce the non-human to its appropriative dimension; the entity is inferiorized to the degree that its other dimensions (e.g., its conatus or natural unfolding, intentionality, needs, etc.) are either unrecognized or ignored. Our calculations regarding the satisfaction of our own ends do not factor in the non-human other and its striving to meet its own. As a result, we humans over-consume and appropriate unnecessary products, destroying species, objects, and environments in the process.

Eco-consumption, on the other hand, is the ecocentric alternative to hyper-consumption. It recognizes how appropriation is necessary for survival-flourishing, both for humans and non-humans; consuming is one of the crucial ways – together with other practices, like instrumentalization, manufacture, etc. – in which reasonable ends are met. Eco-consumption is a modest, self-restrained form of appropriation because it recognizes and seeks to take into account the equality of non-humans and their attempts to fulfill their own ends. Eco-consumption is thus a kind of middle or third way beyond obsessive acquisition and ascetic renunciation.

As with eco-use, we may briefly explore the subject of eco-consumption in terms of *what*, *how*, and *how much* to consume. First of all, given that ecocentric living is geared toward meeting basic-higher ends, we only appropriate those things that meet these needs. We also note that we would be less dependent on material goods (a dependence whose distorted addictive expression is embodied by consumerism), given that Earth-centeredness not only focuses on material needs but also higher ends. We thus applaud White's plea to pursue such ends: "We must increase emphasis on the relatively nonconsumptive activities of education, the arts, contemplation and worship" (1978: 109).

We shall focus here on the specific question of food appropriation because it aptly illuminates a number of aspects of ecocentric consumption. To begin with, this question is often traversed by environmental thinkers (e.g., Callicott 1989: 34; Meyer-Abich 1993: 87). What, then, should we eat? Whether an ecocentric ethos espouses plant-based diets (veganism, vegetarianism) or omnivorism is a much thornier issue than might first appear – if one were to automatically assume that a plant-based diet would be the preferred option. To begin with, from a rigorously Earth-centered perspective, we note how plants are just as valued as sheep and cows and other "livestock": there is less recourse here to criteria like sentience or suffering to determine the most eco-ethical diet. As strange as it may first appear, Rolston reminds us that even vegetarianism (and veganism) is a form of predation (1992: 254; cf. Meyer-Abich 1993: 71). Next, one can't necessarily rely on the assumption that crop-based farming is less impactful on the environment than animal-based agriculture (Callicott 1989: 34–35; Albers, Linder and Nichols 1990; Davis 2003; Archer 2011; Bramble and Fischer 2015; Fischer and Lamey 2018). Additionally, we note how there are more ethically sensitive meat-production alternatives to slaughterhouse farming (Fairlie 2010; Schaefer 2018). Hence, omnivorism cannot be dismissed out-of-hand (Bruckner 2015). Furthermore, geographical context must be taken into account: there are cultures located in places where a plant-based diet is inaccessible/impractical, e.g., the Inuits ("Eskimos" is a derogatory term) live in regions where vegetation is scarce, so meat has to be the major/sole part of their diet (Stefansson 1960; Arnaquq-Baril 2016). Indeed, there are even extreme cases where even cannibalism may be occasionally ethically permissible: consider the 1972 Uruguayan plane crash in the Andes mountains, where starving survivors were compelled to eat dead victims in order to stay alive.

Given the aforementioned observations, how would the thoroughgoing eco-centeredness espoused in the present work construe the dilemma of what to eat? While it would not dogmatically advance strict plant-based consumption, it certainly advocates more of it, and conversely, less meat-eating. Why? I noted earlier that "there is less recourse here to criteria like sentience or suffering to determine the most ethical diet" – *less* recourse rather than *no* recourse: for instance, ecocentrism certainly takes a criterion like "suffering" into account. Rolston himself notes that while vegetarians (and vegans) are "predators of a kind . . . what they eat does not suffer" (1992: 254; of course, as we humans don't know what/how plants experience, we remain open to the possibility of some kind of "suffering"). So eco-centeredness certainly leans toward plant-based diets. However, it would not absolutely universally demand these diets, allowing some room for omnivorism and even carnivorism when they might be the only/main options.

The focus on food provides an exemplary rethinking of *how* we would eco-centrically consume. Once again, this question may be tied to the subject of eco-centered affects/dispositions briefly discussed in the previous chapter. To begin with, eco-consumption is informed by a recognition of the non-human thing's equality with us, but how can this commensurability be reflected in consumptive acts like eating? – after all, complete appropriation appears to exemplify one's absolute domination over the thing being consumed (Adams 1990). While this is true, it's mitigated by the fact that eating is a necessary part of creaturely existence (so it's not automatically or wholly reducible to an act of subjection). Furthermore, the dominative dimension of eating is offset by practices allowing us to exhibit our ecocentric recognition of our ontological equality. These practices are typically premodern and often non-Western, given that we today are thoroughgoing anthropocentrists unaware or dismissive of this equality, licentiously appropriating the non-human other.

This recognition of equality or solidarity is expressed in a number of ways: as gratitude, respect, joy, and so on. For instance, the Haudenosanee league of Native American nations would "thank" the animals that are hunted and consumed (Kalman 2001). (One could argue that religious people often "give thanks" for food, but the thanksgiving is typically directed at a deity for the provision of the food. The plant/animal itself typically remains unthanked in any explicit or direct sense.) Pioneering (homocentric) environmentalist John Passmore notes how Germanic tribes would seek the pardon of the animals they hunted: "There are societies in which the axeman or the slaughterer, before taking up his axe or his knife, would first have begged the tree's or the animal's pardon, explaining the necessity which forced him to destroy it. Indeed, such an attitude to nature lingered on among German foresters as late as the nineteenth century" (Passmore 1974: 10 citing Biese 1905). Callicott hones in on the attitude of deference in previous times and places: "animal flesh was respectfully consumed" (1989: 33). Similarly, Rolston observes the apologetic comportment of considerate campers for merely interrupting the natural unfolding of ants: "The single camper must even suppress an instinctive apology to the ants who scatter from beneath the rock he [sic] moves to realign his hearth" (1986: 224). Likewise, environmental historian James Morton Turner eloquently retraces the growing American trend of minimal-impact camping in the latter half of the twentieth century (2002). This kind of care may be read as reflecting something of the ecocentric spirit.

Meyer-Abich identifies two further responses that may be understood as ways of reflecting our recognition of the equality of the consumed non-human other: "In my opinion we owe it to the plants and animals on which we live to eat them with gratitude and joy" (1993: 87). He goes on to extend enjoyment to other forms of consumption: "Joy in eating and drinking, in love, clothes and holidays: such joy . . . might even be the key to renewal of the industrial society" (1993: 88). But why joy? "Because we live off the other we owe it to nature to eat with joy, artistry and festivity; to use the strength food gives us to contribute our share to nature's whole" (1993: 104).

Having briefly discussed *what* we should consume and *how* we should consume it, we may now briefly address the question of *how much* we should appropriate. Worster asks the very same question: "how much should a people consume? What is sufficient for human fulfillment?" (1980: 46). The keyword here is "sufficient": from an Earth-centered perspective, we should consume as little as possible, consuming to the extent that we meet our basic-higher needs.

And we should also recognize that our acts of appropriation should inhibit as little as possible the goal of non-human beings obtaining their reasonable ends. Worster notes how our knowledge of non-human ends will help us in this regard: "We will also need a much firmer knowledge of what all other species [and inanimate things] require for their unimpeded development" (1980: 46). Purser, Park, and Montuori also focus on the relation between what is appropriated and how much should be appropriated: "genuinely green consumerism . . . would focus on reducing rather than simply changing personal levels of consumption" (1995: 8; cf. Gladwin, Kennelly and Krause 1995: 891). Mathews nicely sums up the response to the *how much* question with the goal of "having fewer and older things" (1999a: 127).

Meyer-Abich is a key contributor to the consumption question – indeed, the "revolution" to which he refers in *Revolution for Nature* is precisely a "peaceful consumer revolution" (1993: 21). He (biocentrically) contends that "The revolution is necessary because the life-threatening course of our economy is the greatest problem facing us, and because the best way of coming to grips with the economy is by removing economic acceptance" (1993: 21). This focus on economics is echoed by McLaughlin's suggestion that "The economic systems that we construct and live within are . . . the primary immediate cause of the relations between society and the rest of nature" (1993: 12). Meyer-Abich contends that a consumer revolution should precede any political transformation: "We must not forget that in reality it is the consumers – all of us – who sanction the economic situation by our purchases, and it is also through us that the economy is able to assert itself politically" (1993: 21). (The questions of the political and economic are partially traversed as we proceed, and more directly engaged toward the end of the chapter.)

There appears to be growing awareness of our hyper-consumptive ways and various efforts are being made to counter them. "Green/sustainable consumerism" has emerged over recent decades (Ekström and Glans 2011; Syse and Mueller 2015). Much of this discourse-practice is motivated by the notion to which Meyer-Abich subscribes – to be further discussed and contested as we proceed – that consumer choice compels producers to move to more sustainable production, leading to the proliferation of eco-friendly goods. There's also the rise of "collaborative consumption" (Felson and Spaeth 1978; Botsman and Rogers 2010; Ertz, Durif and Arcand 2016), whereby consumers barter goods and services with each other (traditionally via swap meets, flea markets, second-hand shopping, etc.), as well as the growth of the technologically assisted "share/sharing economy" (Belk 2014). Somewhat more broadly, White refers to "simplification": "we must engage ourselves in a vast and rapid simplification of the forms of culture in industrialized societies to reduce waste, duplication of effort, and redundant production" (1978: 109). Simplicity is a key theme raised by various other eco-thinkers referenced here (e.g., Devall 1988; Eckersley 1992; McLaughlin 1993; cf. Nisbet 1974). Pioneering Christian ecotheologian James A. Nash refers to "frugality" – which is not to be confused with austere asceticism: "Frugality is an earth-affirming and enriching norm that delights in the non- and less-consumptive joys of the mind and flesh, especially the enhanced lives for human communities and other creatures that only constrained consumption and production can make on a confined planet" (1998: 427). We could also note the emergence of "minimalism" as a counter-consumerist practice (Milburn and Nicodemus 2011, 2015).

On the one hand, such movements and discourses should be praised for challenging materialistic consumerism. However, they have also drawn significant criticism in terms of focusing their critiques on consumption at the expense of other factors (Irvine 1989; Speth 2008; Guckian, De Young and Harbo 2017). For example, environmental lawyer James Gustave Speth correctly identifies a number of the underlying drivers of consumer behavior: "Consumption patterns are powerfully shaped by forces other than a preformed set of individual preferences – forces such as advertising, cultural norms, social pressures, and psychological associations" (2008: 147). Furthermore, Meyer-Abich and other scholars neglect the decisive role of *producers* (a point elaborated in the next section), as well as displaying an excessive confidence in the notion that producers respond to consumer demands: "I have no doubt that it [business] will react flexibly to a consumer revolution, by looking to its profits" (Meyer-Abich 1993: 23). Indeed, even Meyer-Abich expresses doubt regarding the power of consumers, given the apparent lack of collective will: "The real problem is whether we, the general public, really want this change" (1993: 25).

Relatedly, Purser, Park, and Montuori target the "green consumerism" mantra of corporations, making the incisive point that this ideology remains within the dominant anthropocentric paradigm, masking what is truly required for ecological sustenance and flourishing: "Although green consumerism may help to some degree in shifting consumption patterns toward more 'environmentally friendly' products . . . it still sends the message that material acquisition can continue unimpeded" (1995: 1075). The proliferation of "eco-products" excuses us from having to examine our materialistic lifestyles (1995: 1075). Furthermore, as elaborated later, "green consumerism" and its variants place much/all of the onus on customers – nicely captured by the phrase "consumer scapegoatism" coined by sustainable consumption–production scholar Lewis Akenji (2014, 2019).

To the extent that conventional "green consumerism" and other similar efforts are problematic and insufficient, are there any alternative leaderly measures whose implementation would dislodge and replace dominant hyperconsumption with eco-consumption (thus working toward transforming homocentric situations into ecocentric ones) or would allow the maintenance of eco-consumption as the dominant consumptive expression (thus working to maintain eco-centered situations from anthropocentric contestation)? This question will shortly be addressed, but first, we elucidate the notion of ecocentric production.

Eco-Production

As demonstrated in Chapter 2, the "hyper-" in hyper-production signifies several things – once again, expressible in terms of the *what, how,* and
how much: commodities are made that are unnecessary or counterproduc-
tive for the satisfaction of reasonable human ends (a foregrounded example
was cheap mass-produced items); products are often extracted, processed, or
manufactured in ways that are anti-environmental (such as fossil fuels); and
often too many goods are produced (such as food), akin to what White calls
"redundant production" (1978: 109). Bennett traces the relation between too
many products and too much trash: "the sheer volume of products, and the
necessity of junking them to make room for new ones, devalues the thing"
(2004: 350). (Of course, overproduction is correlated with the capitalistic obses-
sions of maximum profit and perpetual economic growth, an ideology-practice
that many scholars have powerfully critiqued, e.g., Daly 1973; Pearce, Markandya and Barbier 1989; McLaughlin 1993; Barbier 2012; Washington and
Twomey 2016).

How, then, does eco-production differ from hyper-production? As with
instrumentalization and consumption, ecocentrism recognizes the necessity of
making: like many other creatures, we humans manufacture goods and services. However, and here we commence with the *what* question, ecocentric
production produces those things that go toward meeting our basic–higher
ends. Meyer-Abich contrasts hyper-production with physiocentric production:
"earnings [and indeed profits] become the overriding goal of work, rather than
the transformation of materials into the necessities of life" (1993: 93). Hence,
we should only produce those goods and services that satisfy these "necessities"
(which, we insist, include both basic and higher requirements). Eco-production
is also mainly antithetical to cheap mass production (there might be a need for
some of these goods).

Ecocentric production also focuses on making eco-friendly goods, with
various dimensions to this kind of manufacture. Manufactured goods would
be thoroughly durable. This goes against the grain of "planned obsolescence,"
whereby items are made to intentionally fail within a relatively short period of
time (Galbraith 1958; Fisher, Griliches and Kaysen 1962; Bulow 1986; Guiltinan 2009; Cooper 2016). Eminent environmental thinkers Charles Birch and
John B. Cobb, Jr. declare: "Manufactured goods will be built to last; durabil-
ity will replace planned obsolescence" (1981: 245). Eminent cultural theorist
Raymond Williams, who later engaged in ecological thinking, advanced the
demand for a shift in "production towards new governing standards of dura-
bility, quality and economy" (1983: 256). Whenever possible, ecocentric production involves making items with biodegradable elements (McDonough and
Braungart 2002). Better and safer products means more longer-lasting products
and healthier consumers, as well as less waste and lower replacement rates,

which means less human intervention into the non-human world and lower environmental impacts.

Next, what might be involved in the *how* of eco-production? First of all, given its topicality, we quickly refer to the generation of energy consumables (oil, electricity, gas, etc.). Earth-centeredness favors renewable energy over fossil fuels: the production of renewable energy is less intrusive than conventional energy production; furthermore, less waste and other harmful by-products are also involved with more eco-friendly energy generation. We also return here to the subject of food and food production. Earth-centeredness calls for the best eco-practices, including biodynamics, aeroponics, organic, indoor, urban, and shared farming (Koepf 1989; Dyck 1994; Podolinsky 2002; Paull 2006, 2011; Gebissa 2010; Kaak 2010, 2012; Menck 2012; Subramaniam and Kong 2012; Strasser 2014; MacDonald 2015; Blok 2018; Holzman 2018).

Of course, the question of the *how* of production is often more complicated than what a brief discussion can convey. This complexity is perhaps most aptly illuminated by focusing on the most controversial mode of food production: hunting. Once again, the assumed response might be that eco-centeredness automatically rejects this practice – but, like the food-consumption question, the response is more nuanced. To begin with, we note with environmental philosopher Gary Varner (1995) that there are three basic types of hunting. A first form is subsistence hunting. As the name clearly indicates, it involves activity that allows the hunter to live. This form of predation is ecocentrically acceptable because it is pursued for the sake of meeting an essential end (sustenance). We could also add that it generally tends to occur at smaller scales, so the environmental impact is relatively low. The Inuit example cited earlier would be classified under this category.

The second type of hunting is undertaken for the greater ecological good, i.e., a species of animal or plant, whose unfolding leads to excessive environmental destruction, is restricted or eradicated in order to protect the broader ecosystem from further destruction (Leopold 1989; Callicott 1989: 21). We could also add here the subcategory whereby the hunted animals can also be a source of food for humans (and others). For example, in parts of Australia where there are overabundant kangaroo herds, their culling not only contributes to land conservation but is also a source of food (Grigg 1987; Grigg, Hale and Lunney 1995; Chapman 2003; Cooney and others 2008; Wilson and Edwards 2008).

The third category of hunting often goes by offensive euphemisms like "game/sport/recreational/trophy hunting." We immediately recognize the profoundly unethical nature of this activity. Apart from an assortment of rigorous arguments against this practice (Caras 1970; Baker 1985; Collard and Contrucci 1988; Kheel 1996; Gunn 2001; Simon 2016; Batavia and others 2018), we (also) reject it according to the present work's ecocentric logic because it does not satisfy basic-higher human needs. Hunting, in this instance, is enacted for a kind of perverted human enjoyment – an exemplary homocentric practice: we humans consider ourselves so superior to non-humans that we hunt them down just to satiate our distorted desires.

We conclude our discussion of eco-production by briefly turning to the question of *how much* production. With Earth-centered production, manufacturing rates are drastically minimized for several reasons. To begin with, as we embrace "the given" or what we already have, there is less demand for the production of more items for additional acquisition or the replacement of used ones. A moderate amount of manufacturing also means a moderate amount of waste. Mathews eloquently identifies the link between eco-centered attachment and lower production rates: "We no longer crave bigger and better houses, cars, roads, cities, whatever. We are instead attached to what is already given. There is thus no call for ever-increasing productivity" (1999a: 127).

Some Leaderly Measures for Eco-Consumption and Eco-Production

Given that consumption and production are deeply interrelated – they essentially constitute two sides of the same process – some key leaderly measures for eco-consumption and eco-production are here identified and examined together. To begin with, we note how Gladwin, Kennelly, and Krause rightly posit that "policy instruments and economic incentives are required to place preemptive constraints on the pursuit of purely market criteria bearing upon natural resource use and satisfaction of basic human needs" (1995: 893). What, then, might be some of the measures Earth-centered leading would institute for more eco-consumptive and eco-productive practices, thus contributing to the ecocentric transformation of homocentric situations and the preservation of more eco-centered ones?

First of all, we recall the broad mechanisms identified during the delineation of eco-instrumentalism above: the mass (re-)education program and the robust population policy. We immediately observe how their implementation would prove highly effective for both consumption and production. To begin with, one of the key learning points of the re-education campaign would be the articulation of truly ecocentric consumption, i.e., appropriating only those things that satisfy our reasonable ends, an appropriation process that also takes into account the recognition that non-humans also have ends they seek to satisfy. The education program would seek to contribute to the transformation of our compulsive consumerism to a modest eco-consumption of the necessary and enlightening. As part of this process, we would be taught about ancient and non-Western practices around food appropriation (giving thanks, etc.), with the aim of cultivating ecocentric attitudes, practices, institutions, and systems.

The other broad measure of population regulation would also be an effective lever for displacing anthropocentric forms of consumption–production and elevating/maintaining ecocentric forms. In the first place, stabilizing human demographic levels would positively impact levels of consumption: the more of us there are, the more we need to consume, so the less of us there are, the lower the levels of appropriation. White identifies the correlation between population growth and hyper-consumption, and how they may be offset by population policy and modifying our consumerist lifestyles (1978: 104). Likewise, McLaughlin explicitly links a growing population rate with greater consumption, which adds to "the strain on local and global ecosystems" (1993: 63). He also identifies the combined impact of hyper-production and population growth: "the expanding human population, especially when coupled with environmentally destructive forms of production, appears as a vast aggression against the rest of nature" (1993: 153).

While eco-pedagogy and population stabilization are significant broad measures for fostering eco-consumption and eco-production, we now turn to a discussion of a specific mechanism regarding production. We introduce the topic by recalling how Meyer-Abich places significant weight on consumers' ability to influence production factors like what is made, how it is made, and how much of it is made. Meyer-Abich states: "I am sure that our capitalist economy could survive such a [consumer] revolution, and could produce goods which consumers who think for themselves would wish to purchase" (1993: 25). During the discussion of eco-consumption, I signaled how the notion (or myth) that consumers hold significant sway over producers would be contested. Esteemed Marxist economist Ernest Mandel succinctly explains how producers dictate most of what is produced: "the bulk of both consumer and producer goods are not produced in any way in response to 'market signals'. . . . The bulk of current production corresponds to established consumption patterns and predetermined production techniques that are largely if not completely independent of the market" (1986: 11). Mandel provides the compelling illustrations of motor vehicles and personal computers as items that have been promoted by producers rather than demanded by consumers: "*the initial push towards them* [products] *never comes from the market or the consumer. . . .* There were businesses . . . launching new products on consumers to create the necessary demand for selling as many of their wares as possible" (1986: 11).

Mandel is basically correct: producers mostly dictate what is produced (as well as how it's made and how much is made). Contrary to Meyer-Abich's discourse, we consumers have limited traction in terms of dictating what is made for consumption. In "free markets," producers are essentially free to produce whatever they desire: the existence of these items, combined with advertising and other forces, foster the consumer's desire to obtain it. But this productive "freedom" contravenes the ecocentric imperative to manufacture only what humankind requires materially and psycho-spiritually. As with the case regarding the unbridled freedom to endlessly procreate versus the counter-obligation to avoid over-population, we have a clash here between liberty and equality: unfettered freedom for producers versus maximizing the flourishing of humans and non-humans. Ecocentrism obviously chooses the latter pathway, so Earth-centered leading would seek to contribute to greater flourishing by restricting the freedom of producers to only make goods and services that meet reasonable human ends.

The measure of restricted production is obviously a provocative one. However, when we're allowed to properly consider it, it doesn't appear as unreasonable as it may first appear to our hardened neoliberal sensibilities. First of all, consider the range of wicked but legalized products permitted today: slaughterhouse meat, factory-farmed eggs, cigarettes, etc. If given the power and opportunity, ethico-reasonable people would prohibit or drastically limit the generation of such products. And the prohibition/restriction of various products is precisely what ecocentric leading would do.

Some of the environmental thinkers engaged throughout this study also intimate stronger controls on the market. We may begin with McLaughlin, who recognizes that "It now seems inescapable that ecological problems will require increasing political regulation of processes once left to markets" (1993: 38) – processes that should include the kinds and quantities of commodities. We also note how Eckersley positively identifies a "nonmarket allocative system" as a process that "ensures ecologically benign production for genuine human need" (1992: 122).

Of course, the provocative measure of circumscribed production opens onto the even more confronting question of the nature of a truly ecocentric economics: restricting the freedom of producers is completely antithetical to free-wheeling neoliberal capitalism (Hayek 1944, 1960; Friedman 1962; for critiques, refer to, e.g., Harvey 2005; Jones 2012). Would an Earth-centered economics have affinities with something like a planned economy, or a "mixed" market-socialist model (such as ecosocialist philosopher André Gorz's idea of a simultaneously planned-and-market economy [1982; cf. 1980]), or perhaps an as-yet-unimagined framework? Obviously, this abyssal question lies beyond the scope of the present work and the capacities of its author (a point elaborated later) – but it's being broached by the growing field of ecological economics (Boulding 1966; Daly 1973, 2007; Mandel 1986; Costanza and Daly 1987; Costanza 1992; Gowdy 1998; van den Bergh 2001; Cato 2009; Ackerman 2012; Washington and Maloney 2020).

I recognize that the measure of moving away from an economy where producers are almost completely free to produce whatever they desire to an economy involving profoundly regulated production is yet another extremely controversial proposition: it runs against the very grain of the all-pervasive capitalist spirit; it runs counter to the unbounded freedom that "we capitalists" cherish. However, if ecocentric leadership is to consistently and faithfully pursue the logic-practice of Earth-centeredness, then it must follow its pathways wherever they lead, even when the destinations are contentious. So, when the question of what kinds of leaderly actions could effectively facilitate the right kind of production, then one of these policies appears to be the implementation of a more ordered, heavily regulated economy.

Eco-Liberation

Before delineating the meaning of eco-liberation, let's briefly recount some key facets of its antithesis, i.e., eco-colonization. While "colonization" typically refers to the domination of peoples as well as lands, eco-colonization denotes the colonization of anything/everything non-human. It denies the free unfolding of non-human things. And in the same way that human colonialism often leads to genocide, eco-colonization often leads to ecocide (discussed later). Eco-colonization is implicitly and explicitly traversed by a number of thinkers recalled in the present work. Leopold, for example, links the domination of the non-human to the process of commodification (the same way a human slave becomes a piece of property): "We abuse land because we regard it as a commodity belonging to us" (1989: viii). Meyer-Abich aptly captures the homocentric-imperialistic imperative: "nature is to be possessed rather than lived" (1993: 129). Likewise, Purser, Park, and Montuori describe how ecosystems are "invaded by humans" (1995: 1071). Eminent eco-lawyer Polly Higgins explicitly employs the term "eco-colonization" (and "ecocide") in a 2012 essay titled "Towards a Garden of Eden: Ecocide, Eco-Colonization and the Sacredness of All Life" (cf. Higgins, Short and South 2013). Of course, like a number of excellent environmental works, the paper is nonetheless confined within biocentrism, as indicated by the subtitle. By contrast, as elaborated in the second chapter and in accordance with the thoroughgoing ecocentrism advanced in this work, the term "eco-colonization" as it's used here is inclusive of the abiotic and constructed.

Now, just as "colonization" is typically employed anthropocentrically, so is "liberation" – even though it has expanded nowadays in a biocentric direction: not only do we readily recognize and endorse human liberation (whether from enslavement, patriarchy, classism, etc.) but also animal liberation (from factory farming and other forms of oppression) (Singer 1975; Callicott 1980; Birch and Cobb 1981; Peet and Watts 1996; Plumwood 1999; Best 2014). But what could be meant by truly ecocentric emancipation? What on Earth do we mean by "eco-liberation," especially as it's inclusive of "inanimate" entities and places? Given the radical expansiveness and inclusiveness of ecocentrism, it follows that the phrase signifies the emancipation *of all things*, both biotic entities and their life-giving milieus but also the abiotic and the constructed. We're familiar with more conventional forms of liberation (of humans, of sexual orientations and behaviors, of animals, etc.), but how, exactly, can abiotic/manufactured things be "freed"?

Given the perplexity of this proposition, we shall seek to articulate it with the assistance of relatively unorthodox conceptual means: by recalling and reflecting on some artistic works. We begin with the notion of the liberation of abiotic or manufactured objects. Let's first establish the rigor of this proposition by visualizing it. The example that immediately comes to my mind is a cinematic one: in the 1999 film *American Beauty*, there's a scene in which one of the protagonists attentively films an ordinary plastic shopping bag whirling around on a windy day (the protagonist anthropomorphically describes its movement as "dancing"); sometimes the bag skims the leaf-covered concrete and sometimes it swirls up above it. I, for one, was/am deeply moved by this scene, and judging by the millions of views the clip has accrued on YouTube, it has struck a chord with many others too: but why does this "banal" scene profoundly resonate with viewers? Could the scene's allure be at least partially explained by the ecocentric notion that the plastic bag – exemplar of the mass-produced/used/disposed object – is no longer in servitude to us humans but freely floating around? We remind ourselves that constructed things like plastic bags also unfold, so at least during the duration of the scene, the bag unfolds unobstructed or less-obstructed by human meddling. Of course, I'm aware that this poignant scenario also depicts pollution: plastic shopping bags would be precisely one of the items that ecocentric leading would seek to ban/restrict – a policy that's already being instituted in some parts of the world. I'm therefore not recommending the "release" of all of the world's shopping bags, which would be an environmental catastrophe. The point I'm making here is the preliminary one of visualizing what we mean by the liberation of abiotic things: the item's unfolding is no longer impeded by human intervention.

To further explicate the notion of eco-liberation, we also turn our attention to entities such as abandoned buildings and ghost towns (a site currently receiving much attention is Chernobyl): I've always been fascinated by them, and I think at least part of the fascination may be traced to the notion that they are no longer under human rule. As is the case with the free-floating bag, abandoned buildings and ghost towns are now allowed to unfold naturally. The excellent television series *Life After People* (2008–2010) is based on the premise that there are no longer humans inhabiting the Earth (the reason/s for our absence are unstated): with the use of amazing CGI effects, we're shown stunning visualizations of structures, built environments, and regions that have been liberated from human colonization. These objects and spaces are now left to freely unfurl – or at least unfold together with other naturally unfolding entities: while this unfolding-together will typically involve both co-operation and competition, at least the abandoned objects no longer experience or endure destructive human intervention. This process is often called "rewilding," which takes place either with or without human assistance (Dave Foreman in Foote 1990; Soulé and Noss 1998; Fraser 2009; Monbiot 2013; Sweeney and others 2019).

We conclude our synopsis of eco-liberation with the following reiteration: as has become apparent throughout the course of this chapter, genuine ecocentric leadership would involve the implementation of some measures that restrict/ban some of our human liberties (the freedom for unlimited procreation; the freedom to produce anything, etc.) – one might therefore mistakenly assume that Earth-centeredness and Earth-centered leading are "anti-liberty." I explained earlier how ecocentrism typically places some restrictions on some reasonable freedoms rather than completely dismantling them (e.g., humans are free to procreate but would be restricted in terms of numbers of children). I also explained how, *if/when* one were forced to choose between the values of liberty and equality, then radically egalitarian ecocentrism would be forced to prioritize the latter. So, all things considered, Earth-centeredness is profoundly pro-freedom, though in a sophisticated, qualified way. But in case doubt persists, the present discussion of eco-liberation – the emancipation of the non-human, including built objects and environments – powerfully proves the degree to which liberty is valued (indeed, loved) by ecocentrism and eco-centered leading. In fact, Earth-centeredness values freedom so much that it seeks it for *everything*, not just humans and other sentient creatures.

Eco-Preservation

Just as eco-liberation counters eco-colonization, eco-preservation counteracts the other homocentric expressions and their destructive consequences. And just like the other Earth-centered expressions discussed in this chapter, eco-preservation is all-inclusive, seeking to preserve the natural and the artifactual. Now, there are various kinds and degrees of preservation: conservation, restoration, recycling, and so on. I turn to brief expositions of some of the most significant forms of eco-preservation.

"Conservation" is employed here as a kind of blanket term for two of the most basic and intensive forms of preservation, fostered, and advanced by the likes of Muir, Pinchot, and other pioneering environmentalists (Hirsch 1971; Heacox 1996; Hall 2014; Westover 2016). The most uncompromising kind is radical conservation: human entry/activity is prohibited or severely restricted to typically large-sized tracts of land or sea, often called "nature/wildlife reserves," "refuges," or "sanctuaries" (Duffey 1974; Allin 1990; McLaughlin 1993; Lester and others 2009; Doyle 2017). The non-human is thus preserved for the aim of its continued existence and unfolding, now and into the future, for its own sake. This is the most literal and basic form of preservation, given that it shields the non-human from human interactivity, which often involves the various destructive anthropocentric expressions outlined earlier. But what does ecocentrism bring to this established discourse-practice? It insists that conservation should not just be reserved for natural (typically "pristine") ecosystems but also for built environments. Today, such an insistence is needed more than ever, given neoliberalism's obsession to destroy the old and replace it with the often-blandly new, especially when it comes to urban structures and environments (Brenner and Theodore 2002; Weber 2002; Harvey 2006). And so, full-blown conservation is the strongest form of eco-preservation: natural and built environments are literally protected and thus saved from anthropogenic devastation. To be sure, radical conservation is an extreme measure but a necessary one, given human supremacism's ever-expanding reach and insatiability.

A second form of conservation is less intensive and more "compromising" in the sense that larger tracts of land and sea are protected but some human intervention is allowed, such as restricted logging, mining, and tourism; these places tend to be called "national/state forests/parks" (Sellars 2009; von Hardenberg and others 2017). To be sure, these parks have problematic histories, such as the displacement of native human inhabitants in order to create them (Spence 1999; Gissibl, Höhler and Kupper 2012; Perez 2018; Gilio-Whitaker 2019). Plumwood reminds us that what we Westerners call "wilderness" "is to these [indigenous-human and non-human] others a home" (1993: 183). So the management of such parks must be undertaken with greater sensitivity to native human dwellers. Now, while some damage is inevitably inflicted on these environments due to human intrusion, the damage does not generally threaten their overall integrity, thereby allowing them to perdure and regenerate – but not only for their own sake but also for human use and consumption.

Given the problematic history and "compromising" dimension of these parks, one could reasonably ask whether Earth-centeredness approves or rejects this form of preservation. However, ecocentric letting-be should not to be confused with "hyperseparated understandings of the concept of wilderness" that "demand apartness of nature to the point of insisting that there can be no human influence at all on the *genuinely* natural" (Plumwood 1993: 162). In contrast to a fundamentalistic ecocentrism (which would dogmatically reject human intrusion, endorsing only radical conservation), a nuanced eco-centeredness ratifies this "compromising" conservation, so long as several conditions are met. We first recall how these regions need to be secured and managed sensitively, taking into account existing inhabitants and circumstances. Next, eco-centeredness insists that human use should be restricted to meeting reasonable human needs. So how, for example, could something like tree-logging be allowed? It might be acceptable if, for instance, certain regions can't access harvested trees for justifiable timber needs. The type and degree of human intervention would need to be strictly monitored to minimize our impact. Furthermore, as is the case with radical conservation, ecocentrism insists that not only natural ecosystems but also built environments be protected in this way: ecocentric conservation is all-inclusive; it does not only apply to natural ecosystems. And so, while Earth-centeredness endorses radical conservation in many cases, it also allows human inhabitation/intervention in some cases. Earth-centered leading does not simplistically privilege full-blown conservation over the more compromising kind – it recognizes that what we require is *more of both kinds of conservation*.

We also note how eco-preservation not only applies to natural and built settings but also to individual creatures. For example, one form of eco-preservation is the placement of bans/restrictions on threatened species. Probably the most famous example is the ban on whale hunting, which is observed by much of the international community, while rogue nations are pressured into ceasing or scaling-back this odious activity, with varying degrees of success (Christol, Schmidhauser and Totten 1976; Andresen 1993; Epstein 2005; Dorsey 2014). From an ecocentric perspective, a practice like whale hunting does not meet the criterion of addressing reasonable human needs, so it would be prohibited. (Of course, the Inuit example cited earlier alerts us to the possibility that there might be occasional exceptions to the general rule.)

Another form of eco-preservation is restoration. It typically refers to the revitalization of places (Bradshaw 1980; Berger 1985; Allen 2003; Clewell and Aronson 2007; Court 2012; Martin 2017). Ecocentrism straightaway recognizes how conservation (especially the radical kind) is more preferable than restoration, given that what is often lost is typically irrevocable, especially ecologies like old-growth forests (Elliot 1982; Katz 1992). After all, conservation is preventative while restoration is curative. But restoration's "deficiency" in this regard does not entail its wholesale rejection (Ladkin 2005): it will often be vastly preferable to no eco-intervention whatsoever.

Now, as with the other Earth-centered expressions unpacked in the present chapter, truly ecocentric restoration seeks to revitalize both the natural *and the artifactual*. Given our acquaintance and endorsement of laudable human attempts to recuperate species and ecologies (e.g., breeding programs seek to repopulate species threatened with extinction; humans often participate in the rewilding of damaged ecosystems), we focus here on the renewal of manufactured products that have naturally deteriorated but are restored to their "former glory." An excellent and popular example of this activity is car restoration (Stubenrauch 1984; Berger 2001; Simeone and others 2012), whereby humans interrupt their anthropocentric, object-ignoring ways and exhibit care – even love – toward the manufactured object. The rejuvenation of built things also mitigates against the homocentric drive to obsessively replace old products with new ones, facilitated by planned obsolescence (discussed earlier). Once again, Mathews is clear in this regard: "we shall have to maintain them [homes, cars, etc.], since we shall need to continue to use and inhabit them. Inhabitation will also call for adaptation and aesthetic enhancement. But this is compatible with a fundamental attitude of letting be . . . rather than insisting upon further cycles of demolition and 'redevelopment'" (1999a: 124).

At this juncture, given our foregrounding of a practice like restoration, we emphatically note how ecocentrism certainly does not privilege the new or renewed but rather embraces the new, the renewed, and the old, while also squarely accepting the realities of death and disintegration for the biotic and abiotic, respectively. We recall how letting-be is also a letting-grow-old – we're reminded here of Mathews' wonderful article title "Letting the Earth Grow Old" – and, by extension, this ethos also affirms a letting-die and a letting-disintegrate. Earth-centeredness is certainly not a denial of aging, death, and decomposition. Ecocentrism recognizes and affirms how "unfolding" does not merely involve emergence and flourishing (i.e., the new and young) but it also involves decline and dissolution, death, and non-existence; one could say that unfolding also involves "de-folding." While our homocentric aesthetic assesses this second crucial stage of unfolding in negative terms (abandoned objects are typically described according to a lexicon of "ruin," "decay," "dilapidation," etc.), an ecocentric aesthetic values and affirms the natural de-folding of things: ceasing-to-be is just as integral to the process of unfolding as coming-to-be. Ecocentrically speaking, the old is just as alluring as the new.

Now, given that we're discussing various forms or methods of eco-preservation, we could ask whether recycling belongs to this category. Like some of the other important subjects discussed in this chapter (eco-education, population stabilization, etc.), we shall only summarily treat this topic in order to keep the study manageable. First of all, recycling is a kind of eco-preservation: while the whole original product might not be saved, elements of it – its constituent parts or "materials" – are conserved in the new object. Furthermore, the recycled thing "sacrifices" itself for other non-human entities in that it saves them from being transformed into things for human use and consumption. But certain conditions need to be met in order for properly ecocentric recycling to take place. Entities should be recycled into eco-friendly items that meet reasonable human requirements. I also think the need for recycling would decline when only necessary and durable products are made, whereas today's recycling industry has an interest in greater recycling because it means bigger profits (Meyer-Abich 1993: 100). Furthermore, recycling should not be construed as a cure-all for *all* manufactured waste: not all waste can be eliminated. One of the world's leading philosophers, Slavoj Žižek, makes this point in his inimitable way: "The ideal of 'recycling' involves the utopia of a self-enclosed circle in which all waste, all useless remainder, is sublated: nothing gets lost, all trash is re-used. . . . [A]lready in nature itself, there is no circle of total recycling, there is un-usable waste" (2010a: 35) – though what I would emphasize here is that nature recycles much more than anthropocentric humanity, and it creates much less waste (McDonough and Braungart 2002).

Žižek discloses another risky dimension of the way recycling is presently framed: it displaces much/most of the responsibility for ecological devastation and reparation from the most powerful – and therefore most potentially effective – agents (governments and corporate producers) to individual citizens–consumers; in other words, conventional anthropocentric recycling is part of a set of "environmental" practices where the onus is placed squarely on the individual. Žižek remarks: "We recycle old paper, we buy organic food, we install long-lasting light bulbs – whatever – just so we can be sure that we are doing something" (2010b). While I propose that this push for recycling is positive insofar as it habituates us into becoming more eco-friendly consumer–citizens, it shifts too much accountability to us individuals, with the risk/reality of turning us into eco-neurotic "consumer scapegoats" – as Akenji memorably puts it (2014, 2019).

Furthermore, we must recognize that recycling is only *one* mechanism for overcoming environmental problems. Herein lies the truth and value of the tripartite eco-mantra "reduce, reuse, recycle." Recycling is graphically and logically preceded by two even more important practices. The first is reduction – especially in terms of the reduction of production, consumption, and use. Re-usage is also key: with greater re-utilization comes less wastage and recycling; fewer non-human others are required to replace disposed objects. But recycling is nevertheless a crucial form of eco-preservation. Hence, despite his reservations about this process, Meyer-Abich is still able to insist that "There is a requirement that we should recycle" (1993: 105) – especially an ecocentric kind of recycling.

As with the case of restoring manufactured things, one could also object that recycling defies the Earth-centered ethos of letting-be in the sense that disposed objects should just be allowed to dematerialize. To reiterate, once again: letting-be is not simply reducible to absolute non-intervention. Mathews herself allows for a moderate interventionism: "as beings with a constitutive interest in our own self-preservation and the preservation of our nearest and dearest, we are on occasion to intervene in these unfoldings" (1999a: 123). These needs often require practices like restoration and recycling to meet basic-higher needs (shelter, transportation, aesthetic development, etc.). Earth-centeredness not only positively endorses the existence of the artifactual (from fax machines to cars) but also the prolonging of their being – whether by restoration or recycling – in order to meet human and non-human needs. *Some* products are maintained to unfold for longer than might naturally be the case, especially when there are good reasons for doing so.

Some Leaderly Measures for Eco-Liberation and Eco-Preservation

Now that we've provided synopses of eco-liberation and eco-preservation, we're able to identify and explore some leaderly measures that would foster these practices, thereby contributing to the transformation of homocentric situations and the maintenance of ecocentric ones. Once again, the two broad policies of eco-education and population stabilization would facilitate the goals of ecocentric emancipation and conservation. First, the re-education program would create awareness of our eco-colonizing and ecocidal ways, and the countervailing forces of eco-liberation and eco-preservation. The pedagogical campaign would teach us that the emancipation of humans and sentient creatures should be extended to the apparently "unfreeable" – exemplified by manufactured objects and built environments, which have hitherto been neglected as entities requiring or deserving emancipation. (We could suggest here that the teaching materials would include the plastic bag scene from *American Beauty* and the series *Life After People*.) After all, the more aware we are of the negative and positive practices, the more likely the prospect of halting the former and fostering the latter. Likewise, the implementation of a sensible demographic policy would likely have a positive impact on eco-centered liberation and preservation. For instance, regulating population numbers would lessen the pressure for us to encroach on uninhabited or relatively uninhabited areas, be they the outskirts of existing cities or wilderness areas. (In this regard, there's a growing body of work linking population growth with urban sprawl; e.g., Congedo and Macchi 2015; Tena 2015; Fertner and others 2016).

Then there are more specific measures concerning ecocentric liberation and preservation. In the first place, how does Earth-centered leadership envisage emancipation? We may commence by stating that we ecocentrists are inspired by the direct action of groups like the Animal Liberation Front, which have often freed imprisoned animals from farms and labs, and we also understand actions like eco-sabotage by groups like Earth First!, who are driven by compassion for the creatures and frustration with the system (Manes 1990; McLaughlin 1993; Rosebraugh 2004; Braggs 2012). We note, however, that practices involving, for example, the destruction of buildings is problematic from a consistently eco-centered perspective: should buildings wherein barbaric activities are undertaken be themselves disfigured in the name of eco-liberation? On the one hand, drastic action is required, which often entails "collateral damage"; on the other hand, we should ask whether/to what extent these kinds of localized acts are effective, in contrast to examining ways in which the broader contexts or "mega-situations" that foster eco-colonization might be transformed. What kinds of political conditions/systems would be conducive for overcoming eco-colonization and realizing eco-liberation? As noted earlier, this massive question cannot be comprehensively broached in this work, though it's traversed to some degree in the next section. In any case, one could propose that ecocentric leading favors neither "piecemeal" direct action nor mega-situational transformation but *both the one and the other.*

We now turn to a brief exposition of some leaderly measures for eco-preservation. To begin with, we note that already-cited measures would contribute to the advancement of this Earth-centered expression; for example, a central aspect of ecocentric education would be fostering the awareness that we need to conserve our natural and built ecologies. In terms of specific strategies drawn from our exploration of eco-preservation, obviously radical conservation would be a/the key measure, whereby Earth-centered leadership would both reinforce and expand the practice. Existing wildlife reserves would be strengthened in terms of providing more defensive/security staff, even mobilizing military forces to protect them from deplorable practices like poaching and the killing of rangers (Joyce 2013; Wilkie 2016; Canney 2017; Nuwer 2018; Losh 2019). Furthermore, wherever possible, existing reserves would be expanded, and new reserves would be established (Noss and others 2012; Wuerthner, Crist and Butler 2015; Wilson 2016). After all, very little of the world is presently protected (15% of land and 4% of oceans; UNEP-WCMC and IUCN 2016; Stuart Pimm in Dell'amore 2014), and we continue to encroach upon more of it at alarmingly rapid rates (McLaughlin 1993: 213–216; Haila and Henle 2014). Eco-centered leading would also seek to extend the coverage of limited-use national parks.

In typical ecocentric fashion, the extension of protection would also apply to built environments. Such a measure would inhibit the incessant march of "re-development." It would allow houses and warehouses and trees to grow old. Hence, under Earth-centered leadership, current heritage practices would be expanded and intensified. For instance, whenever possible, existing old buildings would be vigilantly protected and restored rather than demolished and replaced (and often replaced with drab new structures). Protection and restoration are urgently required in various places – especially in my hometown, Melbourne. While the original settlement obviously resulted from dubious colonialization, during the gold-rush days of the 1800s, it developed into a remarkably opulent city ("Marvelous Melbourne" rivaled the world's most prestigious urban centers), but it has now lost hundreds of its heritage buildings (Roe 1974; Davidson 1978, 2004; Chapman and Stillman 2015; Broome and others 2016). It's becoming – or already has become – a ubiquitous globalized city.

With Earth-centered leading, whatever exists has precedence over the (ill-) conceived, no matter how much more "profitable" the latter may be for property developers and the politicians who work in concert with them (Lorimer 1978; Richmond 2009; Rainford 2015). Of course, ecocentric leadership would not fanatically protect *every* old dwelling: as noted earlier, some structures may not be salvageable or restorable, while others may need to be demolished due to hazardous construction materials. Earth-centeredness is not a "hyper-conservationism-at-any-cost," where human safety and other needs are compromised. Further, eco-preservation certainly allows old buildings such as schools and hospitals to be renovated to modernize their facilities (to expand their carrying capacity, to become more energy efficient, and so on): we repeat Mathews' imperative to "maintain them, since we shall need to continue to use and inhabit them" (1999a: 124). But, of course, any maintenance or alterations would need to be kept to a minimum in order to retain much/most of the original structure and character.

Eco-centered leadership would also seek to implement policies that encourage and enforce the preservation of other constructed things – and not just those objects that have traditionally received the most attention, such as cars, artworks, and furniture. But how do we become enchanted by mundane objects so that we restore them (or allow them to be) rather than trash them and destroy them? Certainly, the re-education program would seek to instill in all of us not just a fascination and concern over more exotic and aesthetically pronounced items but also for the overlooked and underwhelming by, for example, drawing our attention to enchantment-inducing scientific and other discourses like those recalled in the previous chapter. But, certainly, one of the challenges of ecocentric leading would be to find ways of facilitating the re-enchantment of the unenchanted.

Like the other measures foregrounded here, recycling would also be encouraged and intensified – intensified because, despite appearances, there's less recycling occurring than might be assumed by consumer–citizens. For instance, it's estimated that over 90% of plastics ever produced – over 8 billion metric tons – hasn't been recycled (Geyer, Jambeck and Law 2017; Parker 2018). Hence, the need for the intensification of recycling efforts. However, Earth-centered leading would seek to alter the individual-centered recycling discourse, thereby relieving citizen-consumers of the anxieties and neuroses generated by the existing recycling paradigm. We note that measures relating to other eco-expressions would also be influential for restoration and recycling processes. For instance, producers would be obliged to create long-lasting items rather than short-"lived" ones, which means there would be less recycling and restoration required.

I end my discussion of ecocentric expressions and eco-leaderly measures on the following important note: some of the proposed measures identified and briefly discussed earlier – especially population stabilization and production control – are quite radical and confronting in nature. This is unsurprising from the perspective of my basic model, which contends that true leading involves the transformation and maintenance of situations. At both the mundane and societal levels, this will often necessitate bold action. Hence, genuine environmental leading will often require courage – a dimension that has been under-researched but increasingly recognized by leadership scholars (e.g., Moore 1994; Chaleff 1995; ILA 2019).

Now that we've completed outlines of the five key eco-centered expressions and discussed some of the core leaderly measures associated with them, we're at the stage of offering some concluding remarks in relation to them. First, it has become apparent that Earth-centered leading (together with the eco-philosophical ethos that drives it) would condition and permeate all fundamental aspects of society, just as homocentrism and homocentric leading condition and permeate all fundamental aspects of Western and increasingly Westernized cultures. Just as human chauvinism informs our contemporary modes of instrumentalization, consumption, and production, and drives eco-colonization and ecocide, Earth-centered leading would contribute to profoundly altering how we Westerners instrumentalize, consume, and produce, and it would seek to eradicate eco-colonization and ecocide by promoting ecocentric liberation and restoration. Given the preliminary and synoptic nature of the outline, a number of questions remain: the subsequent sections seek to cursorily address two important inquiries, the one concerning the political (i.e., what is the politics of ecocentric leadership?), the other concerning ethical justification (i.e., why is Earth-centered leading ethically preferable?).

The Leaderly and the Political

One of the crucial tasks of this chapter has been to attempt to identify and justify leaderly measures. What has become blatantly obvious is the ambitious and truly disruptive nature of a number of the proposed actions. Their rather radical character inevitably obliges us to entertain the following question: what kinds of political contexts or systems would be most conducive for leading for the Earth? In other words, under what political conditions would the above mechanisms be most likely to be implemented? In sum: what might be the politics of ecocentric leadership?

We straightaway grasp a sense of the magnitude of this line of inquiry – and the inquiry's magnitude is precisely a primary reason for suspending it. Furthermore, my research background lies with *environmental* philosophy rather than *political* philosophy, and the present study is a work in environmental *leadership* rather than environmental *politics*. Of course, there is interrelation and overlap between the leaderly and the political, but I've been proceeding according to the premise that they are somewhat distinguishable. This commonality and differentiation explain why the political question has been "suspended" here in both senses of the word: on the one hand, it has hovered over this study, especially in its discussion of transformative eco-leaderly measures; on the other hand, it has been withheld for the aforementioned reasons (it exceeds my specializations; it may be differentiated from leadership; its suspension acts as a monographic limit).

Another reason why I've refrained from articulating ecocentric leadership's political dimension is that if I were to explicitly theorize it, then it could be argued that the present research would pass over from the field of environmental leadership studies (ELS) toward the domain of environmental political theory (EPT) and even environmental political science (EPS), which are quite distinct from ELS (e.g., Hays and Hays 1987; Pearce 1991; Eckersley 1992; Timberlake 1992; Davis 1996; Salleh 1997; Carter 2001; Meyer 2001, 2018; Miles and others 2002; Schreurs 2002; Kassiola 2003; Andronova 2004; Elliott 2004; Robbins 2004; Betsill, Hochstetler and Stevis 2005; DeSombre 2007; Mitchell 2008; Dauvergne 2012; Dobson 2016; Gabrielson and others 2016; Arias-Maldonado and Trachtenberg 2019).

While I shall retrace the field of ELS in the next chapter (thereby allowing me to situate my model within the discipline), we may briefly identify key differences and commonalities between ELS and environmental political theory.

A leading scholar of EPT, John M. Meyer, succinctly summarizes three core goals of his chosen field. First, EPT derives from the discipline of political theory, which focuses on key concepts such as democracy, justice, freedom, and representation. ELS, on the other hand, emerges from leadership studies, which focuses on notions of transformation, followership, authenticity, and so on. Next, environmental political theory hones in on notions like sustainability, environment, and nature (Meyer 2018: 435). ELS also focuses on these concepts, but not always or exclusively: in the present work, there are also other fundamental notions at play, especially ecocentrism and anthropocentrism.

The third core goal of EPT identified by Meyer is the one that has most common ground with ELS – or at least should have the most common ground: "EPT moves beyond critique to advance normative arguments for alternative arrangements of social and political ideas and institutions" (2018: 435). Like EPT, I think environmental leadership studies is/should be both critical and constructive, descriptive and prescriptive, analytical and ethico-politically oriented. While I have not explicitly provided any content to alternative Earth-centered institutional/systemic arrangements in this study, the requirement for such arrangements is signaled when I suggest contentious measures like a stringent population stabilization policy, a more regulated economy, etc. Of course, there's nothing surprising about the shared normative dimension of ELS and environmental political theory/science: researchers from the various fields share a deep concern for the Earth and the ways in which we humans are disfiguring it.

This concern was originally discursively expressed by a number of the foundational environmental thinkers foregrounded in the present work, who likewise also sought or imagined "alternative arrangements" that would foster a more ecological society. We may quickly retrace here some of their thinking in this regard. To begin with, Leopold, Meyer-Abich, Mathews, and Morton contest the notion and practice of private property (Leopold 1989: viii; Meyer-Abich 1993: 126; Mathews 1999a: 129; Morton 2016: 44). Next, a number of the scholars are critics of consumerist society. As noted earlier, Meyer-Abich advances a consumer revolution, and, in a similar vein, Callicott speculates whether what might be required is "a virtual revolution in prevailing attitudes and lifestyles" (1989: 37–38). Meyer-Abich also provocatively proposes that "the greatest political task is to develop, if not a world state, at least some kind of international solidarity" (1993: 61). While the notion of a "world state" might be contentious (consider the neoliberal "new world order"), I also think it is rigorous, given that many of our ecological challenges are global and appear to require some kind of "new world *eco*-order" (cf. Leinen and Bummel 2019).

Furthermore, some of the foundational thinkers interrogate contemporary forms of democracy. For instance, as noted earlier, White stunningly identifies modern Western democracy as the key driver for the eco-crisis (1967: 1204) – a point that has not been sufficiently emphasized by both his supporters and critics – and instead advocates some kind of Francis-inspired divine democracy (1967: 1206), which I think would operate very differently from contemporary versions. Environmental scholars Ben A. Minteer and Robert E. Manning note how White was among a group of scholars from the 1960s and 1970s who identified democracy as a source of the eco-crisis and thus openly toyed with a more authoritarian alternative sociopolitical arrangement: "The eco-apocalyptic literature of this time often flirted with (and in some cases openly endorsed) an authoritarian political solution to various environmental crises (e.g., Ehrlich 1968; Hardin 1968; Ophuls 1977)" (2005: 170). While authoritarian regimes are rightly often criticized, might not some kind of "benevolent-authoritarian" form of leadership be required to overcome the anthropocentric authoritarianism that is concealed by seductive myths such as "free markets" and "absolute individual freedom"? Of course, the mere posing of this kind of question typically brings the immediate charge of "eco-fascism." Returning to White, we note how he advances socio-economic reform and even contemplates the possibility of radical transformation: "Every part of mankind [sic] needs social and economic reform, and perhaps some need revolution" (1978: 104).

Like White, McLaughlin advocates significant social – especially economic – reform, even though his *Regarding Nature* (1993) is light on details. Given McLaughlin's emphasis on industrialism as a/the root cause of eco-crisis (cf. Leopold 1989: viii; Eckersley 1992: 22–23, discussed shortly), he argues for "fundamentally transforming industrialism" (1993: 198). We note how the eco-philosopher is not recommending industrialization's abolition (in previous pages, he emphasizes that he is not calling for a return to primitivism) but rather modifying it into something profoundly moderate, non-expansionary, post-consumerist, anti-anthropocentric, joyful, and so on. Bookchin also speculates about the possibility/necessity of profound upheaval, though somewhat less tentatively than White or McLaughlin: "I would like to ask if the environmental crisis does not have its roots in the very constitution of society as we know it today, if the changes that are needed to create a new equilibrium between the natural world and the social do not require a fundamental, indeed revolutionary, reconstitution of society along ecological lines" (1980: 74).

Mathews is harder to place when it comes to the economic–political dimension of her ecocentrism. On the one hand, she's suspicious of conventional left-egalitarian ideologies due to their lingering human-centeredness (1999a: 127), so it's unsurprising that she's suspicious of socialist revolutions (1999a: 133–134). On the other hand, she's a critic of capitalism, so, given her aversion to radical politics, she favors a less drastic form of transition, suggesting a kind of withdrawal or effort to "extricate oneself, to a significant degree, from the ideological grid of capitalism," so we effectively "become defectors," even though Mathews rightly questions whether such extrication will undo the system (1999a: 130). Nonetheless, the task is to move toward "an entirely different 'economics', or way of ensuring the satisfaction of our material wants and needs" (1999a: 130). Mathews then entertains the notion of more drastic action, such as reinhabiting places earmarked for capitalist "development," thereby frustrating the developers' goals. With her politics of reinhabitation, Mathews finally accepts that what may be required are both "creative and forceful ways" of disrupting and replacing capitalism (1999a: 131). But, as I say, she dismisses the radicalism of the historical left (1999a: 133); instead, Mathews indicates a third way: "the ethos of letting be reconciles something of the custodial role of the right with something of the moral intent of the left" (1999a: 133).

Like Mathews, Eckersley is suspicious of conventional left-wing radicalism. She notes how orthodox communism did not prove ecologically progressive (1992: 23–25). Like McLaughlin, Eckersley claims that the fundamental eco-culprit is neither capitalism nor communism but industrialization, given that ecological disfiguration occurred across the ideological divide: "the international nature of environmental degradation has lent force to the broader claim by emancipatory theorists that the modern ecological crisis is the quintessential crisis of *industrialism*" (1992: 22–23). Nevertheless, during her summary and analysis of ecosocial thought (citing the likes of Gorz and Martin Ryle [1988]), Eckersley does not shy away from representing controversial topics such as the possible/probable need for a planned economy and a strong state apparatus for undertaking ecocentric goals such as the production and distribution of essential goods (1992: 133). Indeed, she acknowledges that ecosocialism "would also enable ecocentrism to anticipate and address in a more concerted way the various forms of opposition that are likely to be encountered in the attempt to give practical expression to ecocentric emancipatory goals" (1992: 132; key ecosocialist texts include, e.g., Ryle 1988; Pepper 1993; Bari 1995; Thornett 2019).

We may also briefly note here how Eckersley claims that "no emancipatory theorist has been able to come up with an entirely novel social and political arrangement, that is, one that has not already been mooted in modern social and political theory" (1992: 31). We may briefly respond by suggesting that perhaps the aim of emancipatory theory is not to seek something "entirely novel" but rather to reimagine existing models: this is exactly what I do in *Following Reason*, where I re-cast Plato's much-ridiculed theory of "philosopher-rulers" (1974) into the concept of "logicracy" – rule/leadership by a collective Reason. An exposition of this model – especially in terms of its relations or synthesis with ecocentric leadership theory – exceeds the contours of the current study. Certainly, one of the key tasks, then, of both environmentally oriented leadership studies and political theory is to attempt to conceive the kind/s of "social and political arrangements" that would be conducive for genuine, bold, and effective Earth-centered leading and politics.

Of course, another key social arrangement is the economic one. As the above review of Mathews' political thoughts shows, the economic question is just as crucial as the political: what kinds of economics would be conducive for ecocentric existence? While we touched on this subject in relation to the leaderly measure of restricted production and referred to the growing discipline of eco-logical economics, the subject is not further explored here because we have neither the expertise nor the space to explore it, even though, given the radical nature of Earth-centeredness, I tend to side with the environmental thinkers who deeply question the existing economic order (Bookchin 1971, 1980, 1982; Catton 1980; Pearce 1991; Bari 1995; Best 2014). One could posit that emerg-ing disciplines like ecological economics have responded to McLaughlin's 1993 observation that "So far, the role of economic systems in the generation of ecological problems has received relatively little attention by environmental philosophers" (1993: 17), but ELS would also benefit by paying more attention to it.

The Leaderly and the Ethical

As has become patently obvious over the course of the last two chapters, ecocen-trism involves strongly ethical, normative dimensions (i.e., maximal allowing and minimal intervention; demographic stabilization; etc.). Now, the proposi-tion that eco-centered leading is ethical does not contradict the proposition advanced in my book, *Following Reason*, that leadership "as such" is ethically "neutral" (2019: 21, 39, 50). As explained in the work and reiterated earlier in this book, my *general* definition of leadership may be used to determine *whether* leading takes place (by ascertaining whether sufficient situational change or maintenance is attempted) rather than also seeking to evaluate whether *ethi-cal/unethical* leading occurs. As articulated in *Following Reason*, the question of whether leading may or may not be ethical is a "second-order" issue. We emphasize that the expression "second-order" does not in any way imply that the basic question of whether leading occurs is "more significant" than the question of whether ethical or unethical leading occurs; the phrase simply refers to methodological priority: systematic leadership research first needs to ascer-tain whether acts are leaderly before assessing whether they're ethical.

So when investigations of leadership advance beyond the general question and begin to explore the nature and actions of various *kinds* of leading, the ethical question enters the fray. How so? For instance, an assumption in *Fol-lowing Reason* that is not always explicated or defended in any sustained way is that rational leadership is (more) ethical while anti-rational leadership is (more) unethical. The assumption is not heavily defended because I note that the question of the ethical is indeed a deeply complex and complicated one (2019: 7), though I think that the whole of *Following Reason* acts as a kind of implicit running argument for the ethicality of rational leading over the unethicality of anti-rational leading. Finally, the book assumes that its readers are already drawn to rationality at least to some degree, so it follows that the readership itself is likely to favor rational leading over anti-rational leading; in other words, *Following Reason* generally "preaches to the converted" – and to potential converts (2019: 7). (This is not to dogmatically exclude the possibility that skeptics might be swayed by the work.)

Given that this monograph explores a specific environmental mode of leading, it's driven by the same kind of presupposition: that ecocentric leadership is profoundly ethical while anthropocentric leadership is devastatingly unethical. One may rightly wonder whether I've devoted sufficient time to explicating and defending the presupposition – hence, in a sense, it remains a presupposition. But *if* the presupposition has been insufficiently augmented, that is because its augmentation remains secondary to the study's principle task, which is an elementary description of Earth-centered leading. Furthermore, and as I've previously noted, given the nature, extent, and disastrous effects of anti-environmental attitudes, practices, and leading – culminating today in the multipronged eco-crisis – one questions whether a sustained argument in favor of ecocentrism and Earth-centered leadership is absolutely necessary, especially when others have thoroughly documented the deteriorating state of the world (e.g., Meadows and others 1972; ICIDI 1980; WCED 1987; IAP 1994; UNEA 2019). So while I don't justify the privileging of environmental leadership in any sustained way, my hope is that readers will deem it to be a reasonable and empirically obvious one. And like *Following Reason*, we could also propose that the whole monograph acts as a kind of argument for eco-leadership.

On Our Way to Situating the Theory

In the present chapter, I sought to describe five key ecocentric expressions. As explained earlier, situations are constituted or marked by expressions. Hence, if a given situation is pervaded/dominated by either a homocentric or Earth-centered expression, then the situation is more likely to be characterized as either homocentric or ecocentric. So the task for eco-centered leading is to introduce measures that either maintain any/all of the five key ecocentric expressions within situations or replace their "corresponding" antithetical anthropocentric expressions with the ecocentric ones, so that these situations become (more) eco-centered. Some of the measures identified and discussed earlier included a mass environmental re-education program, a population stabilization policy, an economy based on the production of eco-friendly commodities, and so on. I have also briefly addressed other related questions (such as the suspension of the question of the politics of ecocentric leadership). We're now well-placed to attempt the remaining tasks of the study: reviewing some of the most important works in ELS, and comparing and contrasting them with my ecocentric model.

5

REVIEWING THE LITERATURE, SITUATING THE THEORY

The Review's Structure

Now that we've outlined our theory of ecocentric leadership, we're able to situate it within the burgeoning field of environmental leadership studies (ELS). By "situate," I mean a process involving critically comparing and contrasting the conceptualization developed here with *some* of the field's most important English-language texts. (Hence, one of the many questions opened up by this study but can't be addressed by it is whether/to what extent ELS has developed in the non-English-speaking world. Furthermore, given that the present work follows the rigorous postulation innovatively redeveloped in *Following Reason* that leading differs from managing, the review does not include works belonging to the adjacent field of environmental management studies (e.g., Pauchant and Fortier 1990; Hanna 1995; Russo 1999; Darnall and others 2000; Harris and Crane 2002; Fujii and Managi 2016). However, the retracing does identify cases where eco-leadership scholars confuse leading with managing. Another reason why this review is rather limited is because a thorough retracing of the entire field of ELS would be a massive task in itself that would greatly expand the book's already-expansive ambit.

The review is arranged according to three sometimes-overlapping categories, so they should be understood more in terms of a continuum than absolutely distinct classifications: "Early Efforts," "Conservative-Regressive ELS," and "Critical-Progressive ELS." The labels are fairly self-explanatory but require some clarifications and qualifications here. First of all, I reiterate that these are not (always) clear-cut categories; writings may exhibit both regressive and progressive elements (e.g., Vredenburg and Westley 1993; Brymer and others 2010; Bettridge and Whiteley 2013). Turning to the first classification, I pay quite sustained attention to the early works, not only because they often offer a variety of engaging insights but also because some of them appear to have been neglected by more recent research, so the review also acts as a kind of homage to these pioneering works.

The second category ("conservative-regressive ELS") refers to the group of discourses that remain ensconced in dominant, oppressive, and anti-environmental ideological frameworks such as anthropocentrism and neoliberalism, with their myths of "sustainable development" (for critiques, refer to, e.g., Daly 1990; Plant and Plant 1991; Gunderson, Holing and Light 1995; Springett 2003; Banerjee 2004; Monbiot 2012, 2015), "perpetual economic growth" (Harvey 2014; Satyajit 2017), and so on. These writings lack critical awareness and truly eco-ethical prescriptions, as well as also often being conceptually unclear – especially about founding concepts like "leadership" and "management." I substantiate this claim by analyzing three texts to demonstrate their shortcomings. The fact that this group constitutes a large body of work but whose lack of rigor essentially excludes them from this retracing is a further reason why the present review is not absolutely comprehensive. We also note that I insert the term "regressive" in "conservative-regressive" to differentiate the word "conservative" from other, more progressive significations (e.g., "environmental conservation").

Next, there is the third category of "critical-progressive ELS": "critical" refers to the questioning/criticism of conventional leadership and eco-leadership models, and "progressive" refers to works that are more enlightened and forward-thinking, which includes abandoning anthropocentrism and drawing closer to ecocentrism (even critical-progressive ELS tends to remain biocentric). As is the case with the regressive category, I do not survey every significant critical-progressive work but rather highlight a number of the most important writings. And so, the review is more selective than sweeping, even though it remains quite comprehensive within its limited scope: I've been unable to identify a more comprehensive review of ELS (especially its more critical-progressive works). But to reiterate: the retracing does not seek to map *every* contribution to ELS but a number of the most significant ones, and I critically compare a number of them with my theorization. Of course, the discipline warrants a comprehensive history – though the fact that such a project appears to have not yet been undertaken/completed testifies to the still-relatively-nascent character of our field.

For the sake of minimizing repetition, I also use synonymous terms for the two classifications of "conservative-regressive" and "critical-progressive": I occasionally employ the established scholarly categories of "Dominant Social Paradigm (DSP)" and "New Environmental/Ecological Paradigm (NEP)" (Pirages and Ehrlich 1973; Dunlap and van Liere 1978, 1984; Dunlap and others 2000; Boiral, Cayer and Baron 2009) – with the provision that I recognize that even the New Ecological Paradigm may not be so "new," given that it often appears to retain vestiges of anthropocentrism and other dominant mindsets-practices (Lundmark 2007).

Early Efforts

How does a scholarly field emerge? Obviously in different ways, from the relatively quick-forming and organized to the slow-burning and haphazardly coalescing. A perfect example of the first category is the philosophical (and rather ecocentric) school of speculative realism (cited earlier), which has a precise starting-point (a 2007 University of London conference), numerous "charismatic" advocates (e.g., Graham Harman, Quentin Meillasoux, Ray Brassier), a strong Internet presence, and many adherents (Bryant, Srnicek and Harman 2011). ELS, on the other hand, appears to belong to the set of disciplines that have emerged slowly and inchoately, as suggested by the following review.

According to my literature search, the first scholarly work explicitly focusing in a relatively sustained and systematic way on the question and phenomenon of environmental leadership is the multi-authored *Environmental Leadership: A Sourcebook for Staff and Volunteer Leaders of Environmental Organizations* (1984d), with philosopher–environmentalist Stuart Langton editing the work and also writing and co-writing a number of the essays. The present review focuses on the first two chapters and briefly refers to the Introduction, all written by Langton. In the Introduction, he states that his volume "is not a scholarly work," given that it's "primarily written by and for environmental activists" (1984a: ix), a function clearly stipulated by the book's sub-title – though, as I'll show, there are some very scholarly dimensions to Langton's writing.

The first chapter is poignantly titled "The Future of the Environmental Movement" (Langton 1984b). The author rightly observes how the movement in America has been transformed from something more charismatic to something more institutionalized (Weber 1947, 1967), and while others view this transformation with suspicion (including myself, to a certain degree), Langton optimistically/naïvely regards it as a "success" (1984b: 4). During his description of this transformation, he notes: "it is a movement less marked by inspirational leaders and more dominated by leaders who manage" (1984b: 4). Straightaway, we ask whether this notion of "leaders who manage" is not a contradiction, and if not, why not. According to the general theory of leading I formulated in *Following Reason* and have drawn upon to outline a theory of eco-leading here, leading and managing are different and not synonymous. By definition, leaders lead and managers manage. "Leaders who manage" are not leaders but managers. Hence, if Langton's observation of the 1980s American environmental movement rings true (as I think it does), then we're forced to conclude that the environmental movement has been more managed than led, which means that basically anthropocentric situations are maintained in the relative absence of eco-leaderly contestation.

Langton's apparent merging of managing with leading is all-the-more per-plexing because, in the second chapter, he broaches the important question of their difference. He emphasizes that "the two terms are not interchangeable," adding that "This distinction . . . is very important for environmental organi-zations to understand because it clarifies some of their most common needs and difficult problems" (1984c: 13). Langton begins his analysis by acknowledging that the history of leadership and management theory is marked by a plethora of definitions and definitional disagreements. In order to distinguish the two notions-phenomena, Langton performs the classic scholastic move of retrac-ing their etymologies, a strategy that proves to be very productive: he postu-lates that the word "leadership" is derived from the Anglo-Saxon/Celtic word *laeden*, which "means to travel, to go, to move in some way, to set a direction" (1984c: 13). Straightaway, we note that many conventional definitions express the notion of motion (such as Burns's concept of "transformational leadership"), an idea that's also incorporated into our formulation with the concept of situ-ational *change* – though we add that leading can also involve situational *main-tenance*, which is the very opposite of situational transformation. Hence, the etymological investigation is half-right: leadership is a moving, but it's also a kind of stasis or defending-preserving whenever opposing leadership seeks to transform existing states of affairs.

Next, Langton notes that the word "manage" "means something quite the opposite" to leadership-as-movement (1984c: 13). The author explains how "The French *ménage*, for example, means housekeeping. A related word, *manège*, an equestrian term, means to bring under control, as in reining in and controlling a horse" (1984c: 13). Langton's etymological investigation confirms my own proposition that managing is the maintenance of uncontested situa-tions. Now, citing the likes of Burns and the pioneering French management theorist Henri Foyol (1949), Langton draws the following conclusion: "Leader-ship relates to directing or moving the organization to achieve some purpose or to serve some value. . . . Management, on the other hand, is concerned with maintaining order over the resources and practices of the organization" (1984c: 13). Langton's summation of a/the fundamental difference between leading and managing at the organizational level – which I think is generalizable – is synonymous with my own; both of us have arrived at the same/similar finding albeit via different routes. We may also briefly cite here some other common-alities, such as our shared refusal to privilege one activity over the other, and the recognition that leading may often result in failure, but the activity still remains leaderly.

Despite its pioneering insights, Langton's *Environmental Leadership* has rarely been cited by ELS scholars (notable exceptions include Foster 1993; Howardson 2006). While it's not a sustained systematic treatise on the phe-nomenon of eco-leading, the book warrants more recognition, both for fore-grounding the very notion of "environmental leadership" and for its incisive theoretical contributions, especially its etymological retrievals and definitional clarifications.

(As this retracing proceeds chronologically, we may parenthetically cite two works from 1985 here. The first is an article by environmental scientist John Lemons: "Conventional and Alternative Approaches to the Teaching of Leadership in Environmental Programs." The second is a kind of directory or "Who's Who" in environmental leadership: *National Leaders of American Conservation*, which was edited by fisheries scientist Richard H. Stroud. This was an updated, second edition of an original 1971 directory titled *Leaders of American Conservation*, edited by forester Henry Clepper.)

Another piece of writing that deserves citation is resource policy analyst H. William Rockwell's 1991 one-page Commentary for the *Journal of Forestry*, simply titled "Leadership." The text is short but poignant and hard-hitting: it begins by observing that there's a failure of leadership and followership because selfishness reigns today rather than "groupship" – and, according to Rockwell, "Controlling selfishness . . . is exactly what leadership is all about" (1991: 3). This is an extraordinary statement, and while I question whether it applies to leading at the general level (given that I claim that leadership fundamentally has to do with situational transformation/preservation), I think Rockwell's formulation has traction when we consider that there might be a correlation between human supremacism and greed – an important question that I've suspended in the present work. Rockwell also rightly observes that "we call for leadership without understanding what it is" (1991: 3). His observation confirms the point I advanced in *Following Reason* and reiterate in this work that we need to better understand this phenomenon in order to more effectively practice it in its various concrete forms, including the environmental kind. Rockwell concludes by recalling the ethical dimension of (environmental) leading: "It is not just the ethical balancing of established precepts, but the courage and humility to divine, weigh, and balance 'first principles' in the face of tremendous uncertainty" (1991: 3). A balancing act is exactly what occurs with Earth-centeredness: we work in tensions like maximal allowing and minimal intervening, and seeking to fulfill human and non-human needs.

The next notable early work in the field of ELS that I located is a two-volume 1992 publication edited by Donald Snow, a committed environmentalist since the 1970s. He was commissioned in 1989 by the Conservation Fund (founded in 1985) to identify factors for increasing the effectiveness of the environmental movement. The project resulted in two works: *Inside the Environmental Movement: Meeting the Leadership Challenge* (1992), which collates and interprets data from surveys completed by leaders of environmental organizations, and *Voices from the Environmental Movement: Perspectives for a New Era* (1992), which presents articles from some of the participants. Somewhat ironically, while the first volume's title explicitly refers to leadership, the second volume actually devotes more time and space to the subject, even though the contribution is not sustained or extensive.

I begin by briefly citing what is original and laudable about the two volumes. First of all, they categorically seek to identify and explore the relation between good leadership and effective environmentalism. Second, the two works are strongly empirical: they seek to trace what is actually occurring "on the ground," especially with environmental organizations. The venture involved a survey and the analysis of data collated from it: this heavy empirical emphasis becomes a key characteristic of ELS in subsequent years; my philosophically oriented research therefore seeks to contribute to the relatively sparse theoretical space within the field. Relatedly, the Snow volumes seek to be eminently practical and translatable. (My work addresses this dimension with its provision of various eco-leaderly measures discussed in the previous chapter.) Next, given the volumes' focus on organizations, the writings do not limit themselves to the individual agent-centered approach to leadership that was dominant in leadership studies at the time (and still somewhat prevalent), but rather expands the analytical frame to encompass (and primarily focus on) organizations: we could therefore describe the work as being more organization-centered than agent-centered.

Another promising aspect of the two volumes is that they occasionally draw attention to the significance of the political for environmental conservation and reflourishing. For instance, Snow identifies "the careful formulation of policy" as a key characteristic of environmental leadership, as well as "good government, and a massive realignment of ethics and economics" (1992a: xxvi). The instigation of the policies proposed by the present work would certainly facilitate a massive ethico-economic "realignment." Snow also emphasizes how eco-leadership involves a combination of governmental and non-governmental action (1992a: xxxi): this is an excellent point, particularly in/for the present work, where discussions of "measures" or "policies" might be misinterpreted as strictly *governmental* actions. However, "ecocentric leadership" is not reducible to ecocentric political leadership. Ideally, it would involve a powerful mass movement, a process of leading-and-following.

One of the contributors to the volumes, Sally Ann Gumaer Ranney (1992), an environmental leader, also links eco-leadership with radical transformation. Early on in her essay, which focuses on the question of female environmental leaders, Ranney expresses what she considers to be the function of "dynamic" or great leadership, which no doubt applies to the model of eco-leadership advanced in this book: "The ultimate goal: to shift ideologies and actions and steer history" (1992: 110). Ranney also writes about "the power of spontaneous, 'unprofessional' leadership in communities, the majority of which is female" (1992: 124). While Ranney and I thus concur that a mass environmental movement may be required to foster eco-change, Aldemaro Romero, another environmental leader who contributes a chapter to the *Voices* volume, incisively reminds us that eco-leadership may not always involve mass participation, if we go by history: "The big changes in the course of history have occurred thanks to an elite corps of leaders who knew what they had to do and how to do it, and, most important, who to do it" (1992: 142). Mass mobilizations or democratic mechanisms may not always be required for eco-transformation.

We now briskly turn to some of the problematic aspects of the two volumes. While the *Voices* book is more reflective and contains some theorizing, the pair of books are insufficiently theoretical–philosophical. The two volumes rarely cite, critique, or develop existing leadership scholarship. None of the authors seek to define either "leadership" or "environmentalism" and other important concepts, or distinguish related concepts such as "leading" and "managing." In terms of this last question, this is especially surprising, given that Snow introduces the second chapter of the first volume (1992a: 33) with a lengthy quote from John Gardner (1990: 3), who questions the leadership–management distinction; despite the citation, Snow doesn't take up this important question. Likewise, in his introduction to the second volume, G. Jon Roush (1992a), who later became president of the Wilderness Society, recites the famous saying by eminent leadership scholars Warren Bennis and Burt Nanus that "managers are people who do things right and leaders are people who do the right thing" (1985: 21 cited in Roush 1992a: 13) and then asks "how is a leader to know what the 'right thing' is?" (1992a: 13). But Roush only goes on to cite three of the essays in the volume (which aren't reviewed here, given that I'm only analyzing what I consider to be the most important works).

Another indicator of the theoretical "lightness" of the two Snow volumes is that words like "anthropocentrism" and "biocentrism" are rarely mentioned: Snow refers to the former once (1992b: 55), and while Roush refers to it in his main contribution – excellently describing it as "the unsettling idea that as a species, human beings are no more important than other species" (1992b: 8) – he doesn't develop it. Likewise, Snow only refers to biocentrism once (1992a: xxvi). Despite the volumes' flaws, however, one can't deny the collection's significance for ELS, testified by the fact that a number of important scholars cite the works (e.g., Foster 1993; Egri and Herman 2000; Gordon and Berry 2006; Redekop 2010a).

Another trail-blazing ELS work is a 1993 collection of essays by various authors edited by eco-scholars Joyce K. Berry and John C. Gordon titled *Environmental Leadership: Developing Effective Skills and Styles* (1993). As the sub-title indicates with its reference to agential "skills" and "styles," the book is basically agent-centered: the text discusses the kinds of qualities that environment leaders would be said to possess in order to practice effective eco-leadership. Berry and Gordon offer two contributions to the volume: an introductory piece titled "Environmental Leadership: Who and Why" (1993a) and a concluding essay named "Six Insights" (1993b). (Note: while the edited book names Berry first, the introductory and concluding essays reverse the order.) Only the introductory work is reviewed here (the concluding piece is excessively agent-centered and approaches something like the self-help literature that blossomed in the 1990s and which has characterized much leadership discourse.)

To begin with, Gordon and Berry's introductory essay is strong in terms of addressing definitional questions: early on in the piece, the scholars define eco-leading as "the ability of an individual or group to guide positive change toward a vision of an environmentally better future" (1993a: 3). Despite problems like the focus on change (we recall that leading sometimes has to do with preservation) and the ambiguity of phrases like "environmentally better future," the formulation nevertheless has traction on a number of levels, such as the fact that eco-leading can/should take place at the individual and collective levels, which is a timely reminder, given that the present study essentially focuses on eco-leadership on the societal plane. Gordon and Berry then differentiate between "traditional leadership models" and the environmental kind. They insightfully observe how the conventional models have been most frequently derived from politics, the military, and religion, while contemporary leadership studies has been predominantly derived from business and industry. The authors concur that leaderly insights might be gleaned from these social domains, but eco-leadership demands a new kind of understanding, given that these same social domains have created a number of environmental challenges (1993a: 3). Gordon and Berry then register a variety of sensible characteristics of environmental leading, including long-term solutions, a recognition of complexity, science's inability to provide total certainty, and the integration of various epistemologies and concerns (1993a: 4).

The next noteworthy essay in the Berry-Gordon volume is written by Charles H. W. Foster from Harvard's Kennedy School of Government, titled "What Makes a Leader?" (1993). It's an excellent effort that broaches key questions, proceeds systematically, and cites a number of great leadership scholars (e.g., Zaleznik 1966; Burns 1978; Gardner 1990), but it's also marked by shortcomings. The author commences by recalling Langton's etymological study of the keyword (1993: 13). Foster then admirably traverses through a range of leaderly features (including its "essentials," "types," "styles," etc.). He also powerfully reminds us that leadership is often "*dissensual*": "leadership can be expected to generate conflict, sharpen demands, strengthen values, and enhance motives" (1993: 17). This point resonates particularly sharply for us: given that a number of the proposed ecocentric measures are confronting and deeply disruptive, it's reasonable to anticipate that genuine eco-leading will be resisted, which might/may involve conflict with the defenders of anthropocentrism and associated ideologies-systems (such as neoliberalism). Foster sagely observes how "The positive role of dissent is often overlooked and underappreciated in the normal human tendency to avoid trouble" (1993: 17).

Having outlined some of the fundamentals of leadership, Foster is now ready to engage with the question of the nature of environmental leading. According to Foster, eco-leadership refers to "any activity involving the management, use, or protection of natural resources" (1993: 21). Straightaway, we note that this definition is problematic according to my general theorization, given that I contend that leading differs from managing. Furthermore, we note how the formulation remains heavily biocentric, given its focus on *natural* resources, which would exclude human and non-human constructed things like built environments. (Of course, one could also contest the word "resources," but we've insisted that ecocentrism allows for a moderate amount of natural-resource use.) But there are also positive elements to Foster's definition. For example, the incorporation of the terms "use" and "protection" parallel the notions-practices of eco-instrumentalism and eco-preservation (discussed in the previous chapter of this book). As he proceeds, Foster makes some other strong points, such as the need for environmental leadership's translocal and transnational character – a fact that has become more evident with eco-challenges like climate change, which don't observe borders. Foster also notes how environmental leadership will need to become "more consensual" (1993: 23) – this could be construed as contradictory, given that Foster had emphasized leadership's *dissensual* character only a few pages earlier, though one could counter that leading may/will be both dissensual and consensual. But despite any challenges associated with Foster's brief chapter, I think it's one of the best examples of not only early ELS research but of ELS research thus far.

We also briefly note the next essay in the Berry-Gordon collection, which is written by biologist Jack Ward Thomas and titled "Ethics for Leaders": as the heading suggests, the engaging text focuses on questions about eco-leadership ethics. Thomas differentiates between personal, professional, and Leopoldian land ethics. He seems to be an ethical relativist, appearing to accept both anthropocentric and biocentric positions (Thomas 1993: 36–37), while the present work obviously takes – to use quite relativistic language – a less relativistic and more objectivistic stance (or perhaps somewhere between these polarities).

The next essay briskly summarized here is "Managing Conflict" by the environmental mediator Ty Tice. The most interesting thing about this piece is how Tice rightly recognizes how leadership has little to do with conflict mediation, noting that leaders and mediators are different (1993: 70). Indeed, Ty even muses how "Being forever in the middle has a downside. . . . It is with some envy that I see the satisfaction some leaders derive from total commitment to the cause" (1993: 69). I do not dogmatically suggest that environmental leading would *never* involve compromise; however, accommodation does not appear to be a fundamental aspect, given that human chauvinism and ecocentrism are incompatible; they're irresolvable oppositions. On the whole, environmental leadership is/would be an uncompromising phenomenon.

Another noteworthy essay is provided by forestry researcher Henry H. Webster. Titled "Lessons from State and Regional Resource Management" (1993), the first half of the paper focuses on the experiences of environmental organizations, but then it surprisingly turns to the reflective-philosophical question "How does leadership come about?" (1993: 119). Noting the vast amount of literature devoted to the subject, Webster – like a number of esteemed leadership scholars (e.g., Ciulla, Ladkin, etc.) – questions whether there's any "*central* notion" of leading (i.e., a general or universal conception). Admirably, Webster's speculation appears to move beyond the more restricted agent-centered and action-centered models that were dominant during this time. For instance, he provides the following intriguing proposition: "leadership may result from *circumstances* as much as from actions" (1993: 119). Given that our model of leading is somewhat situation-centered, then one could perhaps suggest that there appears to be some commonality here, given the overlap (but not identity) between "circumstances" and "situations": "circumstances" perhaps suggests a higher degree of elements such as contingency and randomness – indeed, Webster judiciously identifies luck as a leadership factor – while the way I employ "situations" doesn't run the risk of ignoring or backgrounding elements like agency, intentionality, and so on. Unfortunately, Webster doesn't deeply probe this question – and nor can I, given the monographic limits – but the fact that he opens up this line of inquiry certainly demonstrates his sophisticated approach to the contemplation of leadership.

The next contribution in the 1993 Berry-Gordon volume that merits some attention in this semi-comprehensive survey is the essay titled "National Leadership" by forestry administrator Jeff M. Sirmon. Like many of the other pieces in the volume, Sirmon commences autobiographically and then reflects on the phenomenon of leadership. He states that "Leaders and leadership come in many forms and styles" (1993: 171). We note two important things about this seemingly "trite" remark. To begin with, Sirmon not only refers to leaders but also to leadership, thereby inferring that leadership is not reducible to individual agents: leading comprises more than those individuals who are "identified" as leaders (nor the followers who follow them). Next, Sirmon correctly observes that there's a variety of leaderly forms – though we would stress that this doesn't imply that we can't identify any conditions or criteria common to all leadership phenomena (such as situational transformation/preservation).

Sirmon then notes how leadership styles have evolved. In the U.S. Forest Service, the dominant authoritarian style – which, he astutely observes, may appear questionable in some ways but was also highly effective (1993: 172) – has given way to more conciliatory approaches. For those of us advancing the claim that more robust eco-leadership is required (a point I've been gradually developing), Sirmon's acknowledgment/confirmation of the effectiveness of more authoritarian methods is a welcomed change from the theorizing that dogmatically rejects any and all forms of authoritarian governance, thereby closing off the question of whether "wicked" problems might require more "wicked" leadership (a question too massive to be addressed here). Indeed, Sirmon himself rigorously speculates that "Leadership in government will become more difficult as competition between resource use and conservation becomes more intense" (1993: 183) – but he backs away from advancing any kind of stern authoritarian style. The question then remains whether a conciliatory approach will be effective, given that it hasn't worked thus far (especially regarding issues such as pollution and climate change).

Sirmon also astutely notes that the nature of followers – especially in the forestry service – has also changed (1993: 182–183). He observes how followers/employees in the forestry service were formerly more homogeneous (mainly male, similar backgrounds, etc.), but there has been growing diversity. Sirmon's discussion of the evolving nature of followers is an important one, especially since leadership studies in general and ELS in particular (including this work) has often tended to excessively focus on the "leader" part of the leader–follower equation.

The next noteworthy essay in the Berry-Gordon volume is "Local Voluntary Organizations" by eco-organizational leader James J. Espy, Jr. (1993). Like Sirmon and a number of the other authors, he commences autobiographically and then turns to reflecting on the question of leadership. He identifies six factors pertinent to his experience as a leader: "job title, vision, inspiration, management, knowledge, and humility" (1993: 204). These are all interesting points for various reasons but I only summarily respond to two of them. To begin with, the first factor ("job title") may/should be criticized, as leadership scholars have convincingly demonstrated that one's position or office does not "maketh the leader," so to speak (e.g., Kotter 1990a; cf. Manolopoulos 2019: 45–46). However, Espy provides us with a timely reminder that, insofar as leadership is related to agency and power, then one's job title *may* facilitate leadership in certain cases. The other leaderly factor discussed by Espy is "management": astutely, he concurs that "leadership (in its broadest sense) and management do require different skills" (1993: 206); however, as is the case with much leadership and management theory, Espy veers toward their fusion when he states that "successful leaders must . . . provide competent management" (1993: 206). But leaders provide leadership, whether competent or otherwise, while managers provide management, whether competent or otherwise.

Another noteworthy essay in the Berry-Gordon volume is "Academic Leadership" by natural resources and planning professor James E. Crawfoot. He explains how he has moved from an agent-based notion of leadership – "basically having the power and expertise to influence people" (1993: 230) – to "ways of being; it is actions that enable life" (1993: 231). He expands/refines this deeply philosophical (but still biocentric) definition: "I conceptualize such leadership" – and we could perhaps state that he's more specifically referring to environmental leading – "as a circle of distinct but interrelated values and behavior" (1993: 231). There are various aspects to this circle but the one that immediately resonates with me is that leadership is "knowing what is and what could be" (1993: 231). This is one way we could describe my own general definition of leadership: it knows what is (for example, given situations are either predominantly anthropocentric or ecocentric) and what could be (anthropocentric situations could be transformed into ecocentric ones, and contested ecocentric ones could remain ecocentric). Crawfoot's foregrounding of knowledge is reiterated when he goes on to cite it as one of the fundamental factors for "preparing for leadership" (1993: 243–244).

Another admirable aspect of Crawfoot's contribution is his emphasis on situations. In a section titled "Specific Situations" (1993: 246–248), he turns to an examination of specific concrete scenarios and identifies leaderly activity therein. There are obvious affinities with the present work's emphasis on situations. Now, I conclude my unfairly short summary of Crawfoot's essay by noting his claim that "Leadership will be challenged to develop new ethics addressing inequity" (1993: 249): in the present study, "inequity" is understood anthropocentrically, while the "new ethics" is Earth-centeredness.

The short review of Crawfoot's contribution concludes our retracing of the 1993 Berry-Gordon volume, but we may also quickly recall the book they wrote thirteen years later: *Environmental Leadership Equals Essential Leadership: Redefining Who Leads and How* (2006). First of all, I'm immediately struck by the title: the authors equate environmental leadership with leading as such, whereas I endorse the common/"intuitive" understanding (i.e., that eco-leading is a specific kind of leading). Hence, the Berry-Gordon equation between general leadership and eco-leading is a problematic one. Its problematic dimension is somewhat diminished when we turn to the book itself and note that the authors qualify and nuance the term "equals": it really refers to the translatability of certain "themes" in environmental leadership to other leaderly contexts (e.g., business, politics, education, and so on). There might be some warrant in this proposition, given that all leading involves situational change/conservation, but any "translatability" should not be overstated: there are different *types* of leading precisely because there are qualitatively *different* situations to be changed or preserved.

To be sure, there are also strengths with the 2006 book. For instance, Gordon and Berry insist – like I do – that leading occurs in the most mundane situations and that we can learn much about leadership at this level (2006: xxv). The book also maintains the empirical thrust of ELS by including a survey of leaders from various social domains. There's also a strong ethical dimension to the volume, and though it's sometimes overstated, it's a refreshing change from the excessively relativistic bent in much academic discourse. For instance, Gordon and Berry claim that "Ethics, a secure and clear knowledge of right and wrong and how to apply it, are a major and tricky component of leadership under uncertainty" and "Successful leaders operate from a strong ethical base" (2006: 3, 7). And so, while the 2006 book may be described as a mix of insights and shortcomings, it is – like the earlier 1993 volume – an important contribution to ELS.

Conservative-Regressive ELS

The above selective review of key foundational ELS works during the 1980s and early-90s has identified some of their strengths and weaknesses. What happens during the subsequent decades? To begin with, the 1990s witnessed strong growth in the discipline, with much/most research being conducted within the parameters of the Dominant Social Paradigm (DSP), which does not question the West's prevailing anthropocentric-neoliberal attitudes-practices (e.g., Dechant and others 1994; Walley and Whitehead 1994; Boyd and others 2009; Adams and others 2011; Kane 2011; Mino and Hanaki 2013; Christensen, Mackey and Whetten 2014; Silvestri and Veltri 2019; etc.). In other words, this significant/dominant current of ELS claims that eco-leadership can transpire in the context of "business as usual"; there's supposedly no fundamental conflict between the status quo and eco-leading. Now, rather than spending an excessive amount of time deconstructing all/many of these works, I focus here on three paradigmatic texts.

We begin with a 1994 paper by renowned management researcher Paul Shrivastava, whose title is deeply resonant for us: "Ecocentric Leadership in the 21st Century" (1994b). The article appeared in a special double-issue on environmental leadership in the prestigious *Leadership Quarterly* (other papers from the issue also feature in this mapping). We may straightaway point out that I have thus far been unable to locate any other English-language academic texts that use the phrase "ecocentric leadership" in their title, so I was delighted to discover it: unfortunately, for reasons outlined shortly, my anticipation was quickly followed by disappointment; the work does not live up to its promising title. But before commencing the analysis, I note that the article – like a number of the texts reviewed here – is extremely short (just over 1,000 words): as critics, we're required to take into account its introductory and declaratory character.

We commence with some of the strengths of the paper. Shrivastava begins by recognizing the "mind-numbing" number of eco-crises and that a "new vision and new leadership" is required to meet these challenges in the twenty-first century (1994b: 224). He also confirms that such leading will involve some radical measures such as "controlling population explosion, ensuring worldwide food security, preserving ecosystem resources, and moderating the type and pace of economic development" (1994b: 224). One admires Shrivastava's veracity, especially when phenomena like climate change (which he mentions at the very beginning of the article) were not as evident as they are becoming today. And given that Shrivastava focuses on both corporations and individuals within them – laudably, not only leaders but also followers (1994b: 225) – his work is inclusive of both organization-centered and agent-centered approaches.

There are, however, several problems with the article. First, it's difficult to determine exactly what Shrivastava means by "ecocentric leadership." He proceeds in quite an unsystematic way, simultaneously fusing and differentiating leading and managing, and automatically reducing the leadership concept to the level of the corporation (i.e., ecocentric corporate leadership) without showing, for example, whether/how he has derived this specific conception from a more general, fundamental one. When Shrivastava first addresses the definitional task, he refers to the "wholesale transformation of companies to ecologically sustainable management practices. In this brief essay, I frame these needs of corporate transformation in the concept of *ecocentric management*. I explain what this implies for corporate leadership" (1994b: 224). Shrivastava later specifies how "'ecocentric' management places ecology at the center of corporate and management concerns, rather than at their periphery" (1994b: 224). He goes on to ask – without really addressing – the following question: "What does leadership mean within this context of Ecocentric Management?" (1994b: 225). We straightaway ask how the meaning of leadership could be determined within the "context" of management? And what does Shrivastava mean by managerial "context"? According to my theorization in *Following Reason*, managing is "derived" from leading in the sense that it's the maintenance of situations that aren't contested (we recall that leadership involves the maintenance of situations in the presence of competing leadership seeking to alter them). Shrivastava reverses this logical-conceptual sequence – which *might* be valid – but he doesn't explain how leadership can be understood from within a managerial "context."

Next, Shrivastava is overly optimistic in placing faith in corporations that they will act eco-ethically – this optimism/naïvete (or worse) is another deeply problematic characteristic of DSP scholarship in various disciplines, including ELS. He remarks: "As the main engines of economic growth, corporations bear special responsibility for these ecological problems, and hold special promise for their resolution" (1994b: 224). Thus far, this "special promise" remains largely unfulfilled – and likely necessarily so. Why? Any reforms remain ensconced within the same underlying, overarching structure of anthropocentrism-neoliberalism. McLaughlin's incisive critique of Rolston can be applied to a number of the early (and contemporary) environmental leadership scholars: according to McLaughlin, Rolston basically offered "recommendations that he thinks businesses should follow, giving no attention to the economic systems within which they operate. In short, he never considers the structure of capitalistic economies that would make it difficult for any individual firm to adopt his moral maxims" (1993: 168). Shrivastava's project remains trapped within the DSP and its various shaky assumptions (perpetual economic growth, sustainable development, etc.).

But Shrivastava and other DSP scholars don't only err in terms of accepting questionable neoliberal assumptions but falter at a broader, deeper level, for neoliberalism is itself embedded within the broader, deeper context of human supremacism. Shrivastava remains constricted within human-centeredness, though it expresses itself in the paper in rather indirect ways; for instance, he remarks that eco-leadership "seeks to fulfill the needs of the present genera-tion, without jeopardizing the ability of future generations to meet their needs" (1994b: 224), which is a reasonable statement, but I wonder whether Shrivas-tava's "future generations" refers to just *human* ones.

I end my short review of Shrivastava's flawed but important paper by not-ing that he also published other articles around environmental questions dur-ing this time (e.g., 1994a, 1995a, 1995b). I don't critique them here not only because they share some of the problems of the "Ecocentric Leadership" paper but also because they more properly belong to the fields of organizational and management studies. However, I cite them to demonstrate how Shrivastava was deeply engaged with the related questions of environmentalism, leadership, and management from the near-beginning of their academic study. Despite the shortcomings of Shrivastava's research, there's no doubt that he's a key figure in the emergence of ELS, indicated by the citation of his work by other scholars (e.g., Gladwin, Kennelly and Krause 1995; Hanna 1995).

Now, it might be considered strange that the other article we survey in this section is written by one of the founders of Greenpeace: Patrick Moore. However, "Hard Choices for the Environmental Movement," which also appeared in the special 1994 double-issue in *Leadership Quarterly*, certainly belongs in the conservative-regressive category: this article perfectly embodies the transformation of the environmental movement from a counter-cultural force to its assimilation into the established (discursive) order. Moore enthusi-astically endorses the collaborative stance of the mainstream movement with the powers-that-be: "A collaborative approach promises to give environmen-tal issue [*sic*] their fair consideration in relation to the traditional economic and social priorities" (1994: 248). The realistic element of eco-leaderly dissent is completely lacking here (a point that's elaborated as we proceed). We also note how Moore – like Shrivastava – employs the lexicon of promise, and thus far, this promise remains woefully unfulfilled – indeed, broken. Next, we observe how it's very simple and easy to appear to *consider* environmental issues – haven't conservative governments and corporations repeatedly gath-ered together to discuss challenges like climate change? – but the eco-crises continue to multiply and intensify. In the actual scheme of things, the "tradi-tional" economic and social priorities – economic growth, profit maximiza-tion, longer working hours for stagnant wages – *are the only ones*. Of course, today we also have the benefit of hindsight, so one can't be too critical of these individuals' misplaced optimism/naïvete.

Returning to Moore's advancement of "collaboration," it's unsurprising – but still unsettling – that he portrays the uncompromising strand of the envi-ronmental movement in such a harsh and condescending way; we also note how he refers to it in the past tense, assuming *somewhat correctly* that it's a thing of the past (1994: 248). In response, we posit the following set of questions: given the spiraling ecological crisis, should eco-leadership today be on the side of "the monkey-wrenchers, tree-spikers, and boat scuttlers" (Moore 1994: 248), or on the side of the professional collaborators? Furthermore, while radical environmentalism is uncompromising, is this not also the case with neoliberalism? Hasn't neoliberalism advanced uncompromisingly – even if often by stealth (Brown 2015)? Might we not assert that the eco-crisis has intensified and diversified not only due to the forces of human supremacism, growing industrialization, population expansion, etc., but also because the environmental movement and its "leadership" have been too accommodative?

We also note Moore's crude rendering of deep ecology: "In the name of 'deep ecology,' many environmentalists have taken a sharp turn to the ultra-left, ushering in a mood of extremism and intolerance" (1994: 248). But deep ecology and ultimately complementary worldviews (e.g., ecofeminism, social ecology, this work's radical ecocentrism) are only considered "extreme" because they sharply contrast with the prevailing anthropocentric-neoliberal mindset. (Ecofeminism exposes the link between the domination of female humans and non-humans; refer to, e.g., Eaubonne 1974; Adams 1993; Salleh 1997; Warren 2000; Nhanenge 2011; social ecology exposes the link between the domination of humans and non-humans; refer to, e.g., Bookchin 1971, 1980, 1982, 1990).

Moore then explains/laments that his endorsement of collaboration has led to his banishment from Greenpeace and the more radical element of the environmental movement. One could perhaps question whether he has been treated too harshly – he recognizes eco-devastation and prophetically notes its impact on humanity "during the coming decades" (1994: 249), and he acknowledges factors like population growth (1994: 248, 251) – but then his increasingly vindictive discourse perhaps vindicates his expulsion. Obviously motivated by emotion rather than rationality, Moore describes the radical wing of the eco-movement as misanthropic, anti-science/technology, anti-organizations, anti-trade, anti-business, and anti-civilization (with the assumption that civilization can only appear in Western-agricultural form); Moore reduces bioregionalism to "ultra-nationalism," and he pro-anthropocentrically ridicules by way of scare quotes those who consider electoral democracy "too 'human-centered'" (1994: 249–250). Vindictive, indeed.

A third work cited in this second part of the review is "The Action Logics of Environmental Leadership: A Developmental Perspective" (2009) by organizational management researchers Olivier Boiral, Mario Cayer, and Charles Baron. In a number of ways, this is a very good article: it therefore exemplifies the way in which both conservative and progressive elements often characterize ELS. This duality is aptly captured in the way the authors broach the question of ecocentrism. To begin with, the fact that they discuss it is a progressive move; however, they provide a distorted and diluted definition, formulating it as "openness to major environmental issues, the promotion of sustainable development, and a reconsideration of the dominant anthropocentric perspective"

(2009: 482). First of all, the word "openness" seems both "soft" and ambiguous: surely clearer and more dynamic terms such as "attentiveness" or "active pursuit" would have been more suitable. Likewise, the term "issues" seems to play down the reality of major environmental problems, crises, and catastrophes. Next, Boiral, Cayer, and Baron employ the problematic phrase "sustainable development": ideally, one would differentiate between existing "sustainable development" as a cover/euphemism for neoliberal economic expansion and, on the other hand, true eco-sustainability. Lastly, the authors undertake more under-stating when they construe ecocentrism as a "reconsideration" of human chauvinism: Earth-centeredness seeks to expose, erase, and replace it.

The conservative dimension of the way the authors treat the question of eco-centrism is further evidenced by the following assessment, which could be construed as closing down discussion of it rather than opening it up: "Although this ecocentric perspective can shed some light on the general values that may be associated with an environmental ethic and its importance to management [and leadership], it remains too nonspecific to really elucidate the modes of thought and action of environmental leaders" (2009: 482). However, there's some truth in the valuation: the "modes of thought and action" of Earth-centeredness remain generally unknown – and that's precisely why the present work has sought to provide sufficient specification in terms of some of the measures that truly environmental leading would seek to implement.

The above critique of these three articles should not be construed as a wholesale dismissal of the conservative-regressive current of ELS: there is often good scholarship at work within these texts, in varying degrees; however, it is precisely what is often left unstated that constitutes their fundamental flaw: the scholars do not question the distorted assumptions that structure their ruminations. And this failure has thus far impacted ELS as a discipline, given that the DSP current has been a major one – even perhaps the dominant one, at least in terms of research output/publication.

Critical-Progressive ELS

I now turn to a semi-comprehensive mapping of ELS literature that moves away from the anthropocentric and other dominant frameworks, and toward more critical-progressive positions. A number of pioneering texts in this more questioning-enlightened branch may be found in the same 1994 special double-issue of *Leadership Quarterly* in which Shrivastava's and Moore's articles appear. I begin by briefly focusing on the two most progressive works from the double-issue; then, I focus on some of the most important texts from the NEP corpus; and I conclude the section by citing some "honorable mentions."

"Leadership for Environmental and Social Change" is the editorial by the guest editors, eco-leadership pioneers Carolyn P. Egri and Peter J. Frost. One is immediately struck by the title's linkage of the ecological and the social: this is a hallmark of NEP scholarship, given that the paradigm recognizes how genuine environmental reparation and rejuvenation is unlikely/impossible to occur without fundamental social transformation. (By contrast, as we have observed earlier, DSP discourses ignore or reject even contemplating the idea/option of fundamental social-systemic change.) Serendipitously, given our category of "critical-progressive," Egri and Frost employ the term "progressive" in the very first sentence, stating that "The theme of this special issue is the nature of leadership needed to bring about progressive changes in humankind's relationships with the natural environment and within social environments" (1994: 195).

Egri and Frost observe: "The articles we received reflect the wide diversity of research being conducted in this new and exciting arena" (1994: 196). This observation confirms our contention that ELS was a new – and already very diverse – discourse by the mid-1990s. They also stress the empirical flavor of the discipline, with its deployment of case studies, interviews, surveys, and so on. But Egri and Frost also remind us "how qualitative research is often an ongoing iterative process requiring self-reflection and numerous adjustments and responses to prior frameworks and understandings" (1994: 196). Another commendable feature of the work is that the editors invited researchers to explore "the essence of leadership," a point that reinforces my insistence that we should attempt to define and theorize leading if we are to practice it and apply it – especially when it comes to leading for the Earth. Egri and Frost identify certain common themes across the various articles in the double-issue, but the very first one is particularly poignant: "egalitarianism" (1994: 199). Unfortunately, they do not proceed to define it (which is somewhat understandable, given that it's a short editorial), but I question whether/to what extent egalitarianism is indeed a foregrounded theme – especially "egalitarianism" understood in its fullest, ecocentric sense.

The other article from the 1994 double-issue that warrants a short synopsis is "Holism: A Philosophy of Organizational Leadership for the Future" by organizational psychologist-philosopher James R. Carlopio. The author offers a fascinating thesis: "I propose that we can better help organizational leaders by offering them alternative guiding philosophies and premises rather than prescriptive theories and complex models" (1994: 298). Carlopio commences by explaining how the majority of leadership and management theories are predicated on a mechanistic framing of the world, whereby organizations and indeed the Earth are composed of discrete parts that can be studied separately and are easily replaceable (on organizations as "machines," refer to, e.g., Wheatley 1992; Allen, Stelzner and Wielkiewicz 1998; Wielkiewicz and Stelzner 2005; on organizations as "organisms," refer to, e.g., Cletzer and Kaufman 2018). Carlopio explains: "Bureaucracies and the 'Fordist' assembly line, for example, are designed in the image of the machine. Peoples' jobs have been decomposed into supposedly simple, independent tasks" (1994: 298). This construal of the material world leaves little/no room for genuine leading: "Leadership roughly equates with a mechanistic, technical process whereby the organization is operated by a management technician in control at the top of the steep organizational hierarchy" (1994: 298).

Carlopio advances the alternative perspective of holism, whereby each entity "simultaneously attempts to function as part of the larger whole and to preserve its individual autonomy and wholeness" (1994: 298). Other examples of this kind of dialectical understanding include rationality and intuition, ying and yang, linear and non-linear, etc. The author transposes this thinking to leadership, whereby two opposing but complementary elements are held in balance: "Problems occur when leaders emphasize one side to the exclusion of the other" (1994: 298). Carlopio claims that organizational theory has focused on the rational at the expense of the "nonrational" – which should not be construed as the *anti*-rational (Manolopoulos 2019: 1) – including "myths, symbols, rituals, intuition, metaphorical analysis" (1994: 299).

Carlopio then identifies how this holistic approach may be applied at the level of organizations (be they corporations, nations, and so on). First, "the task of holistically minded organizational leaders is not to provide specific answers, direction or control but to focus on organizational processes" (1994: 304). Next, a holistic approach involves reciprocity: "you can only take out of a system if you continue to put in to it" (1994: 304–305). Carlopio also emphasizes the role of ethics/values: "Leading holistically also means living one's life motivated by a set of core values that place a high priority on integrity, service, and spiritual as well as monetary profit" (1994: 305). While the article tends toward the abstract, Carlopio fortifies it by referring to the practices of an existing company (The Body Shop, which originated in Australia; this organization has been praised by a number of leadership and management researchers). While more specification would have fortified the text's rigor, it's nevertheless an important piece, given that it foregrounds an alternative philosophical ethics converging/consistent with ecocentrism.

Another important contribution to NEP ELS is the 1995 article "Limits to Anthropocentrism: Toward an Ecocentric Organization Paradigm?" by Purser, Park, and Montuori. The fact that we've already alluded to this text a number of times in the present study signals its significance, and as I now further show, I think it's one of the most important contributions to the discipline, packed with incisive thoughts – too many to be recounted here. To begin with, the authors pursue the definitional question regarding human-centeredness. Coming from the perspective of organization sciences (like sociology and management studies), Purser, Park, and Montuori commence by defining anthropocentrism in terms of "the perception of a fundamental duality between organizations and the natural environment" before proceeding to cite Eckersley's more expansive formulation, i.e., "the belief that there is a clear and morally relevant dividing line between humankind and the rest of nature, that humankind is the only principal source of value or meaning in the world" (Eckersley 1992: 51 cited in Purser, Park and Montuori 1995: 1054). Further on, the researchers provide what I think is an even more precise definition: "humans . . . locate themselves at the apex and center of the natural world" (1995: 1056). The authors then proceed to show how homocentrism informs everything from the early American conservation movement (1995: 1067) to the Rio Declaration at the 1992 Earth Summit (1995: 1054). The writers boldly proclaim that "Anthropocentrism must be recognized and eradicated before fundamental changes can take place in people's attitudes and actions toward the nonhuman world" (1995: 1054).

Purser, Park, and Montuori then trace some of the modern historical phenomena that have facilitated the intensification of homocentrism. The retracing is both fascinating and important, given that an awareness of *how* human supremacism has historically developed and accelerated allows us to better confront it and overcome it. Along the way, the authors echo McLaughlin's and Mathews' insistence that the human is a part of nature: "the human species is organically related to what is conceptually referred to as Nature. In some real biological sense, humans must be part of Nature" (1995: 1057–1058).

The researchers then undertake a sustained critical analysis of the way homocentrism manifests itself in organizational discourse, observing how "anthropocentrism *is* entrenched within organization science and management practice" (1995: 1065). Now, in the same way that my leadership thinking does not privilege leading over management, the researchers are likewise not "anti-management": they will later emphasize that "Ecocentrism is not an attack on management as such but on anthropocentric management" (1995: 1081). Hence, Purser, Park, and Montuori do not recoil from criticizing mainstream management discourse-practice: "environmental management is essentially a policy of reform that avoids the necessity of having to examine the deeper philosophical causes of the ecological crisis and that sidesteps issues regarding fundamental changes in lifestyles, which are virtually unthinkable" (1995: 1065). This observation augments my contention that what we are mainly presently experiencing is conservative-regressive environmental management (the maintenance of existing situations in the absence of competing leadership) rather than genuine environmental leading. This conservative–regressive environmental management passes for leadership, but it's only pseudo-leadership.

Purser, Park, and Montuori seek to redress the anthropocentric distortion by advancing the "competing dimensions of ecology" (1995: 1065–1074). This involves what they call the "ecocentric responsibility paradigm" (ERP). They insightfully point out that "Ecocentric philosophers view the anthropocentric assumptions in our culture as the deeper cause of environmental problems" (1995: 1065). During their engaging extrapolation of ERP, the researchers traverse various subjects that have been broached in the present work. For instance, they address the questions of intrinsic value and instrumentalism: "Traditional philosophies do not consider the inherent worth of nature but simply ascribe instrumental value. Similarly, human beings regard nature only as a 'resource' to exploit, without considering nature as our 'source'" (1995: 1065). Purser, Park, and Montuori also refer to what I've been calling eco-liberation: "Ecocentrists are explicitly concerned with emancipating ecosystems from the effects of human mismanagement, overuse, and exploitation" (1995: 1065). They recall a number of the great biocentric thinkers, including Leopold and Rolston (1995: 1071–1074). In terms of eco-education, they discuss what they call "ecological learning" (1995: 1079–1080). They even broach the political dimension of environmental leadership by advocating "ecological democracy" (albeit within biocentric constraints): "employees and nonhuman lifeforms would not be subjected to being managed, exploited, controlled, or dominated by an elite group (i.e., supervisors or planetary managers) that presumes to occupy a superior position above the systems to which it belongs" (1995: 1080). While I now conclude our short retracing of this article, I think it nonetheless indicates how Purser, Park, and Montuori offer a masterful example of critical-progressive ELS.

The next noteworthy articles were produced by educational leadership scholar Kathleen E. Allen, psychology professor Stephen P. Stelzner, and leadership researcher Richard M. Wielkiewicz. In 1998, they published "The Ecology of Leadership: Adapting to the Challenges of a Changing World," and Wielkiewicz and Stelzner wrote a short follow-up piece in 2005 titled "An Ecological Perspective on Leadership Theory, Research, and Practice." I focus here on the first paper with some reference to the second. As with a number of ELS writings, these pieces are packed with so many insights, postulations, and recommendations that they can't all be cataloged and analyzed here.

The overarching aim of the research is to outline a theory of environmental leadership that departs from the traditional agent-centered "positional" approach to leading, where the focus is on elected officials and corporate heads. (In the second article, the authors articulate how the conventional approach is also inclusive of the mechanistic understanding of organizations that Carlopio had articulated [Wielkiewicz and Stelzner 2005: 326].) The conventional model is criticized by the authors for having led to "the degradation of our environment, an increasing gap between rich and poor, businesses that go bankrupt, and ethical problems in those who hold public office – all signs of failed leadership" (Allen, Stelzner and Wielkiewicz 1998: 63). The researchers' post-agent-centered approach is also edifying for my own "situation-centered" efforts: early on in the 2005 article, Wielkiewicz and Stelzner expound how "Observers from Western cultures seeking to explain the behavior of another person are likely to overestimate the importance of personality factors and underestimate the importance of situational factors" (2005: 327; the authors cite Kelley 1973; Harvey and Weary 1984; Bond and Smith 1996; and Choi, Nisbett and Norenzayan 1999).

Allen, Stelzner, and Wielkiewicz contend that ecology provides a better understanding of organizations and organizational leadership. They identify and foreground four eco-principles as the basis of their model: interdependence; open systems and feedback loops; the cycling of human and non-human resources; and adaptation (cf. Wielkiewicz and Stelzner 2005: 326–327). While these four now-familiar concepts-phenomena may initially appear somewhat abstract, the authors identify a number of their leadership implications and applications, e.g., a recognition of feedback loops entails organizations being receptive to employees and other often-neglected voices (as becomes apparent, this theme emerges as a/the central one in the 1998 paper).

Allen, Stelzner, and Wielkiewicz then proceed to provide a very comprehensive seven-point leadership definition that is premised on the notion that an entity or phenomenon can be better understood by better understanding its broad context (the example they provide is a tree: one must not only study the tree itself but also, say, the forest within which it is situated). The authors produce a detailed formulation of leadership grounded in a broader, ecological perspective: leading is a process emerging from individual and group interactions within and outside an organization; this process occurs within a broader socio-biological context; organizational adaptability depends upon how open they are to feedback loops; leaderly effectiveness is measured by how robustly it responds to challenges arising in its broader ecosystem, recognizing that leaderly actions are best understood over the longer-term; and leaderly responsibility is/should be shared (Allen, Stelzner and Wielkiewicz 1998: 72–73). A/the key difference between conventionally led organizations and ecologically led ones is that the former are closed and the latter are open (1998: 73–76). This contrast becomes the main thrust of the paper and is reiterated in the conclusion, whereby eco-leadership is understood as being receptive to internal and external feedback loops, while positional leadership focuses on "short term feedback loops such as profits, stock price, or a 'bottom line'" (1998: 80).

While both articles are very strong examples of ELS, there are also problematic aspects to them. To begin with, in their eagerness to foreground the processual character of leading, Allen, Stelzner, and Wielkiewicz marginalize its agential, positional aspect: this is exemplified at the beginning of the 1998 paper, when they rigidly assert that "Leadership, therefore, is a process, not the actions of an individual" (1998: 69), though the authors admirably soften their stance as the article proceeds, acknowledging and integrating the agential dimension (1998: 71, 72, 78). Indeed, by the time of the 2005 paper, Wielkiewicz and Stelzner are more inclusive of the positional–agential dimension (2005: 327), even adopting a kind of dialectical understanding: "we see leadership processes as involving a tension between the traditional *industrial* approach [e.g., agent/position-centered, organizations-as-machines] and the more neglected *ecological* approach" (2005: 326).

Another shortcoming is that Allen, Stelzner, and Wielkiewicz don't embrace a fully ecocentric position. This is indicated when they formulate the basic purpose of ecological leadership: "Leadership processes and individual actions should create a community of reciprocal care and shared responsibility and promote harmony with nature thereby providing sustainability for future generations" (1998: 76) – I wonder whether "nature" here includes the artifactual, and I also wonder whether "future generations" (a phrase, we recall, also employed by Shrivastava) is inclusive of the non-human. Despite these shortcomings, the 1998 and 2005 articles are some of the most definitive for critical-progressive ELS.

Apart from my uncompromising ecocentrism, there's another fundamental way in which the research of Allen, Stelzner, and Wielkiewicz differs from mine. The scholars focus on organizations (and not just businesses or corporations), so they foreground a certain understanding or "metaphor" of ecology (1998: 67, 69, 71; Wielkiewicz and Stelzner 2005: 336), and extrapolate from it an exemplary/optimal model for human organizations, i.e., interdependent, open-ended, processual, etc. There are therefore resonances with Carlopio's approach, and it has also been echoed by scholars working at the intersection of conservation science and environmental leadership (e.g., Dietz and others 2004; van Vugt 2004; Manolis and others 2009; Black, Groombridge and Jones 2011; Gutiérrez, Hilborn and Defeo 2011; Warren and Visser 2016; cf. Christensen and others 1996). I duly offer a short critique of this discourse (via a 2015 article by Peter Case and others) and merely highlight here how my approach differs: rather than observing nature and applying these observations in the construction of an eco-leadership model, I observed leadership phenomena and used these observations to construct a general leadership model (i.e., *Following Reason*) and then derived a theory of environmental leadership from the general model (the present monograph). A detailed comparison of the methods and recommendations of the two approaches exceeds the scope of this review, but it would certainly constitute valuable scholarship.

We now turn to the next reviewed text: in 2000, Egri partnered with Susan Herman to produce the article "Leadership in the North American Environmental Sector: Values, Leadership Styles and Contexts of Environmental Leaders and Their Organizations." It's a strong piece of scholarship on several fronts. First of all, the authors attend to the definitional question. They basically reiterate Gordon and Berry's formulation: "we [Egri and Herman] define environmental leadership as the ability to influence individuals and mobilize organizations to realize a vision of long-term ecological sustainability" (2000: 572). They straightaway introduce the Earth-centered dimension to the formulation – later they'll equate ecological sustainability with ecocentrism (2000: 572) – noting how eco-leaders who are "guided by ecocentric values and assumptions . . . seek to change economic and social systems that they perceive as currently and potentially threatening the health of the biophysical environment" (2000: 572). This dense and nuanced sentence warrants more unpacking than can be provided here, but we can flag certain key points. First, we note – and applaud – how this form of leading is *guided* by ecocentrism (we also note the epistemic thrust of the word "assumptions": as I explained in *Following Reason* and reiterated in this book, any ethical system is quite difficult to "ground" or "substantiate"). The ecocentrism advanced in the Egri-Herman article is also comprehensive: note how "biophysical environment" is a very inclusive phrase, even though we note the prefix "bio" pulls it back to biocentrism.

We also observe the baldness – and rigor – of the remark's claim that eco-leadership involves attempts to "change economic and social systems": no doubt, the word "change" is crucial here, for it can mean two diverging acts – reform or replacement. Egri and Herman appear to cognize this division by differentiating "reform environmentalists" from "radical environmentalists" (2000: 599), though their prudent use of nuancing terms such as "more" and "than" indicates more of a spectrum than a strict polarity (cf. Egri and Pinfield 1996). They also prudently note how reform tends to involve "contradictory values, assumptions, and goals" (2000: 599), but they're not quick to dogmatically and totalizingly choose one over the other. In a similar vein, I would propose that maybe a mix of replacement and reform is required, e.g., replacing some aspects of the economy, and reforming others. The nature of different systems or situations – are they presently more anthropocentric or more ecocentric? – will determine whether/to what extent reform or replacement might be required.

Egri and Herman also stipulate that the "primary focus" of the paper is "Delineating the differences between environmental leadership and traditional leadership" (2000: 572). We may assume that what the authors mean by "traditional leadership" is the leading associated with "traditional belief systems" where "the biophysical environment is in service to humankind" (2000: 572). But we can't straightaway presume that all traditional belief systems were/are anthropocentric: we recall the compelling proposition flagged in the second chapter that human supremacism appears to have arisen with agrarianism, so it's reasonable to propose that pre-agricultural leadership was likely often eco-centered leadership. Now, returning to the article, Egri and Herman state that they intend to delineate the differences between the two diverging leadership modes via an empirical study, surveying (following Snow's lead) environmental leaders from a broad variety of environmental organizations. The findings showed that these leaders espoused "ecocentric" (read: biocentric) values and were more open to transformational leadership activity.

The article also recognizes – and one could say even encourages – the ethico-contestational character of eco-leadership: "being environmentally proactive challenges the societal and industrial status quo" (2000: 599). This is confirmed when Egri and Herman conclude that "One challenge for researchers . . . is to find ways to facilitate progress toward environmental sustainability, even though . . . this may take us to 'places we didn't think to go'" (2000: 600). It's hoped that the present work is an example of traveling to these unthought/unthinkable places.

While Egri and Herman offer a strong piece of research – indeed, one of the finest in ELS – there are also problematic aspects to it. Once again, "leadership" is not defined in any specific or rigorous sense; hence, the definition of "environmental leadership" – which, as I noted, has its positives – remains undeveloped, given that the fundamental concept ("leadership") has not been developed or refined. Next, while it's admirable that Egri and Herman draw on the research of leadership luminaries such as Burns and Bernard Bass, any uncritical-unmodified appropriation can lead to problems. For instance, Egri and Herman employ the questionable Burnsian (and Bassian) distinction of "transformational/transactional leadership": as I explained in *Following Reason* (2019: esp. 36–39) "transactional leadership" may be more accurately described as management. But despite the flaws in Egri and Herman's article, it remains cutting-edge, both in terms of originality, rigor, and opening up the question of the ethico-political contestation of the status quo.

We now turn to a very important ELS volume published in 2010: *Leadership for Environmental Sustainability*. It was edited by leadership philosopher Benjamin W. Redekop, who, as will become apparent, is a pivotal figure in critical-progressive ELS, both in terms of his own original thinking and his work in bringing together scholarship in the field. As Redekop notes, *Leadership in Environmental Sustainability* was "the first multidisciplinary treatment of environmental leadership" (2010a: 2). He himself offers three essays in the volume (including introductory and concluding papers), and I shall review Redekop's work collectively at the end of this section (which also signals the conclusion of the retracing). While all of the contributions are academically strong, I focus here on two essays because they are the most relevant/resonant from a thoroughly ecocentric perspective (I also cite "honorable mentions" at the end of the review of the book; we additionally note that the volume also features the 2005 Wielkiewicz and Stelzner article).

The first paper is written by critical theorist Simon Western and titled "Eco-Leadership: Towards the Development of a New Paradigm." Critique is a major part of his project (we note that his 2008 book is titled *Leadership: A Critical Text*) and is now quite a decisive figure in this stream of ELS, with advocates like Redekop and others (e.g., Redekop, Gallagher and Satterwhite 2018a; McManus 2018). Western may also prove influential for the kind of work I'm doing – which might be labeled "radical ELS" (more on this to follow) – given that his work is increasingly foregrounding some of the truly transformational aspects of eco-leadership (2018: 49, 53–54). In this brief retracing, I shall only review the 2010 essay (with occasional reference to the 2018 text), given that it's an excellent representation of his ongoing research into conventional and ecological leadership. To begin with, Western appears to be the first thinker to coin the term "eco-leadership" (2010: 36, 2008). He employs the term in a way that includes but exceeds the common understanding of leading engaged with environmental concerns to encompass "leadership in relation to the ecosystems in which we live and work" (2010: 36). In other words, eco-leading departs from agent-centered and organizations-as-machines perspectives, as it "shifts the focus from individual leaders to leadership, asking of an organization 'how can leadership flourish in this environment?'" (2010: 36). Western's work is therefore somewhat situated within the holistic/systems-thinking current.

However, Western also attempts a meta-critique of leadership studies. He refers to "eco-leadership" as a new discourse that has emerged – defining "discourse" in a broad way, i.e., as "the unconscious and normative assumptions that trap us into a particular way of thinking, speaking, and doing" (2010: 37; cf. Foucault 1972; Butler 1990). Western then identifies the three basic leadership discourses that have defined the discipline: "the controller," "the therapist," and "the messiah" (2010: 37–41). While Western is at pains to stress that these discourses "are not right or wrong, they simply exist within wider social phenomena," he simultaneously entreats us to "'untrap' ourselves" from them (2010: 37).

Western then analyzes the eco-leadership discourse, which he critically embraces and advances. He stipulates its basic aim: "Eco-leadership redistributes leadership and power from the center to the edges, recognizing the impossibility of 'going it alone' when we are interdependent on each other and on planet Earth" (2010: 42). Western then traces the rise of this discourse due to a variety of epistemological and social changes (quantum physics; globalization and technologization; the environmental movement). He also notes how eco-leadership is "not a woolly, feel-good approach to leadership; it is rather a serious and radical approach that challenges the very coordinates of current theory and practice" (2010: 43). This point certainly resonates with the kind of environmental leadership theorized and espoused in the present work, especially in terms of the confronting transformative policies it identifies and advocates.

Western then extrapolates what eco-leadership might mean at the organizational level. No longer rigid and bounded but organic and fluid, organizations are "reimagined as an ecosystem within other ecosystems" (2010: 46). The author foregrounds the ecosystem "metaphor," given that it connotes interdependence and sustainability (2010: 46). Western spells out some of the practical organizational implications of such a reimagining, including workplace diversity and attentiveness to spaces (2010: 47–49). However, the eco-leaderly characteristic that's most relevant in the context of this study is the advancement of some kind of "systemic ethics," a "unifying source" that might be based, for example, in religion, spirituality, nature holism, eco-justice, etc. (2010: 49). Whatever it might be, it must be antithetical to – and Western's specificity here is surprising – neoliberal pioneer Milton Friedman's imperative for ever-increasing corporate profit (2010: 50; Western cites Friedman 1962: 132–133). In other words, this unifying ethic must be stridently anti-neoliberalist. Now, I would argue that *ecocentrism* is precisely this kind of unifying ethic/ethos:

it's broadly consistent with sophisticated versions of the worldviews cited above, and it's antithetical to neoliberalism and hyper-profit – but *even more crucially* it also seeks to dislodge the older, deeper, and broader problem of human supremacism.

The other essay from *Leadership for Environmental Sustainability* that is foregrounded here (we recall that Redekop's entries are reviewed at the end of this section) is "Deep Systems Leadership: A Model for the 21st Century," written by another eco-scholar informed by systems thinking and critical theory: Rian Satterwhite (first cited in our introductory chapter). As we proceed, it will become apparent that he is also another important figure both in terms of his own innovative research and collaborative efforts. Now, in "Deep Systems Leadership," Satterwhite proceeds very systematically. He begins by stating that we need to understand the causes of crises like climate change and other eco-problems, and we need to rethink "our place in this world" (2010a: 230). When reading this proposition, ecocentrism straightaway came to my mind, given that it discloses anthropocentrism as a/the semi-concealed cause-driver of these problems, and Earth-centeredness also renders our true place in egalitarian terms (discussed in Chapters 2 and 3). Returning to Satterwhite's text: interestingly, and without initially articulating the connection, the author immediately introduces the subject of an environmental leadership model, explaining that his model – which is congruent with the eco-leadership paradigm (he later cites Western) – synthesizes four emerging disciplines: "cultural biology, systems theory, Deep Ecology, and selected leadership models" (2010a: 230).

In the first main section of the essay, Satterwhite briskly retraces ELS, citing a number of the authors discussed earlier (including Allen, Stelzner, and Wielkiewicz, and Western). Toward the end of the section, he makes a point that's incredibly significant for my own model of leading; when discussing conservation, he explains that it means "shifting away from the idea that what leaders do is facilitate *change*. In this [deep systems] model, leaders facilitate conservation more than they seek to bring about change" (2010a: 232). Now, we recall that my basic model of leadership is "paradoxical" because it recognizes leading as both a transformational and preservational force (for it has to do with situational change and maintenance). What Satterwhite's work admirably attempts is the foregrounding of the conservational dimension of leading. He commendably uses a language of degree (he refers to conservation "more than" change) to ensure that he's not advancing an exclusively conservational model, for merely replacing transformation with preservation as the main/exclusive dimension would merely reverse the conventional emphasis, whereas the ultimate critical task is to recognize both diverging dimensions.

Satterwhite then discusses cultural biology and its emphasis on conservation. Key concepts-facts of cultural biology are "autopoesis" (self-generation within the limits of an entity's structure – akin to the notion of natural unfolding) and "structural coupling" (whereby congruence emerges between two distinct entities/systems, such as living beings and their environments). Bringing these together, Satterwhite makes the "obvious" yet crucial point that "we must prevent changes in the external environment that threaten the finely tuned interaction between internal self and external world" (2010a: 235). The author nicely sums up how any disruption to nature also disrupts ourselves. The imperative against (unnecessary) disruption aptly ties in with the ecocentric imperative of letting-be.

Satterwhite then draws systems theory into his compelling argument to expand the model beyond local contexts of selves and their immediate environments. He succinctly sums up renowned physicist Fritjof Capra's (1996) pioneering characterization of deep-systems theory: "the shift from the parts to the whole; the ability to move attention back and forth between different systems levels; recognizing emergent properties that can only be found when examining the whole and that are not found in the parts; viewing life as a network of relationships" (Satterwhite 2010a: 236). Systems theory expands any local circle of care to the Earth itself (2010a: 237).

So how does one live according to these notions of autopoesis, structural coupling, and systems theory? Satterwhite proposes that deep ecology articulates this practice. He defines it in opposition to mainstream environmentalism, which perpetuates human domination rather than perceiving humanity's place "*within* nature" (2010a: 237) – which is a tidy way of contrasting anthropocentrism with ecocentrism. Satterwhite offers a nuanced critique of deep ecology, favoring a Naessean perspective that affirms both identification with nature and one's distinction from it (Naess 1986), which is compatible with the cultural–biological and systems-theory perspectives. Satterwhite also notes how a Naessean deep ecology is "leading to a more ecocentric ethic" (2010a: 238). The essay also clarifies the notion of "deep systems": the synthesis of deep ecology and systems theory.

Satterwhite then cites some of the fundamental tenets of "Deep Systems Leadership": a recognition of interconnectedness and interdependence, mindfulness of the overlapping systems within which we are embedded, and relating to one another "in a loving manner" (2010a: 238). The author concludes by citing four fundamental principles. The first states: "Both anthropocentric ethics and eco-ethics demand that we live in a more sustainable manner" (2010a: 238–239). But what the present study has sought to do is show that anthropocentrism is actually an *anti*-ethics; it's irreconcilable with any genuine sustainability. Like other scholars before him, Satterwhite has here diluted or clouded the true meaning of anthropocentrism – which is nothing less than human supremacism. Satterwhite's second core principle involves a shared responsibility "that is blind to hierarchy, position, influence, power, or structure" (2010a: 240). The author immediately enunciates the next core principle without having explained what he means by the word "blind," but it seems that the employment of a totalizing word insinuates that the theory completely dismisses forces such as hierarchy and positionality, whereas a more sophisticated perspective recognizes the range of varying and often competing forces that constitute leadership phenomena. The third key principle emphasizes that both environmental *and social* justice should be pursued. The fourth principle returns us to the point foregrounded at the beginning of the essay: conservation.

Despite the disputable first and second principles, Satterwhite's essay is brilliant: it's difficult for me to identify a piece of ELS writing with which I find more commonality or resonance. The author "builds" his model in a very systematic way; with interdisciplinary acumen, he synthesizes some of the most incisive currents of contemporary knowledge; he challenges conventional understandings of leadership and nature; and he thinks and writes in an engaging critical-theoretical or philosophical style. While the two of us ultimately propose different – though probably not fundamentally conflicting – models, Satterwhite certainly offers a sophisticated – indeed, profound – theory of environmental leadership.

I now quickly turn to the other solo-authored work by Satterwhite reviewed here: "A Case for Universal Context: Intersections of the Biosphere, Systems, and Justice Using a Critical Constructionist Lens" (2018). This is Satterwhite's contribution to *Innovation in Environmental Leadership*, another very important volume, which is co-edited by Satterwhite and Redekop, as well as Deborah Rigling Gallagher, who is discussed shortly. Now, a first striking dimension of the essay is Satterwhite's foregrounding of the tension between the way in which the question of leadership has splintered into many discursive directions and the ongoing task of finding a formulation that applies across contexts. My general model claims to apply across contexts because it proposes that leadership phenomena are characterized by situational transformation/preservation.

But Satterwhite moves in another fascinating direction, proposing three contexts: the biosphere (cf. Evans 2018: 67–68), systems (ecological and otherwise), and justice. Satterwhite notes how our individual backgrounds vary but we all share these three contexts. The first two are self-evidently true (given that they're fundamental physical realities within which we're individually and collectively enmeshed) but they nevertheless need to be foregrounded (as Satterwhite does) – precisely, I would add, because our anthropocentrism has inferiorized them to the extent that they are obscured or forgotten. The justice context is more complex, given that it – like ethics, to which it is related – can be notoriously difficult to define. While the ethical (or just) is construed in the present work according to the ecocentric–anthropocentric polarity, Satterwhite references a range of definitions regarding human justice and then insists that the justice discourse "must now be expanded to include the biospheric level, to the non-human realm" (2018: 43), but he doesn't unpack the details of this expansion. I recognize that the essay is introductory in nature but more specificity would have propelled the argument.

While Satterwhite's thinking is generally nuanced, sophisticated, rigorous, and compelling, various other questions emerge. For example, consider the author's basic definition of leadership – which is located in brackets, perhaps signaling that it should be understood as quite an "informal" one: "how people come together and do coordinated work in order to achieve a mutually beneficial outcome" (2018: 40). How has Satterwhite arrived at this formulation? Is it "thin" enough to cover all leaderly phenomena but does it also provide sufficient specificity to differentiate it from other often-similar phenomena like management? How would the basic definition be developed to describe environmental leadership? And also how is this general formulation related to the universal contexts of the biosphere, systems, and justice? As for the contexts, Satterwhite cautions that they "do not lead to a grand unified theory of leadership; rather, they provide a common language and perhaps a common set of overarching goals across the diversity of leadership theory and research" (2018: 44) – though one could ask whether the provision of a "common language" and even "overarching goals" goes some way to being some kind of "unified theory," albeit a not-so-grand one.

Now, given that the other contributions in *Leadership for Environmental Sustainability* are also strong pieces of scholarship but with different emphases to the present study (i.e., they are more empirical, sociological, etc.), I shall only cite (in order of appearance) those authors whose works most resonate with aspects of my own research: (Williams 2010; Birmingham and LeQuire 2010; Stodola 2010; Jacoby and Xia 2010; McDougall 2010).

The next work foregrounded in this selective review is the magisterial two-volume *Environmental Leadership: A Reference Handbook* (2012). The *Handbook*, which contains almost one hundred entries and is undoubtedly the most ambitious project in ELS thus far, was edited by Gallagher, who has published a number of writings on eco-leading (e.g., 2014, 2016, 2018), and as earlier mentioned, co-edited *Innovation in Environmental Leadership* (2018) together with Redekop and Satterwhite. Going by these herculean efforts, there's no doubt that Gallagher is another pivotal figure in critical-progressive ELS. Now, while there's a large number of essays in the *Handbook*, I shall only review here Gallagher's introductory piece, titled "Why Environmental Leadership?": this is the text that most resonates with my own rethinking of eco-leadership, i.e., it's more philosophically attuned, theoretically oriented, and focused on questions like definition. This is not to say that the other entries are not academically strong: indeed, given such a large collection, the consistency in scholarship is outstanding; Satterwhite also provides a fine paper (2010b), and I also cite below the papers that I find the most engaging and rigorous. However, most of the entries either follow conventional ELS trajectories (empirical/case studies, sociological, historical, etc.) or establish/develop alternative (and welcomed) lines of inquiry (e.g., spiritual-theological trajectories, strong foci on political–governmental dimensions, etc.). Bracketing these texts from this review will allow us to keep the retracing (and the study) within its limits.

Gallagher admirably – and topically from the present study's perspective – commences her introductory essay by pointing out some of the alarming facts regarding human population growth (2012: 3). The fact that authoritative scholars register their own concerns regarding population expansion galvanizes my controversial argument that eco-leadership would seek to stabilize human population numbers in order to thwart growing environmental damage. Gallagher returns to the topic of population when discussing the need for a new definition of eco-leadership: "It must take into account the increased urgency to confront wicked environmental challenges faced by a planet with 7 billion inhabitants" (2012: 5).

Gallagher also raises the possibility of a conceptual framework that offers "a means to consider perspectives on environmental leadership from religion, history, literature, education, the arts, and philosophy alongside detailed examinations of environmental problems and associated case studies of personal, scientific, organizational, and political leadership" (2012: 4). A "critical first step" for building this framework is "to construct a definition of environmental leadership. That definition must be well grounded in leadership studies, itself a young and evolving field" (2012: 4). Gallagher commendably notes how our theory-practice of environmental leading should be philosophically informed. She cites a number of thinkers who have also been foregrounded in the current project (Muir, Leopold, Naess, etc.), and she rightly foregrounds ecofeminist thought. Gallagher's call for reflective thinking strongly resonates: this is precisely what I've attempted to do in this study. Gallagher also points out the inadequacy of the conventional "heroic male" approach and credits the more recent theoretical practice on focusing on "what it means to exercise leadership" (2012: 4) – which is akin to the present work's focus on what (environmental) leadership does/would do (i.e., transform and maintain situations).

Gallagher also summarizes the broad range of leadership theories, ranging from the transformational to the charismatic and destructive. While she recognizes that conventional formulations may contribute to the question of genuine eco-leading, she suggests that "The nascent field of environmental leadership, however, is best served by its own definition, one that is at once comprehensive and concise yet also highlights the collective action necessary to address the uniqueness of the wicked, complex, and intractable environmental problems we now face" (2012: 5). My approach both confirms and deviates from this position: while environmental leading has "its own definition," the definition is nevertheless derived/generated from my general one.

Another strength of Gallagher's essay is that it differentiates leading from managing, drawing on the likes of prominent leadership researchers like Bennis and Nanus, Egri and Herman, and Boiral, Cayer and Baron. Drawing on this distinction, Gallagher compellingly contends that "Environmental management focuses on applying technical solutions to specific environmental problems" while "environmental leadership focuses on influencing followers to jointly and creatively confront diffuse challenges" (2012: 5).

Gallagher also recognizes the limits of existing formulations of eco-leadership: "While these definitions have served the nascent field well for over a decade, in 2012 a new definition of environmental leadership is required" (2012: 5). She then offers her own formulation: "environmental leadership *is a process by which Earth's inhabitants apply interpersonal influence and engage in collective action to protect the planet's natural resources and its inhabitants from further harm*" (2012: 5). I think this is a good conception, given its eco-inclusive character ("Earth's inhabitants"), emphasis on transformation via mass means ("collective action"), and preservational dimension ("protect . . . from harm"). While I'm unsure how Gallagher would then systematically derive and develop a framework or model from the basic definition (certainly a research question worth pursuing), she's clear about what environmental leading involves in practice. She rightly focuses on the way that it cuts across all situations, from the household to the national, from the local to the global. It must negotiate the task of human prosperity with the needs of the ecosphere.

Gallagher also graciously notes the value of contrarians who question whether we are facing ecological crisis and devastation/to what extent (e.g., Simon 1999; Lomborg 2001). Like Gallagher, I endorse open-mindedness, questioning, and testing the claims of environmentalists: a healthy dose of skepticism guards against dogmatism – even of the ecological kind. Open-mindedness is a central theme in my works (e.g., Manolopoulos 2009, 2018, 2019). Now, much of the work of the contrarians involves seeking to undermine admittedly large empirical claims (e.g., is anthropogenic climate change occurring? Is the world over-populated? etc.) but I posit that my own work deflects this risk by more focusing on what is/might be ethical (Earth-centeredness) and unethical (human supremacism). The empirical data that I've referenced in this work and others acts to *support* – rather than *ground* – my assessments, i.e., anthropocentric practice typically entails negative empirical consequences; ecocentric practice typically entails positive empirical consequences. In other words, the present study is basically grounded in the philosophico-ethical and supported by the empirical.

Gallagher then briefly surveys the kind of key social institutions that participate in environmental leadership: government (local, state, national, and international), NGOs (Greenpeace, Friends of the Earth, etc.), and a growing number of corporations (cf. Gallagher 2018). As noted in the previous chapter regarding the political dimension, this study doesn't explore how these actors may contribute to truly ecological leadership; however, given the radical nature of the measures, the involvement of these kinds of actors would certainly facilitate the process. Now, during her discussion of these institutions, Gallagher bravely advances structural transformation in the face of unrestrained neoliberalism: "Environmental leadership is thus transformational, it promotes a societal change from a perspective in which economic growth is valued above all to one that recognizes the limits of natural resources" (2012: 5). Later on, she echoes Foster's point about the dissensual or conflictual nature of genuine leading: "Future environmental leaders will be engaged in an ongoing conflict between economic progress and environmental protection" (2012: 9).

While Gallagher's introduction is relatively short, it makes quite the impact, not only in terms of addressing fundamental issues like defining key terms but also as a kind of pointer for fruitful future pathways for eco-leadership research. When we add Gallagher's editorial efforts to the mix, it becomes obvious that she is one of ELS's pivotal progressive promoters. Regarding the rest of the *Handbook*, I cite here some "honorable mentions" (in order of appearance): (Christensen 2012; Smutko and Addor 2012; Berkey 2012; Satterwhite 2010b; Anderton and Pangbourne 2012; Faruqi 2012; Warren 2012; Margai 2012; Berger 2012; Davis, Bowser and Brown 2012; Moser 2012).

Another work in the field of progressive ELS is *Nature-Centered Leadership: An Aspirational Narrative* (2013) by eco-educational leadership scholars Spencer S. Stober and Tracey L. Brown, and eco-business leadership scholar Sean J. Cullen. It's difficult to assess this book: on the one hand, it traverses a number of important issues in ELS – and thus, some of its foci and concerns are shared by my work (some of which are briefly discussed shortly); on the other hand, it's a kind of sprawling work rather than a systematic treatise (also demonstrated shortly), so it's somewhat difficult to engage from a critical perspective. No doubt, the book's somewhat "post-academic" character is flagged from the very beginning, announcing itself as "an aspirational narrative" (its sub-title) – but it can't decide whether it's predominantly a story, argument, or both. (While the present study introduces itself with a kind of meta-narrative or story, it quickly assumes the mode of a philosophically flavored discourse.) Maybe the (divided) nature of *Nature-Centered Leadership* partially accounts for why it hasn't thus far drawn significant attention. (A notable advocate is Redekop: Redekop, Gallagher and Satterwhite 2018a: 1; Redekop and Thomas 2018: 145 – though even in those essays the work is cited rather than discussed.)

Let's briefly show how *Nature-Centered Leadership* is simultaneously worthy of consideration but also problematic from a "scholarly" perspective. To begin with, at the very beginning of the book, the authors provide a kind of three-part meta-narrative akin to the one I offer in the Introduction to this book: they speak of humans being "over" (dominating), "with" (partially dominating), and "of" (existing with) Nature (capitalized). But what do Stober, Brown, and Cullen mean, exactly, by "Nature" – and why, incidentally, is it capitalized? It's difficult to gauge from definitions such as "referring to all natural phenomena" and "Nature-centered leaders capitalize the word Nature to acknowledge both material and spiritual views of life on Earth" (2013: 2). One is also prone to wondering whether the book privileges non-human nature over the human. Furthermore, the fact that Stober, Brown, and Cullen do not register non-human nature's power and domination over humans lends the work to the charge of portraying non-human nature in overly harmonious, romanticized terms, whereas my version of Earth-centeredness fully recognizes the violent dimensions of the non-human world, such as predation, pandemics, dissolution, and death.

Also in the very first pages of *Nature-Centered Leadership* is another shared theme: the book refers to anthropocentrism, biocentrism, and ecocentrism; Stober, Brown, and Cullen state: "This [Nature-centered] leadership process works to minimize human-centered (anthropocentric) values while promoting Nature-centric (bio- and eco-centric) values" (2013: 2). This is a promising sign but the authors somewhat expand on these notions in snippets (2013: 3, 11, 12, 13, etc.) rather than fully or systematically developing them. This is somewhat surprising, given that "Nature-centered" takes center-stage and is perpetually reiterated. This patchwork approach is also applied to the key concept-phenomenon: "Nature-centered leadership." What do they mean by it? – indeed, what do they mean by "leadership"?

I conclude my review of *Nature-Centered Leadership* on the following note: early in the book, Stober, Brown, and Cullen offer a clear and concise review of various forms of leadership, one of them being "situational leadership" – which is obviously interesting from my perspective, given the centrality of "situations" in my theorization. The authors summarize this form of leading in the following way: "Situations vary and leaders must adjust accordingly to be effective. Nature-centered leaders need to modulate their rhetoric and actions to accommodate changing perspectives on the environment" (2013: 22). While the term "situation" is shared, my approach diverges from this model: the represented perspective is quite diplomatic and flexible, while the version I advance "stands its ground," so to speak, doggedly defending existing Earth-centered situations from anthropocentric contestation, and transforming human-centered situations into more eco-centered ones.

The next piece of writing examined here is "Rethinking Environmental Leadership: The Social Construction of Leaders and Leadership in Discourses of Ecological Crisis, Development and Conservation" (2015) by organizational and leadership scholar Peter Case, environmental governance researcher Louisa S. Evans, and their co-authors. (Other important/related works by these scholars include, e.g., Case, French and Simpson 2013; Evans and others 2015.) The article ranks among the most sophisticated pieces of ELS literature that I've encountered – however (and once again), my review will not do justice to the scope and depth of the text. The paper accomplishes a number of interrelated tasks. It shows when and how the concept of leadership features in conservation science (some discursive references were cited earlier). It also draws on the work of cutting-edge leadership scholar Keith Grint (2001, 2005) to authoritatively problematize the ways in which researchers exclusively/primarily focus on one aspect of the phenomenon, e.g., agential, positional, processual, etc. (2015: 405–412 cf. Grint, Jones and Holt 2016). The authors therefore advocate a thoroughly "pluralistic" understanding of eco-leadership that incorporates the array of perspectives. One may posit that this pluralistic approach resonates to some degree with my method because "situation" somewhat encompasses these various dimensions of leadership phenomena.

While there are certain resonances between the article and my work, the crucial question we may ask but can only respond in a preliminary way is whether/to what extent my research is prone to the various incisive criticisms raised by the article. For instance, Case and his co-authors approach the definitional question from a nuanced skeptical perspective, questioning (but not completely dismissing) conventional formulations of leading. Are, then, my definitions of leading and eco-leading examples of "positivist positions that aim to distil the fundamental laws of leadership"? (Case and others 2015: 400). One could propose that this characterization rings true because I have "distilled" what I consider to be the basic criteria or conditions of leaderly and eco-leaderly phenomena, i.e., efforts to change (anthropocentric) situations and maintain contested (ecocentric) ones. However, my whole approach is suffused by openness, uncertainty, ambiguity, and a tension between a sophisticated essentialism and a moderate constructionism, expressed by the fact that, in *Following Reason*, I repeatedly intentionally note that I have "identified or constructed/construed" leadership's fundamental indicators (2019: 11, 13, 31), implying that they may be either inherent elements or constructed measures (or perhaps a bit of both). My work is too tentative to proclaim that I have discovered something like the "eternal laws" of leadership, though I also think there is enough traction to it that it contributes to our understanding of this perplexing phenomenon, both at the general and environmental levels.

Another important theme in the 2015 article that challenges this study is the authors' questioning/contestation of environmental-crisis narratives. Given that I've referred to the multipronged eco-crisis throughout this work, the article acts as a reminder that this discourse poses risks, including justifying the following practices: imposing solutions that silence alternative perspectives; prioritizing Western-scientific knowledge-action over other local-indigenous knowledges-actions; and implementing strong centralized/globalized governance (Case and others 2015: 399–400). Other criticisms/recommendations in the article by Case and his co-authors are even more plainly pertinent for the present study. For instance, the researchers note that there is very little research in environmental science on the dimension of followership (2015: 414), which also applies to ELS and this monograph. As I explained in my Introduction, while I heavily focused on this question in *Following Reason*, in the present work I've bracketed it in order to restrain an already-expansive project.

I now turn to a review of key texts from *Innovation in Environmental Leadership: Critical Perspectives* (2018c), which was edited by Redekop, Gallagher, and

Satterwhite. It is sophisticated, well-written, and well-argued; it challenges mainstream leadership studies and ELS and offers pathways forward for future research. There's a good mix of more theoretical and more empirical studies. As the retracing shows, this is an excellent volume – perhaps the most rigorous example of critical-progressive ELS, though there are elements of it that are questioned from my radically ecocentric perspective. As with my reviews of other edited volumes, I focus on what I consider to be the most significant from my perspective (i.e., more philosophically oriented; some recourse to the anthropocentric-ecocentric polarity; etc.). As explained earlier, I shall review Redekop's sole-authored contributions to the 2010 and 2018 volumes together (thereby concluding the retracing), so I first turn to the other entries, beginning with a short review of the Introduction and an even shorter review of the Conclusion, which are written by Redekop, Gallagher, and Satterwhite. I also continue my custom of citing "honorable mentions" at the end of the review.

The Introduction begins by stating that the collection is a kind of "sequel" to Redekop's 2010 volume (2018a: 1), so the authors cite key texts since that publication (Gallagher's *Handbook*; Stober, Brown, and Cullen's *Nature-Centered Leadership*; and the 2013 second edition of Western's *Leadership: A Critical Text*). The editors state that works like *Leadership for Environmental Sustainability* and the *Handbook* did not favor any particular method or perspective, while the present volume focuses on "critical, postheroic, and global perspectives" (2018a: 2). Very pointedly, Redekop, Gallagher, and Satterwhite note how conventional leadership scholarship has been largely shaped – and I would add: misled – by "an environmentally unsustainable socio-economic world system" (2018a: 2). The authors immediately explain how critical leadership studies (CLS) has nevertheless emerged from the very same business school environment from which mainstream leadership discourse developed; the rest of the Introduction cites key articles from this emerging current (e.g., Collinson 2011; Collinson and Tourish 2015). The authors define CLS in terms of the ways in which it "critiques essentialist, heroic, and dualistic understandings of leadership, suggesting instead dialectical approaches that acknowledge follower agency and the realities of power and complexity in human and organizational dynamics" (2018a: 2).

Given that my method does not completely dismiss elements of "essentialist, heroic, and dualistic" leadership discourse but also appropriates/parallels aspects of CLS (e.g., it's more-than-agent-centered), one could propose that my work oscillates in the space between (or beyond) conventional and critical camps. Indeed, one could claim that Redekop, Gallagher, and Satterwhite occupy the same/similar space, given that, on the one hand, they question something like heroicism in mainstream leadership studies, but they nevertheless don't seek to abandon it altogether: "it would be naïve to dismiss the role of powerful positional leaders in all walks of life, and thus a critically informed pragmatism is in order" (2018a: 6, cf. 2018b: 242). This inclusive approach is also employed by Western – who is a foundational figure for the volume, as stated by the editors in the Introduction (2018a: 1, 2): "I am firmly of the belief that the individual leader and follower are essential to understanding leadership" (2018: 55–56). I read these statements as a kind of confirmation of the promise of my approach to leading, which doesn't simplistically abandon received leadership studies doctrines but rather critically synthesizes and develops elements of traditional and critical-progressive pathways, thereby constructing something that I've already called "radical ELS." The authors will make the same point about Western's work in their concluding essay: "not simply rejecting outdated forms of leadership entirely, but rather employing those elements in limited ways as needed moving forward" (2018b: 242).

Redekop, Gallagher, and Satterwhite's discerning perspective is also evidenced by the fact that they note how critical leadership studies – which emphasizes various contexts (social, economic, political, etc.) – has nonetheless typically disregarded the environmental context: "The CLS focus on the socio-cultural construction of leadership ignores the fact that we all inhabit a physical/natural universe that is in the end not a human construction – at least not in its fundamental features" (2018a: 3–4). Hence, one of the aims of the volume is to expand the scope of CLS to include the ecological context (2018a: 4) – exemplified by Satterwhite's contribution, which was reviewed earlier. Such an expansion brings progressive ELS closer to radical ELS. The rest of the Introduction summarizes the volume's contributions.

Given that the volume is devoted to *critical* leadership studies, the concluding essay by Redekop, Gallagher, and Satterwhite rightly refocuses on the constructive–prescriptive dimension of the discipline; the authors edifyingly note: "a critical perspective is not one bound by critique alone, but with an eye toward change" (2018b: 241) – though we also recall that my model insists that leading will often also involve *maintaining* existing situations. The editors then review the volume's contributions from this programmatic angle. We now turn to brief examinations of some of the contributions.

Sustainable leadership scholar Jem Bendell, leadership development consultant Richard Little, and organizational theorist Neil Sutherland are the authors of the first chapter, which is provocatively titled "The Seven Unsustainabilities of Mainstream Leadership." On the one hand, the essay is self-assured and deftly destabilizes key conventional leadership mantras. On the other hand, I found the texts' formulations of key concepts problematic. For instance, the authors commence by reciting a definition constructed by Bendell and Little in a previous work: "Leadership is any behavior that has the effect of helping groups of people achieve something that the majority of them are pleased with and which [observers] assess as significant and what they would not have otherwise achieved" (2015: 15). While there are certain strengths to it – e.g., the "pleased with" condition deftly differentiates leading from more coercive practices like dictatorship – one wonders whether it remains too narrow, given its emphasis on the behavioral dimension of the phenomenon. One may also ask how a definition of environmental leading may be derived from the fundamental formulation.

After a whirlwind retracing of key problems associated with mainstream leadership discourse, and after Bendell, Little, and Sutherland provide a list of seven key unsustainable notions associated with conventional leadership concepts and then counter them with sustainable ones (we shall not discuss these points here), the authors provide a definition of sustainable leadership: "*Sustainable leadership is any ethical behavior that has the intention and effect of helping groups of people address shared dilemmas in significant ways not otherwise achieved*" (2018: 26). The most striking thing about the definition for me is the absence of any reference to the non-human world, though the word "dilemmas" encompasses eco-predicaments (this is confirmed in the paragraph after the definition is provided).

The next contribution from *Innovation in Environmental Leadership* briefly highlighted here is "Sustainable Leadership: Toward Restoring the Human and Natural World" by sustainability scholar Tina Lynn Evans. The chapter commences in a striking way for me because it refers to "tiered dualism" (2018: 61), which I call "hierarchical dualism/binarism" – an important notion for the present work (especially the second and third chapters). Evans explains how this hierarchical logic-practice has proliferated among many discourses, including leadership. Evans defines sustainable leadership as "a form of community praxis in which one coalesces and directs the energies of a group toward ends that enhance the long-term health, integrity, and resilience of the community and natural systems of which it is a part" (2018: 62). Straightaway we note the Leopoldian tone, with the formulation's reference to "community" and "integrity" (Leopold 1989: viii, 204, 224–225). During the course of the essay, Evans elaborates on the key themes of health, integrity, and resilience according to a variety of discourses and contexts.

From my perspective, the most admirable aspect of the Evans essay is that it becomes increasingly radical. She first offers relatively vague morsels like "To realize sustainable leadership would entail deep social change that can only happen through a long-term process of cultural change" (2018: 63) but then declares that "The world-system is not sustainable, but predatory and opportunistic" (2018: 63). Evans proceeds to robustly criticize colonialism and the world economic system it spawned. She also makes the following profound observation: "Because most people now live and survive through an unjust and unsustainable capitalist system, we are walking contradictions, supporting ourselves and our families in the short term while participating in the long-term undoing of the natural world as well as the continued breakdown of social justice and coherent, collaborative communities" (2018: 65–66). Evans's boldness is breathtaking, rare, true, and welcomed by us radical ecocentrists.

Another noteworthy contribution to *Innovation in Environmental Leadership* is "Toward an Understanding of the Relationship Between the Study of

Leadership and the Natural World" by leadership scholar Robert M. McManus, co-author with Gama Perruci of the 2015 book, *Understanding Leadership: An Arts and Humanities Perspective*, and also the co-author with David J. Brown of a chapter on followership in the 2018 collection that is not retraced here. The most interesting thing about the essay from my perspective is that McManus outlines the definition of leadership he developed with Perruci in *Understanding Leadership*; they conceptualize leading as a process consisting of five parts: leader, followers, the goal, the context, and influential values and norms (2018: 98; McManus and Perruci 2015: 15). Straightaway we note a certain congruence with my own theorization, given that the five elements (and possibly/ probably others) may be incorporated into the notion of "situation" – this congruence is later confirmed (but not elaborated) by McManus when he states that "Leadership is essentially situational" (2018: 111).

Now, the author prefaces the definition with the plea for leadership scholars to include "the natural world" in our understanding of leadership, so it's unclear whether the plea also applies to his own basic model, given that it's conceivable that "the natural world" could be included under "context" and even "values and norms." However, McManus later confirms that this broad concept-entity (which, as far as I can tell, is not defined in the chapter) be included as a feature or condition of leading in general: "What I am proposing here . . . is that the natural world not be seen as a component of only environmental leadership, but as a vital component of the general phenomenon of leadership" (2018: 100). But should a *general* formulation of leading be required to explicitly include it? My fundamental model doesn't explicitly refer to it – indeed, even my environmental formulation doesn't include it. Why? Because "the natural world" is folded into the concept of ecocentrism, just as "the artifactual world" is also included.

McManus's chapter is packed with insights – too many for all of them to be addressed here. Much of his thinking traverses, parallels, and often departs from mine – in terms of both my general leadership theory and eco-leadership model. For instance, McManus perceives the ubiquity and mundaneness of leadership (2018: 102), points I also make in *Following Reason*. Another commonality is our appropriation of Maslow's schema – albeit for different ends: I draw on it in order to construct an ecocentric ethic/ethos (i.e., non-human needs take precedence over unreasonable human wants), while McManus draws on the notion of a certain prioritization of physiological needs (food, shelter, etc.) over psycho-social ones (love, belonging, etc.) to reinforce his claim of the centrality of the natural world for all leadership theory. This is a rather reasonable point, but I haven't privileged the physiological over the psychological for a number of unstated reasons (e.g., ecocentrism seeks the full formation of individuals and societies, which requires the satisfaction of psychological as well as physiological needs; I think the two are quite interdependent; etc.). To sum up, then: given that McManus's essay focuses on things like definition, the parallels between our general models, the question of human needs, and indeed his insistence on the natural world (problematic though it might be), I consider the text to be an important contribution to critical-progressive ELS.

All of the contributions to *Innovation in Environmental Leadership* are excellent but, as with Gallagher's *Handbook*, I shall only cite some of the more resonant entries (in order of appearance): (Western 2018; Cletzer and Kaufman 2018; Gallagher 2018; Brown and McManus 2018; Redekop and Thomas 2018; Allen 2018; Steffen 2018).

In this last part of the review, I examine the work of Redekop. As noted earlier, he is one of the most important figures in critical-progressive ELS, in terms of both the quality of his output and his editorial achievements. As with other important figures, the retracing doesn't do justice to the scope and depth of his work. Now, I have already surveyed his co-written Introduction and Conclusion to the 2018 volume, and I now examine his three contributions to the 2010 collection: the Introduction, which is titled "Connecting Leadership and Sustainability" (2010a); "Challenges and Strategies of Leading for Sustainability" (2010b); and the Conclusion, titled "Towards a New General Theory of Leadership" (2010c).

As we can tell from the titles of the first two essays, Redekop is focused on the theme of sustainability in his work, but what does he mean by it? From the outset – from the first paragraph of the Introduction – he makes clear that when he's speaking of "sustainability," he's not merely referring to the survivalist dimension of the word-phenomenon but also to its sense of flourishing (2010a: 1, 8; this echoes my just-discussed inclusion of both physiological and psychological needs). In the next paragraph, Redekop adopts the definition by the World (/Brundtland) Commission on the Environment and Development: "meeting the needs of the present without compromising the ability of future generations to meet their own needs" (WCED 1987: 8) – once again, "future generations" is problematic insofar as it typically excludes the non-human (or at least doesn't explicitly include it). Redekop also introduces the work by way of a broad retracing, noting how the discipline of leadership studies had paid scant attention to environmental matters (2010a: 2–5). (Of course, since 2010, ELS has significantly grown, as the present retracing shows.) During his review, Redekop incisively notes how mainstream ELS had been restricted within the capitalist perspective that ignores the broader social and ecological context within which leading takes place (2010a: 3).

Redekop then devotes some time to the definitional question. He expresses a nuanced inclusive understanding of leading. He states that "we [it is unclear whether he is speaking in the royal "we" or representing the group of authors in the volume] do not assume that leadership necessarily resides in a person or position but rather is a quality that can be expressed and shared in myriad ways, times, and places" (2010a: 6). Note the crucial qualifying term "necessarily": one may reasonably infer that Redekop is unwilling to dogmatically reject agent-centered and positional renderings of leading while simultaneously incorporating other perspectives. The author's dialectical "both/and" understanding is explicated in the very next sentence when he states that "Leaders are both born and made" (2010a: 6): this is a welcomed approach in a field when one side is ordinarily prioritized at the expense of the other/others; this inclusive, multipronged strategy is mirrored in my work, given that "situation" gathers up a/the multiplicity of dimensions and perspectives.

Redekop then states that the approach taken in the book (once again, it's unclear whether he's speaking for himself or collectively) "is a more philosophical one" (2010a: 6), which is obviously a welcomed approach from my perspective. But then Redekop straightaway makes the claim that "leadership *by definition* entails environmental concern" (2010a: 6; cf. Redekop 2010c: 243). According to my theory of leadership, this isn't necessarily the case if/to the extent that "concern" has an ethical dimension: I claim that leading has to do with the maintenance and transformation of situations; the question of concern (whether environmental or any other kind) is addressable when we engage with specific kinds of leading and are able to determine whether situational maintenance or transformation is an ethical endeavor (Manolopoulos 2019; Chapter 1 above).

So Redekop begins his explanation of the nature of leadership in a contestable way; however, as he progresses, he develops a solid conception. First of all, he notes how the phenomenon occurs within, and is conditioned by, space and time (cf. Redekop 2010c: 243). This is an excellent point, given that leadership discourse has tended to ignore or insufficiently explicate these dimensions. This may also be true of my work, though the concept of situational change/maintenance implies these factors. Leading on from this point, Redekop then emphasizes context (and the socially constructed dimension of leading), arguing that leadership changes over time and space: he provides the example whereby leading for hunter–gatherers is different from corporate leadership. But I beg to differ: my general model shows how we can identify at least two conditions/criteria of leading across time/times and space/spaces (i.e., situational change/maintenance), while other traits will be context-dependent (such as the nature of the acts that lead to situational change/maintenance). And so, as "paradoxical" as it may appear, I contend that leading is both context-dependent and context-independent. Redekop himself appears to confirm my contention: "To make this suggestion [leadership's context-dependence] is not to argue that there are no fundamental leadership qualities that are widely shared" (2010a: 6) – once again, note how Redekop attempts to maintain a tension, this time between a hyper-essentialistic and hyper-relativistic/constructionist understanding. Later on, the philosopher will suspend the question regarding "*absolutely universal* leadership qualities" (2010a: 8); one can perceive how Redekop is grappling with these confounding questions. The fact that he performs suspensions and employs nuanced language is testament to the fact that it's a *thoughtful* grappling.

Redekop then explains how leading is conditioned by the dimension of time: he immediately states that "good leaders are those people who help the group navigate its way into a desirable future" (2010a: 7). While Redekop includes the ethical dimension of leading into the equation, it's fundamentally sound: leading occurs over time. I therefore strongly concur with Redekop when he stipulates that "Leadership involves, among other things, setting future goals and helping others [followers] to meet them" (2010a: 7). The author then cites the likes of Burns, Bass, and other scholars to support this claim.

Interestingly, Redekop also notes that the trait of future goals is what differentiates leading from managing, which is an excellent way of framing the distinction. He also powerfully explains how the difference is reflected in everyday language: "'to manage' connotes activity in the here and now, while 'to lead' suggests forward motion in both space and time" (2010a: 8). Bracketing the fact that "forward motion" is not the whole story of leading (situational maintenance involves a kind of resistance to the forward motion of competing leadership seeking to change the contested situation), Redekop deftly shows how common language discloses something of the nature of leading.

The next piece of Redekop's writing briefly reviewed here is "Challenges and Strategies of Leading for Sustainability," which is his contribution to the main body of the 2010 volume. While this short work is not as insightful as some of Redekop's other writings, it still provides some noteworthy points. For instance, Redekop insightfully recognizes that a number of environmental challenges "will not be fully felt for decades" (2010b: 55) – anthropogenic climate change immediately comes to mind. He also argues that one of the biggest challenges for eco-leadership is fighting the human tendency for satisfying immediate needs/wants rather than also taking into account the longer-term collective good (2010b: 56). At this stage, Redekop refers to the problem of "unlimited population growth" in the context of "a finite system" (2010b: 56). To overcome human shortsightedness, Redekop turns to environmental psychology and how it can be applied to eco-leadership. Certain laudable suggestions are offered, including re-directing the dominant narrative of "ecological crisis" to "ecological regeneration" (2010b: 59). Another key proposal is framing environmental challenges as justice issues, although Redekop's framing remains narrowly zoocentric: "the more that environmental problems are framed as problems of fairness and justice to other human beings (and perhaps animals), the more people will feel inclined to take responsibility for them" (2010b: 61; cf. Kals and Maes 2002; Hossay 2006; Berkey 2012; Margai 2012; Cripps 2015; Kopnina 2016).

Redekop's Conclusion to the 2010 volume is titled "Towards a New General Theory of Leadership." When I first read the title, I was obviously tantalized by it, given that I myself have sketched the outline of a general theory (Manolopoulos 2019; cf. Chapter 1 above), but I wonder whether the text lives up to the title. First of all, Redekop reiterates a number of the points raised in the

Introduction (such as taking context into account when thinking leadership), and then he promotes discourses like evolutionary theory and psychoanalysis as foundations for a general model (2010c: 243). While I think such discourses have the potential to contribute to our understanding of leading, I question whether they're required as *foundations* for a *general theory*, as my own model doesn't rely on them (it relies on observing leadership phenomena and distilling apparently inherent properties/conditions/criteria). My endeavor therefore flies in the face of Redekop's claim that "it is difficult to see how any truly important and useful theory of leadership will not be informed by evolutionary approaches, including evolutionary psychology" (2010c: 243). What is fascinating is that Redekop immediately warns against applying insights from chaos and complexity theory to our constructions of leadership theory (2010c: 244) – even though he has recommended exactly the same thing with evolutionary biology and psychoanalysis. Another important discourse that Redekop identifies for a general model of leading is systems thinking. As scholars like Satterwhite and others have demonstrated, it's a rich resource for rethinking environmental leadership; but, once again, I question whether/to what extent it's required as a foundation for a fundamental theory.

Redekop also raises the conundrum of reconciling individual freedoms with the collective good (2010c: 245; this subject echoes our discussion of the tension between freedom and equality in the previous chapter). In this regard, he notes how "The difficulty of 'solving' this problem is compounded by the failure of communist and other utopian ideologies to produce a just and workable socioeconomic system, and the attendant revulsion by many segments of the western body politic (particularly in America) to any sort of collectivist thinking" (2010c: 245). Redekop then cites scholars whose theorizations work *within* rather than *against* the market system (Wielkiewicz and Stelzner; Western), though the crucial question here is whether this accommodation could still provide the impetus for launching the kinds of radical leaderly measures I've outlined in the previous chapter. We also note how, during this discussion, Redekop interestingly and skillfully expands "self-interest" to include the self-interest of an organization or system (2010c: 245).

Another element needed for a new general theory sketched by Redekop is "postmodern critical theory" (2010c: 246). I completely agree with Redekop that this set of discourses – which discloses "the subterranean workings of power and the plight of the poor and marginalized" (2010c: 246) – is crucial for leadership studies and ELS, given that the latter discourses have thus far largely ignored or dismissed critical theory and associated epistemic currents (and one could say the same thing about postmodern critical theory)" (followed by a period). The present book has certainly been informed by postmodern thought – albeit often in many implicit ways – as part of its methodology and process (e.g., from its quasi-phenomenological approach to its close deconstructive reading of texts).

Now, I recognize that, in the 2010 Conclusion, Redekop was only marking out a path *toward* a new general theory of leadership (akin to the way this monograph *outlines* a theory of environmental leading). However, I would contend that he proceeds less systematically than I do – or perhaps more accurately: what he attempts to do in the concluding essay is begin to build a theory from pieces provided by the volume's contributors that are quite different in style, content, and method, so his pathway is more synthetic than systematic. I also reiterate that I think Redekop fuses a general theory with an environmental one, whereas I derive/develop the latter from the former. As also just mentioned, there's also the question of Redekop's biocentrism: he remains restricted within life-centered eco-discourse (e.g., 2010a: 1, 2010b: 61). Despite these shortcomings, Redekop displays promise in this early work. In *Innovation in Environmental Leadership*, he doesn't offer a sole-authored contribution, so it's difficult to gauge developments in his own thinking since 2010, though he's very impressed with the progress made by other thinkers like Western.

I conclude this relatively brief survey of ELS by listing some other more-and-less progressively oriented works that weren't reviewed here: (Wheatley 1992; Flannery and May 1994; Portugal and Yukl 1994; Swann 2001; Springett 2003; Starik 2004; Howardson 2006; Skodvin and Andresen 2006; MacNeill 2007; Tranter 2009; Hay 2010; Galaz and others 2011; Schein 2015; Marshall, Coleman and Reason 2017; Heizmann and Liu 2018).

CONCLUSION
Loose Ends and Openings

I noted at the beginning of this work that it does not seek to be a "theory of everything eco-leaderly." However, the study has covered a lot of terrain, from retracing my general theory of leadership (Chapter 1) to intricately describing anthropocentrism and ecocentrism (Chapters 2 and 3) to outlining my theory of eco-centered environmental leadership and some of its measures (Chapter 4) and comparing my model with existing conceptions (Chapter 5). Of course, with such an expansive work, there were questions opened up by it that could not be adequately addressed, such as the issue of ecocentric followership, the correlation between anthropocentrism and egocentrism, the critical appropriation by ELS of contemporary thing-centered philosophies, the politics and economics of Earth-centered leading, and further comparison of my model with other ELS perspectives. But rather than simply interpreting these kinds of suspensions and openings as monographic omissions or shortcomings, it demonstrates the immense richness of ELS as a field of inquiry. In sum: even though I think I've contributed to our understanding of environmental leadership with this treatise, obviously there's so much more we can learn about eco-leading, and hopefully more knowledge of it leads to more manifestations of it.

In the meantime, a crippled Earth continues to be mis/led by an anthropocentric humanity, whose consequences include global pandemics and hellish Australian bushfires. Perhaps we may develop Burns's famous quip about leadership here to describe the current troubling situation: if leadership remains the most observed and least understood phenomenon on Earth, then environmental leadership remains both the least observed and least understood. But I – eternal optimist that I am – conclude on a strangely positive note: eco-leading and its accompanying discipline certainly remain in their infancies, groping around in near-darkness like infants, searching for a better understanding of leading for a thriving Earth – what a challenge, what a responsibility . . . but what a delight.

BIBLIOGRAPHY

Ackerman, Seth. (2012). "The Red and the Black." *Jacobin*. December 20. https://jaco binmag.com/2012/12/the-red-and-the-black

Adams, Carol A., Marielle G Heijltjes, Gavin Jack, Tim Marjoribanks and Michael Powell. (2011). "The Development of Leaders Able to Respond to Climate Change and Sustainability Challenges." *Sustainability Accounting, Management and Policy Journal* 2.1: 165–171.

Adams, Carol J. (1990). *The Sexual Politics of Meat: A Feminist-Vegetarian Critical Theory*. New York: Continuum.

Adams, Carol J., ed. (1993). *Ecofeminism and the Sacred*. New York: Continuum.

Addepalli, Sri, Gerardo Pagalday, Konstantinos Salonitis and Rajkumar Roy. (2018). "Socio-Economic and Demographic Factors that Contribute to the Growth of the Civil Aviation Industry." *Procedia Manufacturing* 19: 2–9.

Agar, Nicholas. (2001). *Life's Intrinsic Value: Science, Ethics, and Nature*. New York: Columbia University Press.

Akenji, Lewis. (2014). "Consumer Scapegoatism and Limits to Green Consumerism." *Journal of Cleaner Production* 63: 13–23.

Akenji, Lewis. (2019). "Avoiding Consumer Scapegoatism: Towards a Political Economy of Sustainable Living." PhD Thesis. University of Helsinki, Helsinki.

Albers, Peter H., Gregory Linder and James D. Nichols. (1990). "Effects of Tillage Practices and Carbofuran Exposure on Small Mammals." *Journal of Wildlife Management* 54.1: 135–142.

Alcraft, Rob. (2000). *Oil Disasters*. Des Plaines: Heinemann Library.

Allen, Edith B. (2003). "New Directions and Growth of Restoration Ecology." *Restoration Ecology* 11.1: 1–2.

Allen, Kathleen E. (2018). "Critical Shifts for Sustainable Leadership." In *Innovation in Environmental Leadership: Critical Perspectives*. Eds. Benjamin W. Redekop, Deborah Rigling Gallagher and Rian Satterwhite. New York: Routledge, 212–224.

Allen, Kathleen E., Stephen P. Stelzner and Richard M. Wielkiewicz. (1998). "The Ecology of Leadership: Adapting to the Challenges of a Changing World." *Journal of Leadership Studies* 5.2: 62–82.

Allhoff, Fritz, Patrick Lin and Daniel Moore. (2010). *What Is Nanotechnology and Why Does It Matter? From Science to Ethics.* Chichester: Wiley-Blackwell.

Allin, Craig, ed. (1990). *International Handbook of National Parks and Nature Reserves.* New York: Greenwood Press.

Alvares, Claude. (1992). *Science, Development and Violence: The Revolt Against Modernity [The Twilight of Modernity].* Delhi: Oxford University Press.

American Beauty. (1999). Feature film. Dir. Sam Mendes. USA: Jinks/Cohen Company.

Anderson, Deborah J. (2019). "Population and the Environment: Time for Another Contraception Revolution." *New England Journal of Medicine* 381: 397–399.

Anderton, Karen and Kate Pangbourne. (2012). "The Significance of Individual Leadership in Complex Governance Arenas: The Case of Transportation and Climate Change." In *Environmental Leadership: A Reference Handbook.* Volume Two. Ed. Deborah Rigling Gallagher. Thousand Oaks: Sage, 746–760.

Andrady, Anthony L., ed. (2003). *Plastics and the Environment.* Hoboken: Wiley-Interscience.

Andresen, Steinar. (1993). "The Effectiveness of the International Whaling Commission." *Arctic* 46.2: 108–115.

Andronova, Liliana B. (2004). *Transnational Politics of the Environment: The European Union and Environmental Policy in Central and Eastern Europe.* Cambridge: MIT Press.

Angry Inuk. (2016). Documentary. Dir. Alethea Arnaquq-Baril. Canada: Alethea Arnaquq-Baril.

Angus, Ian and Simon Butler. (2011). *Too Many People? Population, Immigration, and the Environmental Crisis.* Chicago: Haymarket Books.

Aquinas, Thomas. (1947–1948). *Summa Theologica.* Trans. Fathers of the English Dominican Province. London: Burns & Oates.

Archer, Mike. (2011). "Ordering the Vegetarian Meal? There's More Animal Blood on Your Hands." *The Conversation.* December 16. https://theconversation.com/ordering-the-vegetarian-meal-theres-more-animal-blood-on-your-hands-4659

Arias-Maldonado, Manuel and Zev M. Trachtenberg, eds. (2019). *Rethinking the Environment for the Anthropocene: Political Theory and Socionatural Relations in the New Geological Epoch.* London: Routledge.

Attenborough, David. (2011). "People and Planet." *Royal Society for the Encouragement of Arts,* Manufactures and Commerce President's Lecture. www.youtube.com/watch?v=1sP291B7SCw

Attenborough, David. (2018). "Population Growth Has to Come to an End." *BBC Newsweek.* October 4. www.bbc.com/news/av/science-environment-45741482/sir-david-attenborough-population-growth-has-to-come-to-an-end

Attfield, Robin. (1981). "The Good of Trees." *Journal of Value Inquiry* 15: 35–54.

Australian Institute of Health and Welfare (AIHW) [Australian Government]. (2017). *A Picture of Overweight and Obesity in Australia.* Canberra: AIHW. www.aihw.gov.au/getmedia/172fba28-785e-4a08-ab37-2da3bbae40b8/aihw-phe-216.pdf.aspx?inline=true

Babb, Arnold O. and T. W. Mermel. (1968). *Catalog of Dam Disasters, Failures and Accidents.* Washington, DC: U.S. Department of the Interior, Bureau of Reclamation.

Baker, Ron. (1985). *The American Hunting Myth.* New York: Vantage Press.

Banerjee, S. Bobby. (2004). "Reinventing Colonialism: Exploring the Myth of Sustainable Development." *Situation Analysis* 4: 95–110.

Bansal, Pratima and Hee-Chan Song. (2017). "Similar But Not the Same: Differentiating Corporate Sustainability from Corporate Responsibility." *Academy of Management Annals* 11.1: 105–149.

Barbier, Edward. (2012). *A New Blueprint for a Green Economy*. New York: Routledge.

Bari, Judi. (1995). "Revolutionary Ecology: Biocentrism and Deep Ecology." *Alarm: A Journal of Revolutionary Ecology*. Available at *Capitalism Nature Socialism* (1997) 8.2: 145–149.

Barlow, Jos and others. (2016). "Anthropogenic Disturbance in Tropical Forests Can Double Biodiversity Loss from Deforestation." *Nature* 535: 144–147.

Bar-On, Yinon, Rob Phillips and Ron Milo. (2018). "The Biomass Distribution on Earth." *Proceedings of the National Academy of Sciences of the United States of America* 115.25: 6506–6511.

Bass, Bernard M. (1985). *Leadership and Performance Beyond Expectations*. New York: The Free Press.

Bass, Bernard M. (1990a). *Bass and Stogdill's Handbook of Leadership: Theory, Research, and Managerial Applications*. New York: The Free Press.

Bass, Bernard M. (1990b). "From Transactional to Transformational Leadership: Learning to Share the Vision." *Organizational Dynamics* 18.3: 19–31.

Bass, Bernard M. (1997). "Does the Transactional–Transformational Leadership Paradigm Transcend Organizational and National Boundaries?" *American Psychologist* 52.2: 130–139.

Bass, Bernard M. (2007). "Concepts of Leadership." In *Leadership: Understanding the Dynamics of Power and Influence in Organizations*. Second ed. Ed. Robert P. Vecchio. Notre Dame: University of Notre Dame Press, 1–22.

Bass, Bernard M. and Paul Steidlmeier. (1999). "Ethics, Character, and Authentic Transformational Leadership Behavior." *Leadership Quarterly* 10.2: 181–217.

Batavia, Chelsea, Michael Paul Nelson, Chris T. Dairmont, Paul C. Paquet, William J. Ripple and Arian D. Wallach. (2018). "The Elephant (Head) in the Room: A Critical Look at Trophy Hunting." *Conservation Letters: A Journal of the Society for Conservation Biology* 12.1.

Bate, Jonathan. (2005). *The Song of the Earth*. London: Picador.

Bateson, Gregory. (1972). *Steps to an Ecology of Mind: Collected Essays in Anthropology, Psychiatry, Evolution, and Epistemology*. San Francisco: Chandler Publishing Co.

Baxter, R. M. (1977). "Environmental Effects of Dams and Impoundments." *Annual Review of Ecology and Systematics* 8: 255–283.

Beckerman, Wilfred and Joanna Pasek. (2010). "In Defense of Anthropocentrism." In *Environmental Ethics: The Big Questions*. Ed. David R. Keller. Chichester: Wiley-Blackwell, 83–88.

Belk, Russell. (2014). "You Are What You Can Access: Sharing and Collaborative Consumption Online." *Journal of Business Research* 67.8: 1595–1600.

Belnap, Nuel. (1993). "On Rigorous Definitions." *Philosophical Studies: An International Journal for Philosophy in the Analytic Tradition* 72.2–3: 115–146.

Benagiano, Giuseppe, Carlo Bastianelli and Manuela Farris. (2007). "Contraception: A Social Revolution." *European Journal of Contraception & Reproductive Health Care* 12.1: 3–12.

Bendell, Jem and Richard Litte. (2015). "Seeking Sustainability Leadership." *Journal of Corporate Citizenship* 60: 13–26.

Bendell, Jem, Richard Little and Neil Sutherland. (2018). "The Seven Unsustainabilities of Mainstream Leadership." In *Innovation in Environmental Leadership: Critical*

Perspectives. Eds. Benjamin W. Redekop, Deborah Rigling Gallagher and Rian Satterwhite. New York: Routledge, 13–31.

Bennett, Jane. (2004). "The Force of Things: Steps Toward an Ecology of Matter." *Political Theory* 32.3: 347–372.

Bennett, Jane. (2010). *Vibrant Matter: A Political Ecology of Things.* Durham: Duke University Press.

Bennis, Warren G. (1975). "Where Have All the Leaders Gone?" In *Ethics, Leadership and Interdependence: Three Addresses to Federal Executives.* Ed. Patrick J. Conklin. Charlottesville: Federal Executive Institute. Reprinted in *Contemporary Issues in Leadership.* Second ed. Eds. W. E. Rosenbach and Robert L. Taylor. Boulder: Westview Press, 5–23.

Bennis, Warren G. (1989). *On Becoming a Leader.* New York: Addison Wesley.

Bennis, Warren G. and Burt Nanus. (1985). *Leaders: The Strategies for Taking Charge.* New York: Harper & Row.

Bennis, Warren G. and Burt Nanus. (1997). *Leaders: Strategies for Taking Charge.* Second ed. New York: HarperBusiness.

Berger, John J. (1985). *Restoring the Earth: How Americans Are Working to Renew Our Damaged Environment.* New York: Knopf/Random House.

Berger, Michael L. (2001). *The Automobile in American History and Culture: A Reference Guide.* Westport: Greenwood Press.

Berger, Stephanie G. (2012). "Leading for the Future." In *Environmental Leadership: A Reference Handbook.* Volume Two. Ed. Deborah Rigling Gallagher. Thousand Oaks: Sage, 883–890.

Berkey, Becca. (2012). "Environmental Justice from the Ground Up." In *Environmental Leadership: A Reference Handbook.* Volume One. Ed. Deborah Rigling Gallagher. Thousand Oaks: Sage, 328–335.

Berry, Joyce K. and John C. Gordon, eds. (1993). *Environmental Leadership: Developing Effective Skills and Styles.* Washington, DC: Island Press.

Best, Steven. (2014). *The Politics of Total Liberation: Revolution for the 21st Century.* New York: Palgrave Macmillan.

Betsill, Michele E., Kathryn Hochstetler and Dimitris Stevis, eds. (2005). *Palgrave Advances in International Environmental Politics.* New York: Palgrave Macmillan.

Bettridge, Neela and Philip Whiteley. (2013). *New Normal, Radical Shift: Changing Business and Politics for a Sustainable Future.* London: Routledge.

Bible. (1993). *New Revised Standard Version.* Grand Rapids: Zondervan.

Biese, Alfred. (1905). *The Development of the Feeling for Nature in the Middle Ages and Modern Times.* London: G. Routledge & Sons.

Birch, Charles and John B. Cobb, Jr. (1981). *The Liberation of Life.* Cambridge: Cambridge University Press.

Birmingham, Beth and Stan L. LeQuire. (2010). "Green Heroes Reexamined: An Evaluation of Environmental Role Models." In *Leadership for Environmental Sustainability.* Ed. Benjamin W. Redekop. New York: Routledge, 107–121.

Black, Simon A., Jim J. Groombridge and Carl G. Jones. (2011). "Leadership and Conservation Effectiveness: Finding a Better Way to Lead." *Conservation Letters* 4.5: 329–339.

Blake, Robert R. and Jane Srygley Mouton. (1982). "Theory and Research for Developing a Science of Leadership." *Journal of Applied Behavioral Science* 18.3: 275–291.

Blok, Vincent. (2018). "Technocratic Management Versus Ethical Leadership Redefining Responsible Professionalism in the Agri-Food Sector in the Anthropocene." *Journal of Agricultural and Environmental Ethics* 31.5: 583–591.

Boddice, Rob. (2009). *A History of Attitudes and Behaviours Toward Animals in Eighteenth- and Nineteenth-Century Britain: Anthropocentrism and the Emergence of Animals.* Lewiston: Mellen Press.

Boddice, Rob. (2011). "Introduction: The End of Anthropocentrism." In *Anthropocentrism: Humans, Animals, Environments.* Ed. Rob Boddice. Leiden: Brill, 1–18.

Boesch, Donald D., Carl H. Hershner and Jerome H. Milgram. (1974). *Oil Spills and the Marine Environment.* Cambridge: Ballinger Publishing Co.

Bogost, Ian. (2012). *Alien Phenomenology.* Ann Arbor: Open Humanities Press.

Boiral, Olivier, Mario Cayer and Charles Baron. (2009). "The Action Logics of Environmental Leadership: A Developmental Perspective." *Journal of Business Ethics* 85.4: 479–499.

Bolig, Andy. (2016). "Patina: Caring for the Evidence of Previous Neglect." *Rod Authority.* September 25. www.rodauthority.com/features/editorials-opinions/patina-caring-for-the-evidence-of-previous-neglect/

Bond, Michael Harris and Peter B. Smith. (1996). "Cross-Cultural Social and Organizational Psychology." *Annual Review of Psychology* 47: 205–235.

Bookchin, Murray. (1971). *Post-Scarcity Anarchism.* Berkeley: Ramparts Press.

Bookchin, Murray. (1980). *Toward an Ecological Society.* Montreal: Black Rose Books.

Bookchin, Murray. (1982). *The Ecology of Freedom: The Emergence and Dissolution of Hierarchy.* Palo Alto: Cheshire Books.

Bookchin, Murray. (1990). *Philosophy of Social Ecology: Essays on Dialectical Naturalism.* Montreal: Black Rose Books.

Bookchin, Murray. (1991). "Where I Stand Now." In *Defending the Earth: A Debate.* Eds. Dave Foreman and Murray Bookchin. Montreal: Black Rose Books, 80–88.

Botsman, Rachel and Roo Rogers. (2010). *What's Mine Is Yours: The Rise of Collaborative Consumption.* New York: Harper Business.

Boulding, Kenneth E. (1966). "The Economics of the Coming Spaceship Earth." In *Environmental Quality in a Growing Economy: Resources for the Future.* Ed. Henry Jarrett. Baltimore: Johns Hopkins University Press, 3–14.

Boyd, Brewster, Nina Henning, Emily Reyna, Daniel E. Wang and Matthew D. Welch. (2009). *Hybrid Organizations: New Business Models for Environmental Leadership.* Sheffield: Greenleaf.

Bradshaw, Anthony David. (1980). *The Restoration of Land: The Ecology and Reclamation of Derelict and Degraded Land.* Oxford: Blackwell.

Braggs, Sierra. (2012). "Earth First!: The Rise of Eco-Action." MA Thesis. Humboldt State University, Arcata.

Bramble, Ben and Bob Fischer, eds. (2015). *The Moral Complexities of Eating Meat.* New York: Oxford University Press.

Brannen, Peter. (2017). *The Ends of the World: Volcanic Apocalypses, Lethal Oceans, and Our Quest to Understand Earth's Past Mass Extinctions.* New York: Ecco (HarperCollins).

Brassier, Ray. (2009). *Nihil Unbound: Enlightenment and Extinction.* Basingstoke: Palgrave Macmillan.

Brenner, Neil and Nik Theodore. (2002). "Cities and Geographies of 'Actually Existing Neoliberalism'." *Antipode* 34.3: 349–379.

Broome, Richard, with Richard Barnden, Don Garden, Don Gibb, Elisabeth Jackson and Judith Smart. (2016). *Remembering Melbourne 1850–1960.* Melbourne: Royal Historical Society of Victoria.

Broswimmer, Franz J. (2002). *Ecocide: A Short History of the Mass Extinction of Species.* London: Pluto Press.

Brown, Charles S. and Ted Toadvine, eds. (2003). *Eco-Phenomenology: Back to the Earth Itself.* Albany: State University of New York Press.

Brown, David J. and Robert M. McManus. (2018). "Followers' Self-Perception of Their Role in Addressing Climate Change: A Cultural Comparison." In *Innovation in Environmental Leadership: Critical Perspectives.* Eds. Benjamin W. Redekop, Deborah Rigling Gallagher and Rian Satterwhite. New York: Routledge, 167–184.

Brown, Wendy. (2015). *Undoing the Demos: Neoliberalism's Stealth Revolution.* New York: Zone Books.

Bruckner, Donald D. (2015). "Strict Vegetarianism Is Immoral." *The Moral Complexities of Eating Meat.* Eds. Ben Bramble and Bob Fischer. New York: Oxford University Press, 30–47.

Bryant, Levi. (2011). *The Democracy of Objects.* Ann Arbor: Open Humanities Press.

Bryant, Levi, Nick Srnicek and Graham Harman. (2011). *The Speculative Turn: Continental Materialism and Realism.* Melbourne: re.press.

Brymer, Eric George, Tonia Gray, Wayne Cotton and Cathryn Carpenter. (2010). *Ecological Leadership: A New Perspective on Leadership.* Baulkham Hills: Spirituality, Leadership and Management Conference Proceedings, 84–94.

Bulow, Jeremy. (1986). "An Economic Theory of Planned Obsolescence." *Quarterly Journal of Economics* 101.4: 729–750.

Burchett, Kyle. (2014). "Anthropocentrism and Nature: An Attempt at Reconciliation." *Teoria* 34.2: 119–137.

Burns, James MacGregor. (1978). *Leadership.* New York: Harper & Row.

Burns, James MacGregor. (2003). *Transforming Leadership: A New Pursuit of Happiness.* New York: Atlantic Monthly Press.

Butler, Judith. (1990). *Gender Trouble: Feminism and the Subversion of Identity.* New York: Routledge.

Calder, Nigel. (2005). *Magic Universe: A Grand Tour of Modern Science.* Oxford: Oxford University Press.

Caldwell, John C. (1980). "Mass Education as a Determinant of the Timing of Fertility Decline." *Population and Development Review* 6.2: 225–255.

Callicott, J. Baird. (1980). "Animal Liberation: A Triangular Affair." *Environmental Ethics* 2.4: 311–338.

Callicott, J. Baird. (1984). "Non-Anthropocentric Value Theory and Environmental Ethics." *American Philosophical Quarterly* 21.4: 299–309.

Callicott, J. Baird. (1986). "On the Intrinsic Value of Non-Human Species." In *The Preservation of Species.* Princeton: Princeton University Press, 138–172.

Callicott, J. Baird. (1987a). "Conceptual Resources for Environmental Ethics in Asian Traditions of Thought: A Propaedeutic." *Philosophy East and West* 37.2: 115–130.

Callicott, J. Baird. (1987b). "The Philosophical Value of Wildlife." In *Economic and Social Values of Wildlife.* Eds. Daniel J. Decker and Gary R. Goff. Boulder: Westview Press, 214–221.

Callicott, J. Baird. (1989). *In Defense of the Land Ethic: Essays in Environmental Philosophy.* Albany: State University of New York Press.

Callicott, J. Baird. (1992). "Rolston on Intrinsic Value." *Environmental Ethics* 14.2: 129–143.

Callicott, J. Baird and James McRae, eds. (2014). *Environmental Philosophy in Asian Traditions of Thought.* Albany: State University of New York Press.

Campbell, Colin J. (1991). *The Golden Century of Oil 1950–2050: The Depletion of a Resource.* New York: Springer.

Campbell, Colin J. and Jean H. Laherrère. (1998). "The End of Cheap Oil." *Scientific American*. March: 78–83.

Canney, Susan. (2017). "A Response to 'We Need to Talk About the Militarization of Conservation'." *Wild Foundation*. July 24. www.wild.org/blog/green-european-journal-response/

Capra, Fritjof. (1996). *The Web of Life*. New York: Anchor Books.

Caras, Roger. (1970). *Death as a Way of Life*. Boston: Little, Brown & Co.

Carlopio, James R. (1994). "Holism: A Philosophy of Organizational Leadership for the Future." *Leadership Quarterly* 5.3–4: 297–307.

Carrington, Damian, Niko Kommenda, Pablo Gutiérrez and Cath Levett. (2017). "One Football Pitch of Forest Lost Every Second in 2017, Data Reveals." *The Guardian*. June 27. www.theguardian.com/environment/ng-interactive/2018/jun/27/one-football-pitch-of-forest-lost-every-second-in-2017-data-reveals

Carson, Rachel. (1962). *Silent Spring*. Boston: Houghton Mifflin.

Carter, Neil. (2001). *The Politics of the Environment: Ideas, Activism, Policy*. Cambridge: Cambridge University Press.

Case, Peter, Louisa S. Evans, Michael Fabinyi, Philippa J. Cohen, Christina C. Hicks, Murray Prideau and David J. Mills. (2015). "Rethinking Environmental Leadership: The Social Construction of Leaders and Leadership in Discourses of Ecological Crisis, Development and Conservation." *Leadership* 11.4: 396–423.

Case, Peter, Robert French and Peter Simpson. (2013). "The Philosophy of Leadership." In *Sage Handbook of Leadership*. Eds. Alan Bryman, David Collinson, Keith Grint, Brad Jackson and Mary Uhl-Bien. London: Sage, 242–254.

Casper, Julie Kerr. (2010). *Fossil Fuels and Pollution: The Future of Air Quality*. New York: Facts on File.

Cato, Molly Scott. (2009). *Green Economics: An Introduction to Theory, Policy and Practice*. London: Earthscan.

Catton, William, Jr. (1980). *Overshoot: The Ecological Basis of Revolutionary Change*. Urbana: University of Illinois Press.

Cavell, Stanley. (1972). *The Senses of Walden*. New York: Viking Press.

Ceballos, Gerardo, Paul R. Ehrlich, Anthony D. Barnosky, Andrés García, Robert M. Pringle and Todd M. Palmer. (2015). "Accelerated Modern Human-Induced Species Losses: Entering the Sixth Mass Extinction." *Science Advances* 1.5: e1400253. http://advances.sciencemag.org/content/1/5/e1400253

Chaleff, Ira. (1995). *The Courageous Follower*. San Francisco: Berrett-Koehler.

Chang, Li-ping. (2016). "Spirits in the Material World: Ecocentrism in Native American Culture and Louise Erdrich's *Chickadee*." *Children's Literature in Education* 47.2: 148–160.

Chapman, Heather and Judith Stillman. (2015). *Lost Melbourne*. London: Pavilion.

Chapman, Margaret. (2003). "Kangaroos and Feral Goats as Economic Resources for Graziers: Some Views From South-West Queensland." *Rangeland Journal* 25.1: 20–36.

Choi, Incheol, Richard E. Nisbett and Ara Norenzayan. (1999). "Causal Attribution Across Cultures: Variation and Universality." *Psychological Bulletin* 125.1: 47–63.

Christensen, Lisa Jones, Alison Mackey and David Whetten. (2014). "Taking Responsibility for Corporate Social Responsibility: The Role of Leaders in Creating, Implementing, Sustaining, or Avoiding Socially Responsible Firm Behaviors." *Academy of Management Perspectives* 28.2: 164–178.

Christensen, Norman L., Jr. (2012). "Environmental Leadership as a Practice." In *Environmental Leadership: A Reference Handbook*. Volume One. Ed. Deborah Rigling Gallagher. Thousand Oaks: Sage, 11–16.

Christensen, Norman L., Jr., Ann M. Bartuska, James H. Brown, Stephen Carpenter, Carla D'Antonio, Rober Francis, Jerry F. Franklin, James A. MacMahon, Reed F. Noss, David J. Parsons, Charles H. Peterson, Monica G. Turner and Robert G. Woodmansee. (1996). "The Report of the Ecological Society of America Committee on the Scientific Basis for Ecosystem Management." *Ecological Applications* 6.3: 665–691.

Christol, Carl Q., John R. Schmidhauser and George O. Totten. (1976). "The Law and the Whale: Current Developments in the International Whaling Controversy." *Case Western Reserve Journal of International Law* 8.1: 149–167.

Chun, Rosa. (2005). "Ethical Character and Virtue of Organizations: An Empirical Assessment and Strategic Implications." *Journal of Business Ethics* 57.3: 269–284.

Ciulla, Joanne B. (2004). "Ethics and Effective Leadership." In *The Nature of Leadership*. Eds. John Antonakis, Anna T. Cianciolo and Robert J. Sternberg. Thousand Oaks: Sage, 302–327.

Clark, Simon. (1999). "Capitalist Competition and the Tendency to Overproduction: Comments on Brenner's 'Uneven Development and the Long Downturn'." *Historical Materialism* 4.1: 57–72.

Clausen, Rebecca and Brett Clark. (2005). "The Metabolic Rift and Marine Ecology: An Analysis of the Ocean Crisis Within Capitalist Production." *Organization & Environment* 18.4: 422–444.

Clepper, Henry, ed. (1971). *Leaders of American Conservation.* New York: Ronald Press.

Cletzer, D. Adam and Eric K. Kaufman. (2018). "Eco-Leadership, Complexity Science, and 21st-Century Organizations." In *Innovation in Environmental Leadership: Critical Perspectives.* Eds. Benjamin W. Redekop, Deborah Rigling Gallagher and Rian Satterwhite. New York: Routledge, 80–96.

Clewell, Andre F. and James Aronson. (2007). *Ecological Restoration: Principles, Values, and Structure of an Emerging Profession.* Washington, DC: Island Press.

Coates, Peter. (1998). *Nature: Western Attitudes Since Ancient Times.* Berkeley: University of California Press.

Cocks, Samuel and Steven Simpson. (2015). "Anthropocentric and Ecocentric: An Application of Environmental Philosophy to Outdoor Recreation and Environmental Education." *Journal of Experiential Education* 38.3.

Coghlan, Simon. (2014). "Australia and Live Animal Export: Wronging Nonhuman Animals." *Journal of Animal Ethics* 4.2: 45–60.

Cohen, Joel E. (1995). *How Many People Can the Earth Support?* New York: W. W. Norton.

Collard, Andred and Joyce Contrucci. (1988). *The Rape of the Wild: Man's Violence Against Animals and the Earth.* Bloomington: Indiana University Press.

Collinson, David. (2011). "Critical Leadership Studies." *The SAGE Handbook of Leadership.* Eds. Alan Bryman, David Collinson, Keith Grint, Brad Jackson and Mary Uhl-Bien. Thousand Oaks: Sage.

Collinson, David and Dennis Tourish. (2015). "Teaching Leadership Critically: New Directions for Leadership Pedagogy." *Academy of Management Learning & Education* 14.4: 576–594.

Congedo, Luca and Silvia Macchi. (2015). "The Demographic Dimension of Climate Change Vulnerability: Exploring the Relation Between Population Growth and Urban Sprawl in Dar es Salaam." *Current Opinion in Environmental Sustainability* 13: 1–10.

Conly, Sarah. (2016). *One Child: Do We Have a Right to More?* New York: Oxford University Press.

Cooney, Rosie, Alex Baumber, Peter Ampt and George Wilson. (2008). "Sharing Skippy: How Can Landholders Be Involved in Kangaroo Production in Australia?" *Rangeland Journal* 31.3: 283–292.

Cooper, Tim. (2016). "Repair or Replace? How to Fight Constant Demands for 'New Stuff'." *The Conversation*. October 6. https://theconversation.com/repair-or-replace-how-to-fight-constant-demands-for-new-stuff-66299

Costanza, Robert, ed. (1992). *Ecological Economics: The Science and Management of Sustainability*. New York: Columbia University Press.

Costanza, Robert and Herman E. Daly, eds. (1987). "Special Issue on Ecological Economics." *Ecological Modelling* 38.1–2.

Cotton, Ulysses. (1986). *Oil Spills, 1976–85: Statistical Report*. Washington, DC: U.S. Dept of the Interior, Minerals Management Service.

Court, Franklin E. (2012). *Pioneers of Ecological Restoration: The People and Legacy of the University of Wisconsin Arboretum*. Madison: University of Wisconsin Press.

Crawfoot, James E. (1993). "Academic Leadership." In *Environmental Leadership: Developing Effective Skills and Styles*. Eds. John C. Gordon and Joyce K. Berry. Washington, DC: Island Press, 223–251.

Cripps, Elizabeth. (2015). "Climate Change, Population, and Justice: Hard Choices to Avoid Tragic Choices." *Global Justice: Theory Practice Rhetoric* 8.2. www.research.ed.ac.uk/portal/files/21633037/Cripps_GJTPR2015_population_and_justice.pdf

Cripps, Elizabeth. (2017). "Population and Environment: The Impossible, the Impermissible, and the Imperative." In *The Oxford Handbook of Environmental Ethics*. Eds. Stephen M. Gardiner and Allen Thompson. New York: Oxford University Press, 380–390.

Crook, Martin, Damien Short and Nigel South. (2018). "Ecocide, Genocide, Capitalism and Colonialism: Consequences for Indigenous Peoples and Glocal Ecosystems Environments." *Theoretical Criminology* 22.3.

Crossan, Mary, Daina Mazutis, Mark Reno and Peter Rea. (2017). "Leadership Virtues and Character: A Perspective in Practice." In *Handbook of Virtue Ethics in Business and Management*. Eds. Alejo José G. Sison, Gregory R. Beabout and Ignacio Ferrero. Dordrecht: Springer, 509–519.

Crowther, T. W. and others. (2015). "Mapping Tree Density at a Global Scale." *Nature* 525: 201–205.

Crutzen, Paul J. and Eugene F. Stoermer. (2000). "The Anthropocene." *Global Change Newsletter* 41.1: 17–18. [Also refer to "Opinion: Have We Entered the 'Anthropocene'?" www.igbp.net/news/opinion/opinion/haveweenteredtheanthropocene.5.d8b4c3c12bf3be638a8000578.html]

Dallmayr, Fred. (2014). *Mindfulness and Letting Be: On Engaged Thinking and Acting*. Lanham: Lexington Books.

Daly, Herman E., ed. (1973). *Toward a Steady-State Economy*. San Francisco: W. H. Freeman.

Daly, Herman E. (1990). "Sustainable Growth: A Bad Oxymoron." *Environmental Carcinogenesis Reviews* 8.2: 401–407.

Daly, Herman E., ed. (2007). *Ecological Economics and Sustainable Development: Selected Essays of Herman Daly*. Cheltenham: Edward Elgar.

Daly, Mary. (1978). *Gyn/ecology: The Metaethics of Radical Feminism*. Boston: Beacon Press.

Dark Waters. (2019). Feature film. Dir. Todd Haynes. USA: Participant/Killer Films/Focus Features.

Darnall, Nicole and others. (2000). "Environmental Management Systems: Opportunities for Improved Environmental and Business Strategy." *Environmental Quality Management* 9.3: 1–10.

Daston, Lorraine. (2008). "On Scientific Observation." *Isis* 99.1: 97–110.

Dauvergne, Peter, ed. (2012). *Handbook of Global Environmental Politics.* Cheltenham: Edward Elgar.

Davidson, Graeme. (1978). *The Rise and Fall of Marvellous Melbourne.* Carlton: Melbourne University Press.

Davidson, Graeme. (2004). *The Rise and Fall of Marvellous Melbourne.* Second ed. Carlton: Melbourne University Press.

Davis, Elizabeth, Gillian Bowser and Mark Brown. (2012). "Creating the Global Leader and Global Mind-Set." In *Environmental Leadership: A Reference Handbook.* Volume Two. Ed. Deborah Rigling Gallagher. Thousand Oaks: Sage, 891–899.

Davis, Steven L. (2003). "The Least Harm Principle May Require That Humans Consume a Diet Containing Large Herbivores, Not a Vegan Diet." *Journal of Agricultural and Environmental Ethics* 16.4: 387–394.

Davis, Steven M. (1996). "Environmental Politics and the Changing Context of Interest Group Organizations." *Social Science Journal* 33.4: 343–357.

de Beauvoir, Simone. (1989). *The Second Sex.* Trans. H. Parshley. New York: Vintage Books.

Dechant, Kathleen and others. (1994). "Environmental Leadership: From Compliance to Competitive Advantage." *Academy of Management Executive* 8.3: 7–27.

Deffeyes, Kenneth S. (2005). *Beyond Oil: The View from Hubbert's Peak.* New York: Hill & Wang.

Delio, Ilia. (2003). *A Franciscan View of Creation: Learning to Live in a Sacramental World.* St. Bonaventure: The Franciscan Institute.

Dell'amore, Christine. (2014). "Species Extinction Happening 1,000 Times Faster Because of Humans?" *National Geographic.* May 30. www.nationalgeographic.com/news/2014/5/140529-conservation-science-animals-species-endangered-extinction/

Derraik, José G. B. (2002). "The Pollution of the Marine Environment by Plastic Debris: A Review." *Marine Pollution Bulletin* 44.9: 842–852.

Derrida, Jacques. (1976). *Of Grammatology.* Trans. Gayatri Chakravorty Spivak. Baltimore: Johns Hopkins University Press.

Derrida, Jacques. (1995). *Points . . . Interviews, 1974–1994.* Ed. Elisabeth Weber. Trans. Peggy Kamuf and others. Stanford: Stanford University Press.

Derrida, Jacques. (2008). *The Animal That Therefore I Am.* Ed. Marie-Louise Mallet. Trans. David Wills. New York: Fordham University Press.

Desai, Meghnad. (2001). "Consumption and Pollution." In *The Consumer Society.* Eds. I. R. C. Hirst and W. Duncan Reekie. London: Routledge, 23–36.

Descartes, René. (1960). *Discourse on Method and Meditations.* Trans. Laurence J. Lafleur. New York: Bobbs-Merrill.

DeSilver, Drew. (2016). "What's On Your Table? How America's Diet Has Changed Over the Decades." *Fact Tank.* Pew Research Center. December 13. www.pewresearch.org/fact-tank/2016/12/13/whats-on-your-table-how-americas-diet-has-changed-over-the-decades/

DeSombre, Elizabeth R. (2007). *Global Environment and World Politics.* London: Continuum.

Devall, Bill. (1988). *Simple in Means, Rich in Ends.* Salt Lake City: Gibbs-Smith.

de Vos, Jurriaan M., Lucas N. Joppa, John L. Gittleman, Patrick R. Stephens and Stuart L. Pimm. (2015). "Estimating the Normal Background Rate of Species Extinction." *Conservation Biology* 29.2: 452–462.

Diamond, Jared M. (1989). "The Present, Past and Future of Human-Caused Extinctions." *Philosophical Transactions of the Royal Society B Biological Sciences* 325.1228: 469–476.

Diamond, Jared M. (2005). *Collapse: How Societies Choose to Fail or Succeed*. New York: Viking Press.

Dietz, James M., Rina Aviram, Sophia Bickford, Karen Douthwaite, Amy Goodstine, Jose-Luis Izursa, Stephanie Kavanaugh, Katie MacCarthy, Michelle O'Herron and Keri Parker. (2004). "Defining Leadership in Conservation: A View From the Top." *Conservation Biology* 18.1: 274–278.

Dixon, Bernard. (1976). "Smallpox – Imminent Extinction, and an Unresolved Dilemma." *New Scientist* 69.989: 430–432.

DiZegera, Gus. (1996). "Towards an Ecocentric Political Economy." *The Trumpeter: Journal of Ecosophy* 13.4. http://trumpeter.athabascau.ca/index.php/trumpet/article/view/242/349

Dobson, Andrew. (2016). *Environmental Politics: A Very Short Introduction*. Oxford: Oxford University Press.

Dolgin, Elie. (2019). "The Secret Social Lives of Viruses." *Nature*. June 18. www.nature.com/articles/d41586-019-01880-6

Donovan, Josephine. (1990). "Animal Rights and Feminist Theory." *Signs: Journal of Women in Culture and Society* 15.2: 350–375.

Dorsey, Kurk. (2014). *Whales and Nations: Environmental Diplomacy on the High Seas*. Seattle: University of Washington Press.

Doyle, Catherine. (2017). "Captive Wildlife Sanctuaries: Definition, Ethical Considerations and Public Perception." *Animal Studies Journal* 6.2: 55–85.

Drexler, K. Eric. (1986). *Engines of Creation: The Coming Era of Nanotechnology*. Garden City: Doubleday.

Dryzek, John. (1987). *Rational Ecology: Environment and Political Economy*. New York: Basil Blackwell.

Duffey, Eric. (1974). *Nature Reserves and Wildlife*. London: Heinemann Educational.

Dugan, John P. (2017). *Leadership Theory: Cultivating Critical Perspectives*. San Francisco: Jossey-Bass.

Dunlap, Riley E. and Kent D. van Liere. (1978). "The 'New Environmental Paradigm': A Proposed Measuring Instrument and Preliminary Results." *Journal of Environmental Education* 9.4: 10–19.

Dunlap, Riley E. and Kent D. van Liere. (1984). "Commitment to the Dominant Social Paradigm and Concern for Environmental Quality." *Social Science Quarterly* 65: 1013–1028.

Dunlap, Riley E., Kent D. van Liere, Angela G. Mertig and Robert Emmet Jones. (2000). "Measuring Endorsement of the New Ecological Paradigm: A Revised NEP Scale." *Journal of Social Issues* 56.3: 425–442.

Dyck, Bruno. (1994). "From Airy-Fairy Ideas to Concrete Realities: The Case of Shared Farming." *Leadership Quarterly* 5.3–4: 227–246.

Eaubonne, Françoise d'. (1974). *Féminisme ou la Mort*. Paris: P. Horay.

Eberbach, Catherine and Kevin Crowley. (2009). "From Everyday to Scientific Observation: How Children Learn to Observe the Biologist's World." *Review of Educational Research* 79.1.

Eberbach, Catherine and Kevin Crowley. (2017). "From Seeing to Observing: How Parents and Children Learn to See Science in a Botanical Garden." *Journal of the Learning Sciences* 26.4.

Eckersley, Robyn. (1992). *Environmentalism and Political Theory: Toward an Ecocentric Approach*. London: UCL Press.

Edgell, Stephen, Kevin Hetherington and Alan Warde, eds. (1996). *Consumption Matters: The Production and Experience of Consumption*. Oxford: Blackwell.

Egerton, Frank N. (2012). *Roots of Ecology: Antiquity to Haeckel*. Berkeley: University of California Press.

Egri, Carolyn P. and Peter J. Frost. (1994). "Leadership for Environmental and Social Change." *Leadership Quarterly* 5.3–4: 195–200.

Egri, Carolyn P. and Susan Herman. (2000). "Leadership in the North American Environmental Sector: Values, Leadership Styles and Contexts of Environmental Leaders and Their Organizations." *Academy of Management Journal* 43.4: 571–604.

Egri, Carolyn P. and Lawrence T. Pinfield. (1996). "Organizations and the Biosphere: Ecologies and Environments." In *Handbook of Organisation Studies*. Eds. Stewart R. Clegg, Cynthia Hardy and Walter R. Nord. London: Sage, 459–483.

Ehrenfeld, David. (1978). *The Arrogance of Humanism*. New York: Oxford University Press.

Ehrlich, Paul. (1968). *The Population Bomb*. New York: Ballan.

Ekström, Karin M. and Kay Glans, eds. (2011). *Beyond the Consumption Bubble*. New York: Routledge.

Elliot, Robert. (1982). "Faking Nature." *Inquiry* 25.1: 81–93.

Elliott, Lorraine. (2004). *The Global Politics of the Environment*. Washington Square: New York University Press.

Elton, Charles S. (1958). *The Ecology of Invasions by Animals and Plants*. London: Methuen.

Epstein, Charlotte. (2005). *The Power of Words in International Relations: Birth of an Anti-Whaling Discourse*. Cambridge: MIT Press.

Ertz, Myriam, Fabien Durif and Manon Arcand. (2016). "Collaborative Consumption: Conceptual Snapshot at a Buzzword." *Journal of Entrepreneurship Education* 19.2: 1–23.

Espy, James, Jr. (1993). "Local Voluntary Organizations." In *Environmental Leadership: Developing Effective Skills and Styles*. Eds. Joyce K. Berry and John C. Gordon. Washington, DC: Island Press, 200–210.

Evans, Louisa S., Christina C. Hicks, Philippa J. Cohen, Peter Case, Murray Prideaux and David J. Mills. (2015). "Understanding Leadership in the Environmental Sciences." *Ecology and Society* 20.1: 50. www.ecologyandsociety.org/vol20/iss1/art50/

Evans, Tina Lynn. (2012). *Occupy Education: Living and Learning Sustainably*. New York: Peter Lang.

Evans, Tina Lynn. (2018). "Sustainable Leadership: Toward Restoring the Human and Natural World." In *Innovation in Environmental Leadership: Critical Perspectives*. Eds. Benjamin W. Redekop, Deborah Rigling Gallagher and Rian Satterwhite. New York: Routledge, 61–79.

Fairhurst, Gail T. and Heather M. Zoller. (2008). "Resistance, Dissent and Leadership in Practice." In *Dissent and the Failure of Leadership*. Ed. Stephen P. Banks. Northampton: Edward Elgar, 135–148.

Fairlie, Simon. (2010). *Meat: A Benign Extravagance*. White River Junction: Chelsea Green Publishing.

Falk, Pasi. (1994). *The Consuming Body*. Thousand Oaks: Sage Publications.

Falkowski, Paul G. (2015). *Life's Engines: How Microbes Made Earth Habitable*. Princeton: Princeton University Press.

Faruqi, Mehreen. (2012). "Embracing Complexity to Enable Change." In *Environmental Leadership: A Reference Handbook*. Volume Two. Ed. Deborah Rigling Gallagher. Thousand Oaks: Sage, 772–781.

Felson, Marcus and Joe L. Spaeth. (1978). "Community Structure and Collaborative Consumption." *American Behavioral Scientist* 21.4: 614–624.

Ferrando, Francesca. (2016). "The Party of the Anthropocene: Post-Humanism, Environmentalism and the Post-Anthropocentric Paradigm Shift." *Relations: Beyond Anthropocentrism* 4.2: 159–173.

Fertner, Christian, Gertrud Jørgensen, Thomas Alexander Sick Nielsen and Kjell Svenne Bernhard Nilsson. (2016). "Urban Sprawl and Growth Management: Drivers, Impacts and Responses in Selected European and US Cities." *Future Cities and Environment* 2.9.

Fieser, James. (1993). "Callicott and the Metaphysical Basis of Ecocentric Morality." *Environmental Ethics* 15.2: 171–180.

Fischer, Bob and Andy Lamey. (2018). "Field Deaths in Plant Agriculture." *Journal of Agricultural and Environmental Ethics* 31.4: 409–428.

Fisher, Franklin M., Zvi Griliches and C. Kaysen. (1962). "The Costs of Automobile Model Changes Since 1949." *American Economic Review* 52.2: 259–261.

Flannery, Brenda L. and Douglas R. May. (1994). "Prominent Factors Influencing Environmental Leadership: Application of a Theoretical Model in the Waste Management Industry." *Leadership Quarterly* 5.3–4: 201–222.

Foltz, Bruce V. (1995). *Inhabiting the Earth: Heidegger, Environmental Ethics, and the Metaphysics of Nature.* New Jersey: Humanities Press.

Food and Agriculture Organization of the United Nations (FAO). (2002). *The State of the World Fisheries and Aquaculture.* Rome: FAO. www.fao.org/3/a-y7300e.pdf

Food and Agriculture Organization of the United Nations (FAO). (2003). *World Agriculture: Towards 2015/2030.* Rome: FAO. www.fao.org/docrep/005/y4252e/y4252e00.htm#TopOfPage

Food and Agriculture Organization of the United Nations (FAO). (n.d.). *Save Food: Global Initiative on Food Loss and Waste Reduction (Key Findings).* www.fao.org/save-food/resources/keyfindings/en/

Foote, Jennifer. (1990). "Trying to Take Back the Planet." *Newsweek.* February 5: 24.

Foster, Charles H. W. (1993). "What Makes a Leader?" In *Environmental Leadership: Developing Effective Skills and Styles.* Eds. John C. Gordon and Joyce K. Berry. Washington, DC: Island Press, 13–27.

Foucault, Michel. (1972). *The Archaeology of Knowledge.* New York: Pantheon Books.

Fox, Warwick. (1989). "The Deep Ecology-Ecofeminism Debate and Its Parallels." *Environmental Ethics* 11.1: 5–25.

Fox, Warwick. (1990). *Toward a Transpersonal Ecology: Developing New Foundations for Environmentalism.* Boston: Shambhala.

Foyol, Henri. (1949). *General and Industrial Management.* London: Pitman.

Fraser, Caroline. (2009). *Rewilding the World: Dispatches from the Conservation Revolution.* New York: Metropolitan Books.

Frey, R. G. (1980). *Interests and Rights: The Case Against Animals.* Oxford: Clarendon Press.

Friedman, Milton. (1962). *Capitalism and Freedom.* With Rose D. Friedman. Chicago: University of Chicago Press.

Frye, Marilyn. (1983). *The Politics of Reality.* New York: Crossing Press.

Fujii, Hidemichi and Shunsuke Managi. (2016). "Trends in Corporate Environmental Management Studies and Databases." *Environmental Economics and Policy Studies* 18: 265–272.

Gabrielson, Teena, Cheryl Hall, John M. Meyer and David Schlosberg, eds. (2016). *The Oxford Handbook of Environmental Political Theory.* Oxford: Oxford University Press.

Galaz, Victor, Fredrik Moberg, Eva-Karin Olsson, Eric Paglia and Charles Parker. (2011). "Institutional and Political Leadership Dimensions of Cascading Ecological Crises." *Public Administration* 89.2: 361–380.

Galbraith, John K. (1958). *The Affluent Society.* Boston: Houghton Mifflin.

Gallagher, Deborah Rigling. (2012). "Why Environmental Leadership?" In *Environmental Leadership: A Reference Handbook.* Volume One. Ed. Deborah Rigling Gallagher. Thousand Oaks: Sage, 3–10.

Gallagher, Deborah Rigling. (2014). "The United Nations Global Compact: Forum for Environmental Leadership." In *Sustainable Development: The UN Millennium Development Goals, the UN Global Compact, and the Common Good.* Ed. Oliver F. Williams. Notre Dame: University of Notre Dame Press, 271–281.

Gallagher, Deborah Rigling. (2016). "Climate Change Leadership as Sustainability Leadership: From the C-Suite to the Conference of the Parties." *Journal of Leadership Studies* 9.4: 60–64.

Gallagher, Deborah Rigling. (2018). "Heroes No More: Businesses Practice Collaborative Leadership to Confront Climate Change." In *Innovation in Environmental Leadership: Critical Perspectives.* Eds. Benjamin W. Redekop, Deborah Rigling Gallagher and Rian Satterwhite. New York: Routledge, 128–144.

Gardner, John W. (1990). *On Leadership.* New York: The Free Press.

Gebissa, Ezekiel. (2010). "Leadership from Below: Farmers and Sustainable Agriculture in Ethiopia." In *Leadership for Environmental Sustainability.* Ed. Benjamin W. Redekop. New York: Routledge, 158–169.

Geyer, Roland, Jenna R. Jambeck and Kara Lavender Law. (2017). "Production, Use, and Fate of All Plastics Ever Made." *Science Advances* 3.7. https://advances.sciencemag.org/content/3/7/e1700782

Gilio-Whitaker, Dina. (2019). "The Story We've Been Told About America's National Parks Is Incomplete." *Time.* April 2. https://time.com/5562258/indigenous-environmental-justice/

Gissibl, Bernhard, Sabine Höhler and Patrick Kupper. (2012). *Civilizing Nature: National Parks in Global Perspective.* New York: Bergahn Books.

Gladwin, Thomas A., James J. Kennelly and Tara-Shelomith Krause. (1995). "Shifting Paradigms for Sustainable Development: Implications for Management Theory and Research." *Academy of Management Review* 20.4: 874–907.

Goethals, George R. and Georgia L. J. Sorenson eds. (2006). *The Quest for a General Theory of Leadership.* Cheltenham: Edward Elgar.

Goldsmith, Edward and Nicholas Hildyard. (1984–1992). *The Social and Environmental Effects of Large Dams.* Three vols. Camelford: Wadebridge Ecological Centre.

Goodkind, Daniel. (1995). "Vietnam's One-or-Two-Child Policy in Action." *Population and Development Review* 21.1: 85–111.

Goodpaster, Kenneth E. (1978). "On Being Morally Considerable." *Journal of Philosophy* 75: 308–325.

Gordon, John C. and Joyce K. Berry. (1993a). "Environmental Leadership: Who and Why." In *Environmental Leadership: Developing Effective Skills and Styles.* Eds. John C. Gordon and Joyce K. Berry. Washington, DC: Island Press, 3–12.

Gordon, John C. and Joyce K. Berry. (1993b). "Six Insights." In *Environmental Leadership: Developing Effective Skills and Styles.* Eds. John C. Gordon and Joyce K. Berry. Washington, DC: Island Press, 270–274.

Gordon, John C. and Joyce K. Berry. (2006). *Environmental Leadership Equals Essential Leadership: Redefining Who Leads and How.* New Haven: Yale University Press.

Gorz, André. (1980). *Ecology as Politics.* Trans. Patsy Vigderman and Jonathan Cloud. London: Pluto.

Gorz, André. (1982). *Farewell to the Working Class: An Essay in Post-Industrial Socialism.* Trans. Malcolm Imrie. London: Pluto.

Gössling, Stefan and Paul Upham. (2009). *Climate Change and Aviation: Issues, Challenges and Solutions.* London: Earthscan.

Gowdy, John M, ed. (1998). *Limited Wants, Unlimited Means: A Reader on Hunter-Gatherer Economics and the Environment.* Washington, DC: Island Press.

Graen, George B. and Mary Uhl-Bien. (1995). "Relationship-Based Approach to Leadership: Development of Leader-Member Exchange (LMX) Theory Over 25 Years: Applying a Multi-Level Multi-Domain Perspective." *Leadership Quarterly* 6.2: 219–247.

Graham, Jill W. (1988). "Chapter 3 Commentary: Transformational Leadership: Fostering Follower Autonomy, Not Automatic Followership." In *Emerging Leadership Vistas.* Eds. James Gerald Hunt, B. Rajaram Baliga, H. Peter Dachler and Chester A. Schriesheim. Lexington: Lexington Books, 73–79.

Graham, Jill W. (1995). "Leadership, Moral Development, and Citizenship Behavior." *Business Ethics Quarterly* 5.1: 43–54.

Grear, Anna, ed. (2012). *Should Trees Have Standing? 40 Years On.* Cheltenham: Edward Elgar Publishing.

Greenberg, Joy H. and Gregory Greenberg. (2013). "Native American Narratives as Ecoethical Discourse in Land-Use Consultations." *Wicazo Sa Review* 28.2: 30–59.

Greenhalgh, Susan. (2008). *Just One Child: Science and Policy in Deng's China.* Berkeley: University of California Press.

Greer, Germaine. (1970). *The Female Eunuch.* London: MacGibbon & Kee.

Grey, William. (1993). "Anthropocentrism and Deep Ecology." *Australasian Journal of Philosophy* 71.4: 463–475.

Grigg, Gordon. (1987). "Kangaroo Harvesting: A New Approach." *Australian Natural History* 22.5: 204–205.

Grigg, Gordon, Peter Hale and Daniel Lunney, eds. (1995). *Conservation Through Sustainable Use of Wildlife.* St Lucia: Centre for Conservation Biology, University of Queensland.

Grint, Keith. (2001). *The Arts of Leadership.* Oxford: Oxford University Press.

Grint, Keith. (2005). *Leadership: Limits and Possibilities.* New York: Palgrave Macmillan.

Grint, Keith, Owain Smolovic Jones and Clare Holt. (2016). "What Is Leadership: Person, Result, Position or Process, or All or None of These?" In *The Routledge Companion to Leadership.* Eds. John Storey, Jean Hartley, Jean-Louis Denis, Paul 't Hart and Dave Ulrich. Abingdon: Routledge, pp. 3–20.

Gronn, Peter. (2000). "Distributed Properties: A New Architecture for Leadership." *Educational Management and Administration* 28.3: 317–338.

Guckian, Meaghan, Raymond De Young and Spencer Harbo. (2017). "Beyond Green Consumerism: Uncovering the Motivations of Green Citizenship." *Michigan Journal of Sustainability* 5.1.

Guha, Ramachandra and J. Martinez-Alier. (1997). *Varieties of Environmentalism: Essays North and South.* London: Earthscan.

Guiltinan, Joseph. (2009). "Creative Destruction and Destructive Creations: Environmental Ethics and Planned Obsolescence." *Journal of Business Ethics* 89: 19–28.

Gunderson, Lance H., C. S. Holing and Stephen S. Light, eds. (1995). *Barriers and Bridges to the Renewal of Ecosystems and Institutions.* New York: Columbia University Press.

Gunn, Alastair S. (2001). "Environmental Ethics and Trophy Hunting." *Ethics and the Environment* 6.1: 68–95.

Gutiérrez, Nicolás L., Ray Hilborn and Omar Defeo. (2011). "Leadership, Social Capital and Incentives Promote Successful Fisheries." *Nature* 470.7334: 386–389.

Haeckel, Ernst. (1866). *Generelle Morphologie der Organismen: Allgemeine Grundzüge der organischen Formen-Wissenschaft, mechanisch begründet durch die von Charles Darwin reformirte Descendenz-Theorie.* Berlin: G. Reimer.

Haila, Yrjo and Klaus Henle. (2014). "Uncertainty in Biodiversity Science, Policy and Management: A Conceptual Overview." *Nature Conservation* 8.3: 27–43.

Halden, Rolf U. (2010). "Plastics and Health Risks." *Annual Review of Public Health* 31.1: 179–194.

Hall, David A. (1987). "On Seeking a Change of Environment: A Quasi-Taoist Proposal." *Philosophy East and West* 37.2: 160–171.

Hall, Dewey W. (2014). *Romantic Naturalists, Early Environmentalists: An Ecocritical Study.* Burlington: Ashgate.

Hall, Matthew. (2011). *Plants as Persons: A Philosophical Botany.* Albany: State University of New York Press.

Hanna, Mark D. (1995). "Environmentally Responsible Managerial Behavior: Is Ecocentrism a Prerequisite?" *Academy of Management Review* 20.4: 796–799.

Hardin, Garrett. (1968). "The Tragedy of the Commons." *Science* 162.3859: 1243–1248.

Harman, Graham. (2002). *Tool-Being: Heidegger and the Metaphysics of Objects.* Chicago: Open Court.

Harman, Graham. (2018a). *Object-Oriented Ontology: A New Theory of Everything.* London: Pelican Books.

Harman, Graham. (2018b). *Speculative Realism: An Introduction.* Medford: Polity.

Harris, Lloyd C. and Andrew Crane. (2002). "The Greening of Organizational Culture: Managers' Views on the Depth, Degree and Diffusion of Change." *Journal of Organizational Change Management* 15.3: 214–234.

Harrison, Peter. (1999). "Subduing the Earth: Genesis 1, Early Modern Science, and the Exploitation of Nature." *Journal of Religion* 79.1: 86–109.

Harrison, Ruth. (1964). *Animal Machines: The New Factory Farming Industry.* London: Vincent Stuart.

Hartshorne, Charles. (1979). "The Rights of the Subhuman World." *Environmental Ethics* 1.1: 49–60.

Harvey, David. (2005). *A Brief History of Neoliberalism.* Oxford: Oxford University Press.

Harvey, David. (2006). "Neo-Liberalism as Creative Destruction." *Geografiska Annaler, Series B, Human Geography* 88.2: 145–158.

Harvey, David. (2014). *Seven Contradictions and the End of Capitalism.* Oxford: Oxford University Press.

Harvey, John H. and Gifford Weary. (1984). "Current Issues in Attribution Theory." *Annual Review of Psychology* 35: 427–459.

Hatton, Celia. (2013). "No Siblings: A Side-Effect of China's One-Child Policy." *BBC News Magazine.* November 22. www.bbc.com/news/magazine-25035280

Haugeland, John. (2007). "Letting Be." In *Transcendental Heidegger.* Eds. Steven Crowell and Jeff Malpas. Stanford: Stanford University Press, 93–103.

Hawking, Stephen. (1988). *A Brief History of Time: From the Big Bang to Black Holes.* Toronto: Bantam Books.

Hawkins, Gay. (2009). "More-than-Human Politics: The Case of Plastic Bags." *Australian Humanities Review* 46. http://australianhumanitiesreview.org/2009/05/01/more-than-human-politics-the-case-of-plastic-bags/

Hay, Robert. (2010). "The Relevance of Ecocentrism, Personal Development and Transformational Leadership to Sustainability and Identity." *Sustainable Development* 18: 163–171.

Hayek, Friedrich A. von. (1944). *The Road to Serfdom*. London: G. Routledge & Sons.

Hayek, Friedrich A. von. (1960). *The Constitution of Liberty*. Chicago: University of Chicago Press.

Hays, Samuel P. and Barbara D. Hays. (1987). *Beauty, Health, and Permanence: Environmental Politics in the United States, 1955–1985*. Cambridge: Cambridge University Press.

Hayward, Tim. (1996). "Anthropocentrism: A Misunderstood Problem." *Environmental Values* 6.1: 49–63.

Heacox, Kim. (1996). *Visions of a Wild America: Pioneers of Preservation*. Washington, DC: National Geographic Society.

Hegel, Georg Wilhelm Friedrich. (2003). *The Phenomenology of Mind*. Trans. J. B. Baillie. Mineola: Dover Publications.

Heidegger, Martin. (1966a). *Being and Time: A Translation of Sein und Zeit*. Trans. Joan Stambaugh. Seventh ed. Albany: State University of New York Press.

Heidegger, Martin. (1966b). *Discourse on Thinking*. Trans. John M. Anderson and E. Hans Freund. New York: Harper & Row.

Heidegger, Martin. (1971). "The Origin of the Work of Art." In *Poetry, Language, Thought*. Trans. Albert Hofstadter. New York: Harper & Row, 15–86.

Heizmann, Helena and Helena Liu. (2018). "Becoming Green, Becoming Leaders: Identity Narratives in Sustainability Leadership Development." *Management Learning* 49.1: 40–58.

Heller, Trudy and Jon Van Til. (1982). "Leadership and Followership: Some Summary Propositions." *Journal of Applied Behavioral Science* 18.3: 405–414.

Hemphill, John K. (1949). *Situational Factors in Leadership*. Columbus: Ohio State University.

Hersey, Paul and Ken H. Blanchard. (1977). *Management of Organizational Behavior: Utilizing Human Resources*. Third ed. New Jersey: Prentice Hall.

Hettinger, Ned and Bill Throop. (1999). "Refocusing Ecocentrism: De-Emphasizing Stability and Defending Wildness." *Environmental Ethics* 21.1: 3–21.

Higgins, Polly. (2010). *Eradicating Ecocide: Laws and Governance to Prevent the Destruction of Our Planet*. London: Shepheard-Walwyn.

Higgins, Polly. (2012). "Towards a Garden of Eden: Ecocide, Eco-Colonization and the Sacredness of All Life." In *Wild Law: A Reader in Earth Jurisprudence*. Ed. Peter Burdon. Adelaide: Wakefield Press, 305–312.

Higgins, Polly, Damien Short and Nigel South. (2013). "Protecting the Planet: A Proposal for a Law of Ecocide." *Crime, Law and Social Change* 59.3: 251–266.

Hill, Reuben, J. Mayone Stycos and Kurt W. Back. (1959). *The Family and Population Control: A Puerto Rican Experiment in Social Change*. Chapel Hill: University of North Carolina Press.

Hirsch, S. Carl. (1971). *Guardians of Tomorrow: Pioneers in Ecology*. New York: Viking Press.

Hoffman, Andrew J. and Lloyd E. Sandelands. (2005). "Getting Right with Nature: Anthropocentrism, Ecocentrism, and Theocentrism." *Organization & Environment* 18.2.

Hollander, Edwin P. (1992). "The Essential Interdependence of Leadership and Followership." *Current Directions in Psychological Science* 1.2: 71–75.

Holzman, Frank. (2018). *Radical Regenerative Gardening and Farming: Biodynamic Principles and Perspectives*. Lanham: Rowman & Littlefield.

Hossay, Patrick. (2006). *Unsustainable: A Primer for Global Environmental and Social Justice*. London: Zed Books.

House, Robert J., William D. Spangler and James Woycke. (1991). "Personality and Charisma in the U.S. Presidency: A Psychological Theory of Leader Effectiveness." *Administrative Science Quarterly* 36.3: 364–396.

Hovardas, Tasos. (2011). "Towards a Critical Re-Appraisal of Ecology Education: Scheduling an Educational Intervention to Revisit the 'Balance of Nature' Metaphor." *Science & Education* 20.10: 1039–1053.

Hovardas, Tasos. (2012). "A Critical Reading of Ecocentrism and Its Meta-Scientific Use of Ecology: Instrumental Versus Emancipatory Approaches in Environmental Education and Ecology Education." *Science & Education* 22.6.

Howardson, Jacqueline Kirstine. (2006). "Teachers for the Earth: Profiles of Inspired Environmental Leadership." MA Thesis. University of Victoria, Victoria.

Howell, Jane M. and Boas Shamir. (2005). "The Role of Followers in the Charismatic Leadership Process: Relationships and Their Consequences." *Academy of Management Review* 30.1: 96–112.

Hubbert, M. King. (1962). *Energy Resources: A Report to the Committee on Natural Resources of the National Academy of Sciences – National Research Council*. Washington, DC: National Academy of Sciences – National Research Council.

Hunt, W. Murray. (1980). "Are *Mere Things* Morally Considerable?" *Environmental Ethics* 2.1: 59–66.

Husserl, Edmund. (1982). *General Introduction to a Pure Phenomenology*. Trans. F. Kersten. The Hague: Martinus Nijhoff.

Husserl, Edmund. (1983). *Ideas Pertaining to a Pure Phenomenology and to a Phenomenological Philosophy: First Book*. Trans. F. Kersten. The Hague: Martinus Nijhoff.

Husserl, Edmund. (2001). *Logical Investigations*. Two vols. Trans. J. N. Findlay. London: Routledge.

Independent Commission on International Development Issues (ICIDI). (1980). *North-South, A Program for Survival: Report of the Independent Commission on International Development Issues* [Brandt Report]. Cambridge: MIT Press.

InterAcademic Partnership (IAP). (1994). *IAP Statement on Population Growth*. www. interacademies.org/10878/13940.aspx

International Civil Aviation Organization (ICAO) [UN Specialized Agency]. (2017). *Traffic Growth and Airline Profitability Were Highlights of Air Transport in 2016*. January 2. www.icao.int/Newsroom/Pages/traffic-growth-and-airline-profitability-were-highlights-of-air-transport-in-2016.aspx

International Energy Agency (IEA). (2018). *Oil Market Report*. www.iea.org/oilmarket report/omrpublic/

International Leadership Association (ILA). (2019). *Leadership: Courage Required*. Twenty-First Annual Global Conference, Ottawa, Canada.

Introna, Lucas D. (2013). "Otherness and the Letting-Be of Becoming: Or, Ethics Beyond Bifurcation." In *How Matter Matters: Perspectives on Process Organization Studies*. Eds. Paul R. Carlile, David Nicolini, Ann Langley and Haridimos Tsoukas. Oxford: Oxford University Press, 260–287.

Irvine, Sandy. (1989). *Beyond Green Consumerism*. London: Friends of the Earth.

Jacoby, Jill B. and Xia Ji. (2010). "Artists as Transformative Leaders for Sustainability." In *Leadership for Environmental Sustainability*. Ed. Benjamin W. Redekop. New York: Routledge, 133–144.

Jamieson, Dale, ed. (1996). *A Companion to Environmental Philosophy*. Malden: Blackwell.

Jamison, Andrew. (2011). "Ecology and the Environmental Movement." In *Ecology Revisited: Reflecting on Concepts, Advancing Science*. Eds. Astrid Schwarz and Kurt Jax. Dordrecht: Springer, 195–204.

Jankelson, Claire. (2005). "An Engagement with the Phenomenology of Leadership." PhD Thesis. University of Western Sydney, Hawkesbury.

Jax, Kurt and Astrid Schwarz. (2011). "Competing Concepts." In *Ecology Revisited: Reflecting on Concepts, Advancing Science*. Eds. Astrid Schwarz and Kurt Jax. Dordrecht: Springer, 154–159.

Jobin, William. (1999). *Dams and Disease: Ecological Design and Health Impacts of Large Dams, Canals and Irrigation Systems*. London: CRC Press.

Johnson, Andrew. (1991). *Factory Farming*. Oxford: Blackwell.

Johnston, Douglas M. (2006). "The Challenge of International Ocean Governance: Institutional, Ethical and Conceptual Dilemmas." In *Towards Principled Oceans Governance: Australian and Canadian Approaches and Challenges*. Eds. Donald R. Rothwell and David L. VanderZwaag. Abingdon: Routledge, 349–399.

Jones, Daniel Stedman. (2012). *Masters of the Universe: Hayek, Friedman, and the Birth of Neoliberal Politics*. Princeton: Princeton University Press.

Joyce, Christopher. (2013). "Elephant Poaching Pushes Species to Brink of Extinction." *National Public Radio*. March 6. www.npr.org/2013/03/06/173508369/elephant-poaching-pushes-species-to-brink-of-extinction

Kaak, Paul. (2010). "The Agrarian Mind and Good Leadership: Harvesting Insights From the Literary Field of Wendell Berry." In *Leadership for Environmental Sustainability*. Ed. Benjamin W. Redekop. New York: Routledge, 145–157.

Kaak, Paul. (2012). "Leadership for Sustainable Food Systems." In *Environmental Leadership: A Reference Handbook*. Volume Two. Ed. Deborah Rigling Gallagher. Thousand Oaks: Sage, 760–771.

Kaku, Michio. (2008). *Physics of the Impossible: A Scientific Exploration into the World of Phasers, Force Fields, Teleportation, and Time Travel*. New York: Doubleday.

Kalman, Bobbie. (2001). *Life in a Longhouse Village*. New York: Crabtree Publishing Company.

Kals, Elisabeth and Jürgen Maes. (2002). "Sustainable Development and Emotions." In *Psychology of Sustainable Development*. Eds. Peter Schmuck and Wesley P. Schultz. Boston: Kluwer Academic Publishers, 97–122.

Kane, Gareth. (2011). *The Green Executive: Corporate Leadership in a Low Carbon Economy*. London: Routledge.

Kassiola, Joel J., ed. (2003). *Explorations in Environmental Political Theory: Thinking About What We Value*. Armonk: M. E. Sharpe.

Katz, Eric. (1992). "The Big Lie: Human Restoration of Nature." *Research in Philosophy and Technology* 12: 231–241.

Kheel, Marti. (1996). "The Killing Game: An Ecofeminist Critique of Hunting." *Journal of the Philosophy of Sport* 23.1: 30–44.

Keim, Brandon. (2018). "The Surprisingly Complicated Math of How Many Wild Animals Are Killed in Agriculture." *Anthropocene Magazine*. July 18. www.anthropocenemagazine.org/2018/07/how-many-animals-killed-in-agriculture/

Kelley, Harold H. (1973). "The Process of Causal Attribution." *American Psychologist* 28: 107–128.

Kelley, Robert E. (1991). "Combining Followership and Leadership Into Partnership." In *Making Organizations Competitive: Enhancing Networks and Relationships Across Traditional Boundaries*. Eds. Ralph H. Kilmann, Ines Kilmann and Associates. San Francisco: Jossey-Bass, 195–220.

Kierkegaard, Søren. (1987). *Either/Or*. Two vols. Eds. and trans. Howard Hong and Edna Hong. Princeton: Princeton University Press.

Kissling, Frances, Jotham Musinguzi and Peter Singer. (2018). "Talking About Overpopulation Is Still Taboo. That Has to Change." *Washington Post*. June 19. www.

washingtonpost.com/opinions/talking-about-overpopulation-is-still-taboo-that-has-to-change/2018/06/18/ca7c1838-6e6f-11e8-afd5-778aca903bbe_story.html

Koepf, Herbert H. (1989). *The Biodynamic Farm: Agriculture in the Service of the Earth and Humanity*. Hudson: Anthroposophic Press.

Kolbert, Elizabeth. (2014). *The Sixth Extinction: An Unnatural History*. New York: Henry Holt & Co.

Koonin, Eugene V. and Petro Starokadomskyy. (2016). "Are Viruses Alive? The Replicator Paradigm Sheds Decisive Light on an Old But Misguided Question." *Studies in History and Philosophy of Biological and Biomedical Sciences* 59: 125–134.

Kopnina, Helen. (2013). "Evaluating Education for Sustainable Development (ESD): Using Ecocentric and Anthropocentric Attitudes Toward the Sustainable Development (EAATSD) Scale." *Environment, Development and Sustainability* 15.3: 607–623.

Kopnina, Helen. (2016). "Of Big Hegemonies and Little Tigers: Ecocentrism and Environmental Justice." *Journal of Environmental Education* 47.2: 139–150.

Kopnina, Helen and Mickey Gjerris. (2015). "Are Some Animals More Equal Than Others? Animal Rights and Deep Ecology in Environmental Education." *Canadian Journal of Environmental Education* 20:109–123.

Kotter, John P. (1990a). *A Force for Change: How Leadership Differs From Management*. New York: The Free Press.

Kotter, John P. (1990b). "What Leaders Really Do." *Harvard Business Review* 68.3: 103–111.

Kotter, John P. (1996). *Leading Change*. Boston: Harvard Business School Press.

Kotter, John P. (2013). "Management Is (Still) Not Leadership." *Harvard Business Review*. January 9. https://hbr.org/2013/01/management-is-still-not-leadership.%20html

Kotterman, James. (2006). "Leadership Versus Management: What's the Difference?" *The Journal for Quality and Participation* 29.2: 13–17.

Küpers, Wendelin M. (2013). "Embodies Inter-Practices of Leadership: Phenomenological Perspectives on Relational and Responsive Leading and Following." *Leadership* 9.3.

Kureethadam, Joshtrom Isaac. (2017). *The Philosophical Roots of the Ecological Crisis: Descartes and the Modern Worldview*. Newcastle upon Tyne: Cambridge Scholars Publishing.

Ladkin, Donna. (2005). "Does 'Restoration' Necessarily Imply the Domination of Nature?" *Environmental Values* 14.2: 203–219.

Ladkin, Donna. (2010). *Rethinking Leadership: A New Look at Old Leadership Questions*. Northampton: Edward Elgar.

Langton, Stuart. (1984a). "Introduction." In *Environmental Leadership: A Sourcebook for Staff and Volunteer Leaders of Environmental Organizations*. Ed. Stuart Langton. Lexington: Lexington Books, ix–x.

Langton, Stuart. (1984b). "The Future of the Environmental Movement." In *Environmental Leadership: A Sourcebook for Staff and Volunteer Leaders of Environmental Organizations*. Ed. Stuart Langton. Lexington: Lexington Books, 1–12.

Langton, Stuart. (1984c). "Dilemmas of Leadership and Management in Environmental Organizations." In *Environmental Leadership: A Sourcebook for Staff and Volunteer Leaders of Environmental Organizations*. Ed. Stuart Langton. Lexington: Lexington Books, 13–19.

Langton, Stuart, ed. (1984d). *Environmental Leadership: A Sourcebook for Staff and Volunteer Leaders of Environmental Organizations*. Lexington: Lexington Books.

Lankester, E. Ray. (1913). *Science from an Easy Chair*. New York: Henry Holt & Co.

Larsen, Janet. (2003). "Iran: A Model for Family Planning?" *The Globalist.* August 3. www.theglobalist.com/iran-a-model-for-family-planning/

Latour, Brian. (2005). *Reassembling the Social: An Introduction to Actor-Network-Theory.* Oxford: Oxford University Press.

Lawton, Graham. (2019). "We Need to Talk About How Population Growth Is Harming the Planet." *New Scientist.* May 22. www.newscientist.com/article/mg24232310-100-we-need-to-talk-about-how-population-growth-is-harming-the-planet/

Leinen, Jo and Andreas Bummel. (2019). "The Need for a Global Government: Democracy in the Planetary Age." *Cadmus* 3.6: 156–162. http://cadmusjournal.org/article/volume-3/issue-6/need-global-government-democracy-planetary-age

Leiss, William. (1972). *The Domination of Nature.* New York: George Braziller.

Lélé, Sharachchandra M. (1991). "Sustainable Development: A Critical Review." *World Development* 19.6: 607–621.

Lemons, John. (1985). "Conventional and Alternative Approaches to the Teaching of Leadership in Environmental Programs." *Environmental Education and Information* 4.4: 244–251.

Leonard, Annie. (2010). *The Story of Stuff: How Our Obsession With Stuff Is Trashing the Planet, Our Communities, and Our Health – and a Vision for Change.* New York: The Free Press.

Leopold, Aldo. (1989). *A Sand County Almanac and Sketches Here and There.* Special Commemorative Edition. New York: Oxford University Press.

Lester, Sarah E. and others. (2009). "Biological Effects Within No-Take Marine Reserves: A Global Synthesis." *Marine Ecology Progress Series* 384: 33–46.

Levay, Charlotta. (2010). "Charismatic Leadership in Resistance to Change." *Leadership Quarterly* 21.1: 127–143.

Levine, Joel S. and Rudy E. Schild, eds. (2010). *The Human Mission to Mars: Colonizing the Red Planet.* Cosmology.com (Online).

Liddell-Scott-Jones Greek-English Lexicon (Online). (n.d.). "Oikos." Project director Maria Pantelia. http://stephanus.tlg.uci.edu/lsj/#eid=74700

Life After People. (2008–2010). Documentary series. Creator David de Vries. United States: Flight 33 Productions.

Linkenbach, Antje. (1994). "Ecological Movements and the Critique of Development: Agents and Interpreters." *Thesis Eleven* 39: 63–85.

Lipovetsky, Giles. (2011). "The Hyperconsumption Society." In *Beyond the Consumption Bubble.* Eds. Karin M. Ekström and Kay Glans. New York: Routledge, 25–36.

Litzinger, William and Thomas Schaefer. (1982). "Leadership Through Followership." *Business Horizons* 25.5: 78–81.

Liu, Helena. (2015). "Reimagining Ethical Leadership as a Relational, Contextual and Political Practice." *Leadership* 13.3: 343–367.

Liu, Xiaogan. (1991). "Wuwei (non-action): From Laozi to Huainanzi." *Taoist Resources* 3: 4156.

Lomborg, Bjørn. (2001). *The Skeptical Environmentalist: Measuring the Real State of the World.* Cambridge: Cambridge University Press.

Lorimer, James. (1978). *The Developers.* Toronto: James Lorimer.

Losh, Jack. (2019). "Central Africa's Rangers Are as Threatened as the Animals They Guard." *Foreign Policy.* October 6. https://foreignpolicy.com/2019/10/06/central-africas-rangers-are-as-endangered-as-the-animals-they-guard/

Lundmark, Carina. (2007). "The New Ecological Paradigm Revisited: Anchoring the NEP Scale in Environmental Ethics." *Environmental Education Research* 13.3: 329–347.

Lunenberg, Fred C. (2011). "Leadership Versus Management: A Key Distinction – At Least in Theory." *International Journal of Management, Business, and Administration* 14.1: 1–5.

Lyotard, Jean-François. (1984). *The Postmodern Condition: A Report on Knowledge*. Trans. Geoff Bennington and Brian Massumi. Minneapolis: University of Minnesota Press.

MacDonald, Fiona. (2015). "This Indoor Farm is 100 Times More Productive Than Outdoor Fields." *ScienceAlert*. January 13. www.sciencealert.com/this-indoor-farm-is-100-times-more-productive-than-an-outdoor-one

MacNeill, Jim. (2007). "Leadership for Sustainable Development." In *Institutionalizing Sustainable Development* 9: 19–23. Paris: Organisation for Economic Co-operation and Development.

Malthus, Thomas Robert. (1798). *An Essay on the Principle of Population*. London: J. Johnson.

Mandel, Ernest. (1986). "In Defence of Socialist Planning." *New Left Review* 1.159: 5–37.

Manes, Christopher. (1990). *Green Rage: Radical Environmentalism and the Unmaking of Civilization*. Boston: Little Brown.

Manes, Christopher. (1996). "Nature and Silence." In *The Ecocriticism Reader*. Eds. Cheryl Glotfelty and Harold Fromm. Athens: University of Georgia Press, 15–29.

Manolis, Jim C., Kai M. Chan, Myra E. Finkelstein, Scott Stephens, Cara R. Nelson, Jacqueline B. Grant and Michael P. Dombeck. (2009). "Leadership: A New Frontier in Conservation Science." *Conservation Biology* 23.4: 879–886.

Manolopoulos, Mark. (2009). *If Creation Is a Gift*. Albany: State University of New York Press.

Manolopoulos, Mark. (2013). "Caputo in a Nutshell: Two Introductory (and Slightly Critical) Lectures." *Postmodern Openings* 4.2: 21–42. http://postmodernopenings.com/wp-content/uploads/2013/07/3_Mark-MANOLOPOULOS_PO-Vol-4-No-2.pdf

Manolopoulos, Mark. (2018). *Radical Neo-Enlightenment: Passionate Reason, Open Faith, Thoughtful Change*. Newcastle upon Tyne: Cambridge Scholars Publishing.

Manolopoulos, Mark. (2019). *Following Reason: A Theory and Strategy for Rational Leadership*. New York: Routledge.

Manson, Neil A. (2000). "Anthropocentrism and the Design Argument." *Religious Studies* 36.2: 163–176.

Marangudakis, Manussos. (2001). "The Medieval Roots of Our Environmental Crisis." *Environmental Ethics* 23.3: 243–260.

Margai, Florence M. (2012). "Exploring Leadership Pathways in Global Environmental Health and Social Justice." In *Environmental Leadership: A Reference Handbook*. Volume Two. Ed. Deborah Rigling Gallagher. Thousand Oaks: Sage, 823–837.

Marland, Gregg and Ralph M. Rotty. (1984). "Carbon Dioxide Emissions from Fossil Fuels: A Procedure for Estimation and Results for 1950–1982." *Tellus B: Chemical and Physical Meteorology* 36.4: 232–261.

Marsh, George P. (1864). *Man and Nature: Or, Physical Geography as Modified by Human Action*. New York: Charles Scribner.

Marshall, Judi, Gill Coleman and Peter Reason. (2017). *Leadership for Sustainability: An Action Research Approach*. Abingdon: Routledge.

Martin, David M. (2017). "Ecological Restoration Should Be Redefined for the Twenty-First Century." *Restoration Ecology* 25.5: 668–673.

Martin, Teresa Castro. (1995). "Women's Education and Fertility: Results From 26 Demographic and Health Surveys." *Studies in Family Planning* 26.4: 187–202.

Marx, Karl and Frederick [Friedrich] Engels. (1888/1910). *Communist Manifesto.* Chicago: Charles H. Kerr & Co.

Maslow, Abraham H. (1943). "A Theory of Human Motivation." *Psychological Review* 50.4: 370–396.

Mathews, Freya. (1996). "The Soul of Things." *Terra Nova* 1.4: 55–64.

Mathews, Freya. (1999a). "Letting the Earth Grow Old: An Ethos of Countermodernity." *Worldviews: Global Religions, Culture, and Ecology* 3.2: 119–137.

Mathews, Freya. (1999b). "Becoming Native: An Ethos of Countermodernity II." *Worldviews: Environment, Culture, Religion* 3.3: 243–271.

Mathews, Freya. (2003a). *For Love of Matter: A Contemporary Panpsychism.* Albany: State University of New York Press.

Mathews, Freya. (2003b). "Letting the World Do the Doing." *Australian Humanities Review* 33. http://australianhumanitiesreview.org/2004/08/01/letting-the-world-do-the-doing/

Mathews, Freya. (2005). *Reinhabiting Reality: Towards a Recovery of Culture.* Sydney: UNSW Press.

McCarthy, E. Jerome. (1960). *Basic Marketing: A Managerial Approach.* Homewood: R. D. Irwin.

McCrary, Justin and Heather Royer. (2011). "The Effect of Female Education on Fertility and Infant Health: Evidence From School Entry Policies Using Exact Date of Birth." *The American Economic Review* 101.1: 158–195.

McCully, Patrick. (2001). *Silenced Rivers: The Ecology and Politics of Large Dams.* London: Zed Books.

McDaniel, Jay. (1990). *Earth, Sky, Gods and Mortals: Developing an Ecological Spirituality.* Mystic: Twenty-Third Publications.

McDonough, William and Michael Braungart. (2002). *Cradle to Cradle: Remaking the Way We Make Things.* New York: North Point Press.

McDougall, Heather R. (2010). "Protest, Power, and 'Political Somersaults': Lessons From the German Green Party." In *Leadership for Environmental Sustainability.* Ed. Benjamin W. Redekop. New York: Routledge, 184–200.

McGraw, Matthew S. (2016). "A Phenomenological Inquiry of Leadership Competency Perceptions Among Community College Leaders in South Central Appalachia." PhD Thesis. Old Dominion University, Norfolk.

McGregor, Robert Kuhn. (1988). "Deriving a Biocentric History: Evidence From the Journal of Henry David Thoreau." *Environmental Review* 12.2: 117–126.

McLaughlin, Andrew. (1993). *Regarding Nature: Industrialism and Deep Ecology.* Albany: State University of New York Press.

McManus, Robert M. (2018). "Toward an Understanding of the Relationship Between the Study of Leadership and the Natural World." In *Innovation in Environmental Leadership: Critical Perspectives.* Eds. Benjamin W. Redekop, Deborah Rigling Gallagher and Rian Satterwhite. New York: Routledge, 97–115.

McManus, Robert M. and Gama Perruci. (2015). *Understanding Leadership: An Arts and Humanities Perspective.* New York: Routledge.

Meadows, Donella H., Dennis L. Meadows, Jørgen Randers and William W. Behrens III. (1972). *The Limits to Growth: A Report for the Club of Rome's Project on the Predicament of Mankind.* New York: Universe Books.

Meillasoux, Quentin. (2008). *After Finitude: An Essay on the Necessity of Contingency.* London: Continuum.

Menck, Claire. (2012). "Urban Agriculture in the Face of Disaster and Environmental Change." In *Environmental Leadership: A Reference Handbook.* Volume Two. Ed. Deborah Rigling Gallagher. Thousand Oaks: Sage, 663–672.

Merchant, Carolyn. (1992). *Radical Ecology: The Search for a Livable World.* New York: Routledge.

Meyer, John M. (1997). "Gifford Pinchot, John Muir and the Boundaries of Politics in American Thought." *Polity* 30.2: 267–284.

Meyer, John M. (2001). *Political Nature: Environmentalism and the Interpretation of Western Thought.* Cambridge: MIT Press.

Meyer, John M. (2018). "Environmental Political Theory." In *Companion to Environmental Studies.* Eds. Noel Castree, Mike Hulme and James D. Proctor. London: Routledge, 435–438.

Meyer-Abich, Klaus Michael. (1984). *Wege zum Frieden mit der Natur: Praktische Naturphilosophie für die Umweltpolitik.* Munich: C. Hanser.

Meyer-Abich, Klaus Michael. (1993). *Revolution for Nature: From the Environment to the Co-Natural World.* Cambridge/Denton: White Horse/University of North Texas Press.

Meyer-Abich, Klaus Michael. (1997). "Humans in Nature: Towards a Physiocentric Philosophy." In *Technological Trajectories and the Human Environment.* Eds. Jesse H. Ausubel and H. Dale Langford. Washington, DC: National Academy Press, 168–184.

Milburn, Joshua Fields and Ryan Nicodemus. (2011). *Minimalism: Live a Meaningful Life.* Columbia: Asymmetrical Press.

Milburn, Joshua Fields and Ryan Nicodemus. (2015). *Essentials: Essays by the Minimalists.* Missoula: Asymmetrical Press.

Miles, Edward E., Steinar Andresen, Elaine M. Carlin, Jon Birger Skjærsen, Arild Underdal and Jørgen Wettestad, eds. (2002). *Environmental Regime Effectiveness: Confronting Theory with Evidence.* Cambridge: MIT Press.

Miner, John B. (1975). "The Uncertain Future of the Leadership Concept: An Overview." In *Leadership Frontiers.* Eds. James G. Hunt and Lars L. Larson. Kent: Kent State University Press, 197–208.

Mino, Takashi and Keisuke Hanaki, eds. (2013). *Environmental Leadership Capacity Building in Higher Education: Experience and Lessons From Asian Program for Incubation of Environmental Leaders.* Tokyo: Springer.

Minteer, Ben A. and Robert E. Manning. (2005). "An Appraisal of the Critique of Anthropocentrism and Three Lesser Known Themes in Lynn White's 'The Historical Roots of Our Ecologic Crisis'." *Organization & Environment* 18.2: 163–176.

Mitchell, Ronald B., ed. (2008). *International Environmental Politics.* Thousand Oaks: Sage.

Mizzoni, John. (2004). "St. Francis, Paul Taylor, and Franciscan Biocentrism." *Environmental Ethics* 26.1: 41–56.

Mizzoni, John. (2008). "Franciscan Biocentrism and the Franciscan Tradition." *Ethics and the Environment* 13.1: 121–134.

Monastersky, Richard. (2014). "Biodiversity: Life – A Status Report." *Nature* 516.7530. www.nature.com/news/biodiversity-life-a-status-report-1.16523

Monbiot, George. (2012). "Rio+20 Draft Text Is 283 Paragraphs of Fluff." *The Guardian.* June 22. www.theguardian.com/environment/georgemonbiot/2012/jun/22/rio-20-earth-summit-brazil

Monbiot, George. (2013). *Feral: Searching for Enchantment on the Frontiers of Rewilding.* London: Allen Lane.

Monbiot, George. (2015). "Consume More, Conserve More: Sorry, But We Just Can't Do Both." *The Guardian.* November 25. www.theguardian.com/commentisfree/2015/nov/24/consume-conserve-economic-growth-sustainability

Moore, Bryan L. (2008). *Ecology and Literature: Ecocentric Personification From Antiquity to the Twenty-First Century.* New York: Palgrave Macmillan.

Moore, Bryan L. (2017). *Ecological Literature and the Critique of Anthropocentrism.* New York: Springer.

Moore, Patrick. (1994). "Hard Choices for the Environmental Movement." *Leadership Quarterly* 5.3–4: 247–252.

Morito, Bruce. (2003). "Intrinsic Value: A Modern Albatross for the Ecological Approach." *Environmental Values* 12.3: 317–336.

Morrison, Susan Signe. (2015). *Literature of Waste: Material Ecopoetics and Ethical Matter.* New York: Palgrave Macmillan.

Morrison, Susan Signe. (2019). "Dynamic Dirt: Medieval Holy Dust, Ritual Erosion, and Pilgrimage Ecopoetics." *Open Library of Humanities* 5.1. https://olh.openlibhums.org/articles/10.16995/olh.373/?fbclid=IwAR33Ox-DUlTfIAk9bAqNKjBO-uYRr907Ofpue5KfgwmILav4uZJQM50QwNI

Morton, Timothy. (2007). *Ecology Without Nature: Rethinking Environmental Aesthetics.* Cambridge: Harvard University Press.

Morton, Timothy. (2013). "She Stood in Tears Amid the Alien Corn: Thinking Through Agrilogistics." *Diacritics* 41.2: 90–113.

Morton, Timothy. (2016). *Dark Ecology: For a Logic of Future Coexistence.* New York: Columbia University Press.

Morton, Timothy. (2017). *Humankind: Solidarity with Nonhuman People.* London: Verso.

Moser, Susanne C. (2012). "Getting Real About It: Meeting the Psychological and Social Demands of a World in Distress." In *Environmental Leadership: A Reference Handbook.* Volume Two. Ed. Deborah Rigling Gallagher. Thousand Oaks: Sage, 900–908.

Muir, John. (1901). *Our National Parks.* Boston: Houghton Mifflin.

Muir, John. (1911). *My First Summer in the Sierra.* Boston: Houghton Mifflin.

Muir, John. (1997). *Nature Writings.* Ed. William Cronon. New York: Library of America.

Myers, Ransom A. and Boris Worm. (2003). "Rapid Worldwide Depletion of Predatory Fish Communities." *Nature* 423: 280–283.

Myers, Steven Lee, Jin Wu and Claire Fu. (2019). "China's Looming Crisis: A Shrinking Population." *New York Times.* January 21. www.nytimes.com/interactive/2019/01/17/world/asia/china-population-crisis.html

Mylius, Ben. (2013). "Toward the Unthinkable: Earth Jurisprudence and an Ecocentric Episteme." *Australian Journal of Legal Philosophy* 38: 102–122.

Naess, Arne. (1973). "The Shallow and the Deep, Long-Range Ecology Movement: A Summary." *Inquiry* 16.1: 95–100.

Naess, Arne. (1986). "The Deep Ecology Movement." In *Deep Ecology for the 21st Century.* Ed. George Sessions. Boston: Shambhala Publications, 64–84.

Naess, Arne. (1989). *Ecology, Community and Lifestyle: Outline of an Ecosophy.* Trans. David Rothenberg. New York: Cambridge University Press.

Nash, James A. (1998). "On the Subversive Virtue: Frugality." In *Ethics of Consumption.* Eds. David A. Cricker and Toby Linden. Lanham: Rowman & Littlefield, 416–436.

Nash, Roderick Frazier, ed. (1988). *American Environmentalism: Readings in Conservation History.* New York: McGraw-Hill.

Nash, Roderick Frazier. (1989). *The Rights of Nature: A History of Environmental Ethics.* Madison: University of Wisconsin Press.

Nashawi, Sami, Adel Malallah and Mohammed Al-Bisharah. (2010). "Forecasting World Crude Oil Production Using Multicyclic Hubbert Model." *Energy Fuels* 24.3: 1788–1800.

Nava, Mica, Andrew Blake, Iain MacRury and Barry Richards, eds. (1997). *Buy This Book: Studies in Advertising and Consumption.* Abingdon: Routledge.

Nhanenge, Jytte. (2011). *Ecofeminism: Towards Integrating the Concerns of Women, Poor People, and Nature Into Development.* Lanham: University Press of America.

Nietzsche, Friedrich. (1966). *Beyond Good and Evil: Prelude to a Philosophy of the Future.* New York: Vintage Books.

Nietzsche, Friedrich. (1967). *On the Genealogy of Morals.* Trans. Walter Kaufmann and R. J. Hollingdale. New York: Vintage Books.

Nimmo, Richie. (2011). "The Making of the Human: Anthropocentrism in Modern Social Thought." In *Anthropocentrism: Humans, Animals, Environments.* Ed. Rob Boddice. Leiden: Brill, 59–79.

Nisbet, Robert. (1974). *The Social Philosophers: Community and Conflict in Western Thought.* London: Heinemann.

Norris, Stephen P. (1984). "Defining Observational Competence." *Science Education* 68.2: 129–142.

Norris, Stephen P. (1985). "The Philosophical Basis for Observation in Science and Science Education." *Journal of Research in Science Teaching* 22.9: 817–833.

Noske, Barbara. (1997). *Beyond Boundaries: Humans and Animals.* Montreal: Black Rose Books.

Noss, Reed F. and others. (2012). "Bolder Thinking for Conservation." *Conservation Biology* 26.1: 1–4.

Nothwehr, Dawn M., ed. (2002). *Franciscan Theology of the Environment: An Introductory Reader.* Quincy: Franciscan Press.

Nuwer, Rachel. (2018). "Meet the 'Brave Ones': The Women Saving Africa's Wildlife." *BBC Future.* September 27. www.bbc.com/future/article/20180926-akashinga-all-women-rangers-in-africa-fighting-poaching

Ohrem, Dominik and Roman Bartosch, eds. (2017). *Beyond the Human-Animal Divide: Creaturely Lives in Literature and Culture.* New York: Palgrave Macmillan.

Ophuls, William. (1977). *Ecology and the Politics of Scarcity.* San Francisco: W. H. Freeman & Co.

Ospina, Sonia and Georgia L. J. Sorenson. (2006). "A Constructionist Lens on Leadership: Charting New Territory." In *The Quest for a General Theory of Leadership.* Eds. George R. Goethals and Georgia L. J. Sorenson. Cheltenham: Edward Elgar, 188–204.

Ottoni, Eduardo B. and Patricia Izar. (2008)."Capuchin Monkey Tool Use: Overview and Implications." *Evolutionary Anthropology* 17.4: 171–178.

Owen, Nick A., Oliver R. Inderwildi and David A. King. (2010). "The Status of Conventional World Oil Reserves: Hype or Cause for Concern?" *Energy Policy* 38.8: 4743–4749.

Oxford English Dictionary. (2016). Online. Third ed.

Parker, Laura. (2018). "A Whopping 91% of Plastic Isn't Recycled." *National Geographic.* December 20. www.nationalgeographic.com/news/2017/07/plastic-produced-recycling-waste-ocean-trash-debris-environment/

Pascal, Blaise. (1958). *Pascal's Pensées*. Trans. W. F. Trotter. New York: E. P. Dutton & Co.

Passmore, John. (1974). *Man's Responsibility for Nature: Ecological Problems and Western Traditions*. London: Duckworth.

Pauchant, Thierry C. and Isabelle Fortier. (1990). "Anthropocentric Ethics in Organizations, Strategic Management and the Environment: A Typology." In *Advances in Strategic Management*, Volume Six. Eds. Paul Shrivastava and Robert B. Lamb. Greenwich: JAI Press, 99–114.

Paull, John. (2006). "The Farm as Organism: The Foundational Idea of Organic Agriculture." *Elementals: Journal of Bio-Dynamics* 83: 14–18.

Paull, John. (2011). "Attending the First Organic Agriculture Course: Rudolf Steiner's Agricultural Course at Koberwitz, 1924." *European Journal of Social Sciences* 21.1: 64–70.

Pearce, David W., Anil Markandya and Edward B. Barbier. (1989). *A Blueprint for a Green Economy*. London: Earthscan.

Pearce, Fred. (1991). *Green Warriors: The People and the Politics Behind the Environmental Revolution*. London: Bodley Head.

Pearce, Fred. (2015). "Global Extinction Rates: Why Do Estimates Vary So Wildly?" *Yale Environment 360*. August 17. https://e360.yale.edu/features/global_extinction_rates_why_do_estimates_vary_so_wildly

Peet, Richard and Michael Watts, eds. (1996). *Liberation Ecologies: Environment, Development, Social Movements*. London: Routledge.

Pepper, David. (1993). *Eco-Socialism: From Deep Ecology to Social Justice*. London: Routledge.

Perez, Padmapani L. with BUKLURAN (Philippine ICCA Consortium). (2018). "Living with the Problem of National Parks: Indigenous Critique of Philippine Environmental Policy." *Thesis Eleven* 145.1: 58–76.

Pezze, Barbara Dalle. (2006). "Heidegger on *Gelassenheit*." *Minerva: An Internet Journal of Philosophy* 10: 94–122.

Pfeffer, Jeffrey. (1977). "The Ambiguity of Leadership." *Academy of Management Review* 2.1: 104–112.

Pinchot, Gifford. (1910). *The Right for Conservation*. New York: Doubleday, Page & Co.

Pinchot, Gifford. (1998). *Breaking New Ground*. Washington, DC: Island Press.

Pirages, Dennis and Paul R. Ehrlich. (1973). *Ark II: Social Response to Environmental Imperatives*. San Francisco: W. H. Freeman.

Plant, Christopher and Judith Plant, eds. (1991). *Green Business: Hope or Hoax? Toward an Authentic Strategy for Restoring the Earth*. Santa Cruz: New Society Publishers.

Plato. (1974). *The Republic*. Second ed. Trans. Desmond Lee. Harmondsworth: Penguin Books.

Plumwood, Val. (1991). "Ethics and Instrumentalism: A Response to Janna Thompson." *Environmental Ethics* 13: 139–149.

Plumwood, Val. (1993). *Feminism and the Mastery of Nature*. London: Routledge.

Plumwood, Val. (1999). "Paths Beyond Human-Centeredness: Lessons from Liberation Struggles." In *An Invitation to Environmental Philosophy*. Ed. Anthony Weston. New York: Oxford University Press, 69–106.

Plumwood, Val. (2002). *Environmental Culture: The Ecological Crisis of Reason*. London: Routledge.

Plumwood, Val. (2012). *The Eye of the Crocodile*. Ed. Lorraine Shannon. Canberra: Australian National University E Press.

Podolinsky, Alex. (2002). *Living Knowledge*. Lecture to the Australian Bio-Dynamic Agricultural Association of Australia. www.demeter.org.au/electures/Living%20Knowledge.pdf

Portugal, Ed and Gary Yukl. (1994). "Perspectives on Environmental Leadership." *Leadership Quarterly* 5.3–4: 271.276.

Povilitis, Anthony. (1980). "On Assigning Rights to Animals and Nature." *Environmental Ethics* 2.1: 67–72.

Purser, Ronald E., Changkil Park and Alfonso Montuori. (1995). "Limits to Anthropocentrism: Toward an Ecocentric Organization Paradigm?" *Academy of Management Review* 20.4: 1053–1089.

Pye, Gillian, ed. (2010). *Trash Culture: Objects and Obsolescence in Cultural Perspective*. Oxford: Peter Lang.

Rainford, John. (2015). "The Best Politicians That Money Can Buy." *Green Left Weekly* Issue 1041. February 13. www.greenleft.org.au/content/best-politicians-money-can-buy

Ranney, Sally Ann Guamer. (1992). "Heroines and Hierarchy: Female Leadership in the Conservation Movement." In *Voices From the Environmental Movement: Perspectives for a New Era*. Ed. Donald Snow. Washington, DC: Island Press, 110–136.

Redekop, Benjamin W. (2010a). "Introduction: Connecting Leadership and Sustainability." In *Leadership for Environmental Sustainability*. Ed. Benjamin W. Redekop. New York: Routledge, 1–16.

Redekop, Benjamin W. (2010b). "Challenges and Strategies for Leading in Sustainability." In *Leadership for Environmental Sustainability*. Ed. Benjamin W. Redekop. New York: Routledge, 55–66.

Redekop, Benjamin W. (2010c). "Towards a New General Theory of Leadership." In *Leadership for Environmental Sustainability*. Ed. Benjamin W. Redekop. New York: Routledge, 243–248.

Redekop, Benjamin J. and Morgan Thomas. (2018). "Climate Change Leadership: From Tragic to Comic Discourse." In *Innovation in Environmental Leadership: Critical Perspectives*. Eds. Benjamin J. Redekop, Deborah Rigling Gallagher and Rian Satterwhite. New York: Routledge, 145–166.

Redekop, Benjamin W., Deborah Rigling Gallagher and Rian Satterwhite. (2018a). "Introduction." In *Innovation in Environmental Leadership: Critical Perspectives*. Eds. Benjamin J. Redekop, Deborah Rigling Gallagher and Rian Satterwhite. New York: Routledge, 1–12.

Redekop, Benjamin W., Deborah Rigling Gallagher and Rian Satterwhite. (2018b). "Conclusion." In *Innovation in Environmental Leadership: Critical Perspectives*. Eds. Benjamin J. Redekop, Deborah Rigling Gallagher and Rian Satterwhite. New York: Routledge, 241–244.

Redekop, Benjamin W., Deborah Rigling Gallagher and Rian Satterwhite, eds. (2018c). *Innovation in Environmental Leadership: Critical Perspectives*. New York: Routledge.

Regan, Tom. (1975). "The Moral Basis of Vegetarianism." *Canadian Journal of Philosophy* 5.2: 181–214.

Regan, Tom. (1980). "Animal Rights, Human Wrongs." *Environmental Ethics* 2.2: 99–120.

Regan, Tom. (1982). *All That Dwell Therein: Animal Rights and Environmental Ethics*. Berkeley: University of California Press.

Regan, Tom. (1983). *The Case for Animal Rights*. Berkeley: University of California Press.

Regan, Tom and Peter Singer, eds. (1976). *Animal Rights and Human Obligations*. Englewood Cliffs: Prentice-Hall.

Renehan, Robert. (1981). "The Greek Anthropocentric View of Man." *Harvard Studies in Classical Philology* 85: 239–259.

Richmond, Ruth. (2009). *The Stench in This Parliament: The Authorised Biography of John Hatton AO*. Mulwala: Ruth Richmond.

Riley, Matthew T. (2014). "The Democratic Roots of Our Ecologic Crisis: Lynn White, Biodemocracy, and the Earth Charter." *Zygon* 49.4: 938–948.

Robbins, Paul. (2004). *Political Ecology: A Critical Introduction*. Cornwall: Blackwell.

Robinson, Viviane M. J. (2001). "Embedding Leadership in Task Performance." In *Leadership for Quality Schooling: International Perspectives*. Eds. Kam-cheung Wong and Colin W. Evers. London: Falmer Press, 90–102.

Rockwell, H. William, Jr. (1991). "Leadership." *Journal of Forestry* 89.2: 3.

Rodman, John. (1980). "Paradigm Change in Political Science: An Ecological Perspective." *American Behavioral Scientist* 24.1: 49–78.

Roe, Jill. (1974). *Marvellous Melbourne: The Emergence of an Australian City*. Sydney: Hicks Smith & Sons.

Rolston III, Holmes. (1986). *Philosophy Gone Wild*. Buffalo: Prometheus.

Rolston III, Holmes. (1987). "Can the East Help the West to Value Nature?" *Philosophy East and West* 37.2: 172–190.

Rolston III, Holmes. (1988). *Environmental Ethics: Duties to and Values in the Natural World*. Philadelphia: Temple University Press.

Rolston III, Holmes. (1992). "Disvalues in Nature." *The Monist* 75.2: 250–278.

Romero, Aldemaro. (1992). "International Conservation Leadership and the Challenges of the Nineties." In *Voices From the Environmental Movement: Perspectives for a New Era*. Ed. Donald Snow. Washington, DC: Island Press, 137–150.

Roossinck, Marilyn J. (2016). *Virus: An Illustrated Guide to 101 Incredible Microbes*. Princeton: Princeton University Press.

Rosebraugh, Craig. (2004). *Burning Rage of a Dying Planet: Speaking for the Earth Liberation Front*. New York: Lantern Books.

Roser, Max. (2014/2017). "Fertility Rate." *Our World in Data*. https://ourworldindata. org/fertility-rate

Roser, Max, Hannah Ritchie and Esteban Ortiz-Ospina. (2013/2019). "World Population Growth." *Our World in Data*. https://ourworldindata.org/world-population-growth

Rost, Joseph C. (1991). *Leadership for the Twenty-First Century*. New York: Praeger.

Roush, G. Jon. (1992a). "Introduction." In *Voices From the Environmental Movement: Perspectives for a New Era*. Ed. Donald Snow. Washington, DC: Island Press, 1–20.

Roush, G. Jon. (1992b). "Conservation's Hour – Is Leadership Ready?" In *Voices From the Environmental Movement: Perspectives for a New Era*. Ed. Donald Snow. Washington, DC: Island Press, 21–40.

Routley, Richard. (1973). "Is There a Need for a New, an Environmental, Ethic?" *Proceedings of the XVth World Congress of Philosophy*. Varna: Sophia Press, 205–210.

Routley, Richard and Val Routley. (1979). "Against the Inevitability of Human Chauvinism." In *Ethics and Problems of the 21st Century*. Eds. K. E. Goodpaster and K. M. Sayre. Notre Dame: University of Notre Dame Press, 36–59.

Routley, Richard and Val Routley. (1980). "Human Chauvinism." In *Environmental Philosophy*. Eds. D. S. Mannison, M. A. McRobbie and Richard Sylvan. Canberra:

Australian National University (Department of Philosophy, Research School of Social Sciences), 96–189.

Rowe, J. Stan. (1994). "Ecocentrism: The Responsive Chord." *The Trumpeter* 11.2: 106–107. http://trumpeter.athabascau.ca/index.php/trumpet/article/view/330/508

Ruddiman, William F. (2005). *Plows, Plagues, and Petroleum: How Humans Took Control of Climate*. Princeton: Princeton University Press.

Ruether, Rosemary Radford. (1992). *Gaia and God: An Ecofeminist Theology of Earth Healing*. San Francisco: Harper San Francisco.

Russo, Michael V., ed. (1999). *Environmental Management: Readings and Cases*. Boston: Houghton Mifflin.

Ryder, Richard. (1974). *Speciesism: The Ethics of Vivisection*. Edinburgh: Scottish Society for the Prevention of Vivisection.

Ryle, Martin. (1988). *Ecology and Socialism*. London: Century Hutchinson.

Sagan, Carl. (1980). *Cosmos*. New York: Random House.

Sahlins, Marshall. (1967). *Stone-Age Economics*. New York: de Gruyter.

Salleh, Ariel. (1997). *Ecofeminism as Politics*. London: Zed Books.

Samuelsson, Lars. (2010). "On the Demarcation Problem and the Possibility of Environmental Ethics: A Refutation of 'A Refutation of Environmental Ethics'." *Environmental Ethics* 32.2: 247–265.

Sanford, Filmore H. (1950). *Authoritarianism and Leadership*. Philadelphia: Institute for Research in Human Relations.

Sankar, Y. (2003). "Character Not Charisma Is the Critical Measure of Leadership Excellence." *Journal of Leadership and Organizational Studies* 9.4: 45–55.

Santmire, H. Paul. (1985). *The Travail of Nature: The Ambiguous Ecological Promise of Christian Theology*. Philadelphia: Fortress Press.

Satterwhite, Rian. (2010a). "Deep Systems Leadership: A Model for the 21st Century." In *Leadership for Environmental Sustainability*. Ed. Benjamin W. Redekop. New York: Routledge, 230–242.

Satterwhite, Rian. (2010b). "Halting the Decline: How Leadership Theory and Practice Can Address Global Biodiversity Loss." In *Environmental Leadership: A Reference Handbook*. Volume Two. Ed. Deborah Rigling Gallagher. Thousand Oaks: Sage, 577–585.

Satterwhite, Rian. (2018). "A Case for Universal Context: Intersections of the Biosphere, Systems, and Justice Using a Critical Constructionist Lens." In *Leadership for Environmental Sustainability*. Ed. Benjamin W. Redekop. New York: Routledge, 32–47.

Satyajit, Das. (2017). *The Age of Stagnation: Why Perpetual Growth Is Unattainable and the Global Economy Is in Peril*. Amherst: Prometheus Books.

Sayan, Roy. (2016). "A Critique on Current Paradigms of Economic 'Growth' and 'Development' in the Context of Environment and Sustainability Issues." *Consilience: The Journal of Sustainable Development* 16.1: 74–90.

Schaefer, G. Owen. (2018). "Lab-Grown Meat: Beef for Dinner – Without Killing Animals or the Environment." *Scientific American*. September 14. www.scientificamerican.com/article/lab-grown-meat/

Scharping, Thomas. (2003). *Birth Control in China 1949–2000: Population Policy and Demographic Development*. London: Routledge.

Schedlitzki, Doris and Gareth Edwards. (2014). *Studying Leadership: Traditional and Critical Approaches*. London: Sage.

Schein, Steve. (2015). *A New Psychology for Sustainability Leadership: The Hidden Power of Ecological Worldviews*. Sheffield: Greenleaf Publishing Limited.

Schmalemsee, Richard, Thomas M. Stoker and Ruth A. Judson. (1998). "World Carbon Dioxide Emissions: 1950–2050." *Review of Economics and Statistics* 80.1: 15–27.

Schmidt, Stanley and Robert Zubrin. (1996). *Islands in the Sky: Bold New Ideas for Colonizing Space*. New York: Wiley.

Schmidtz, David. (2011). "Respect for Everything." *Ethics, Policy and Environment* 14.2: 127–138.

Schreurs, Miranda A. (2002). *Environmental Politics in Japan, Germany, and the United States*. New York: Cambridge University Press.

Schürmann, Reiner. (1973). "Heidegger and Meister Eckhart on Releasement." *Research in Phenomenology* 3: 95–119.

Schuyler, Robert Livingston. (1948). "Man's Greatest Illusion." *Proceedings of the American Philosophical Society* 92.1: 46–50.

Schwarz, Astrid and Kurt Jax. (2011). "Etymology and Original Sources of the Term 'Ecology'." In *Ecology Revisited: Reflecting on Concepts, Advancing Science*. Eds. Astrid Schwarz and Kurt Jax. Dordrecht: Springer, 145–147.

Schweitzer, Albert. (1974). "Kultur und Ethik." In *Gesammelte Werke*. Volume Two. Five vols. Ed. R. Grabs. Munich: C. H. Beck.

Sellars, Richard West. (2009). *Preserving Nature in the National Parks: A History*. New Haven: Yale University Press.

Senseman, Charles J. (1993). *Ecocentrism: A Normative Inquiry for an Environmental Ethic*. Bloomington: Indiana State University.

Sessions, George. (1987). "The Deep Ecology Movement: A Review." *Environmental Review* 11.2: 105–125.

Shepard, Paul. (1982). *Nature and Madness*. San Francisco: Sierra Club Books.

Shrivastava, Aseem. (2012). *Churning the Earth: The Making of Global India*. New Delhi: Penguin.

Shrivastava, Paul. (1994a). "Castrated Environment: Greening Organizational Studies." *Organization Studies* 15.5: 705–726.

Shrivastava, Paul. (1994b). "Ecocentric Leadership in the 21st Century." *Leadership Quarterly* 5.3–4: 223–226.

Shrivastava, Paul. (1995a). "Ecocentric Management for a Risk Society." *Academy of Management Review* 20.1: 118–137.

Shrivastava, Paul. (1995b). "The Role of Corporations in Achieving Ecological Sustainability." *Academy of Management Review* 20.4: 936–960.

Shriver, Joachim, ed. (2017). *Fossil Fuels and Pollution*. Valley Cottage: Scitus Academic.

Silvestri, Antonella and Stefania Veltri. (2019). "Exploring the Relationships Between Corporate Social Responsibility, Leadership, and Sustainable Entrepreneurship Theories: A Conceptual Framework." *Corporate Social Responsibility and Environmental Management* 27.2: 585–594.

Simeone, Fred and others. (2012). *The Stewardship of Historically Important Automobiles*. Philadelphia: Coachbuilt Press.

Simon, Alexander. (2016). "Against Trophy Hunting: A Marxian-Leopoldian Critique." *Monthly Review*. September 1. https://monthlyreview.org/2016/09/01/against-trophy-hunting/

Simon, Julian. (1999). *Hoodwinking the Nation*. New Brunswick: Transaction.

Sinclair, Amanda. (1998). *Doing Leadership Differently: Gender, Power and Sexuality in a Changing Business Culture*. Carlton South: Melbourne University Press.

Sinclair, Amanda. (2007). *Leadership for the Disillusioned: Moving Beyond the Myths and Heroes to Leading That Liberates.* Crows Nest: Allen & Unwin.

Singer, Peter. (1975). *Animal Liberation: A New Ethics for Our Treatment of Animals.* New York: New York Review.

Singer, Peter and Peter Kissling. (2017). "Rethinking the Population Taboo." *Project Syndicate.* August 4. www.project-syndicate.org/commentary/rethinking-population-control-taboo-by-peter-singer-and-frances-kissling-2017-08?barrier=accesspaylog

Sirmon, Jeff M. (1993). "National Leadership." In *Environmental Leadership: Developing Effective Skills and Styles.* Eds. Joyce K. Berry and John C. Gordon. Washington, DC: Island Press, 165–184.

Skodvin, Tora and Steinar Andresen. (2006). "Leadership Revisited." *Global Environmental Politics* 6.3: 13–27.

Slade, Giles. (2006). *Made to Break: Technology and Obsolescence in America.* Cambridge: Harvard University Press.

Slingerland, Edward. (2000). "Effortless Action: The Chinese Spiritual Ideal of Wu-Wei." *Journal of the American Academy of Religion* 68.2: 293–328.

Smalley, Andrea L. (2017). *Wild by Nature: North American Animals Confront Colonization.* Baltimore: Johns Hopkins University Press.

Smith, Michael B. (1998). "The Value of a Tree: Public Debates of John Muir and Gifford Pinchot." *The Historian* 60.4: 757–778.

Smith, William. (2017). "Deep Ecology and Secondary Schooling: Exploring Ecocentric Alternatives." PhD Thesis. Royal Melbourne Institute of Technology, Melbourne.

Smith, William and Annette Gough. (2015). "Deep Ecology as a Framework for Student Eco-Philosophical Thinking." *Journal of Philosophy in Schools* 2.1: 38–55.

Smutko, L. Steven and Mary Lou Addor. (2012). "The Resilience and Power of Heterarchical Leadership." In *Environmental Leadership: A Reference Handbook.* Volume One. Ed. Deborah Rigling Gallagher. Thousand Oaks: Sage, 237–245.

Snow, Donald, ed. (1992a). *Inside the Environmental Movement: Meeting the Leadership Challenge.* Washington, DC: Island Press.

Snow, Donald, ed. (1992b). *Voices From the Environmental Movement: Perspectives for a New Era.* Washington, DC: Island Press.

Soppelsa, Peter. (2011). "The Instrumentalization of Horses in 19th Century Paris." In *Anthropocentrism: Humans, Animals, Environments.* Ed. Rob Boddice. Leiden: Brill, 245–264.

Sosik, John J. (2006). *Leading with Character: Stories of Valor and Virtue and the Principles They Teach.* Greenwich: Information Age Publishing.

Souba, Wiley W. (2014). "The Phenomenology of Leadership." *Open Journal of Leadership* 3: 77–105.

Soulé, Michael and Reed Noss. (1998). "Rewilding and Biodiversity: Complementary Goals for Continental Conservation." *Wild Earth* 8: 19–28.

Spence, Mark David. (1999). *Dispossessing the Wilderness: Indian Removal and the Making of the National Parks.* New York: Oxford University Press.

Speth, James Gustave. (2008). "Consumption: Living with Enough, Not Always More." In *The Bridge at the End of the World: Capitalism, the Environment, and Crossing From Crisis to Sustainability.* New Haven: Yale University Press, 147–164.

Springett, Delyse. (2003). "Business Conceptions of Sustainable Development: A Perspective from Critical Theory." *Business Strategy and the Environment* 12.2: 71–86.

Starik, Mark. (2004). "Holistic Environmental Leadership: Living Sustainably Beyond 9-to-5." *Human Ecology Review* 11.3: 280–284.

Stefansson, Vilhjalmur. (1960). *The Fat of the Land.* New York: Macmillan.

Steffen, Seana Lowe. (2018). "From Peril to Possibility: Restorative Leadership for a Sustainable Future." In *Innovation in Environmental Leadership: Critical Perspectives.* Eds. Benjamin W. Redekop, Deborah Rigling Gallagher and Rian Satterwhite. New York: Routledge, 225–240.

Steiner, Gary. (2010). *Anthropocentrism and Its Discontents: The Moral Status of Animals in the History of Western Philosophy.* Pittsburgh: University of Pittsburgh Press.

Sterba, James P. (2010). "Kantians and Utilitarians and the Moral Status of Nonhuman Life." In *Environmental Ethics: The Big Questions.* Ed. David R. Keller. Chichester: Wiley-Blackwell, 182–192.

Stober, Spencer S., Tracey L. Brown and Sean J. Cullen. (2013). *Nature-Centered Leadership: An Aspirational Narrative.* Champaign: Common Ground Publishing.

Stodola, Denise. (2010). "Communicating Leadership for Environmental Sustainability: The Rhetorical Strategies of Rachel Carson and Al Gore." In *Leadership for Environmental Sustainability.* Ed. Benjamin W. Redekop. New York: Routledge, 122–132.

Stogdill, Ralph Melvin. (1948). "Personal Factors Associated With Leadership: A Survey of the Literature." *Journal of Psychology* 25.1: 35–71.

Stogdill, Ralph Melvin. (1974). *Handbook of Leadership: A Survey of Theory and Research.* New York: The Free Press.

Stone, Christopher D. (1972). "Should Trees Have Standing? – Toward Legal Rights for Natural Objects." *Southern California Law Review* 45: 450–501.

Strasser, Annie-Rose. (2014). "The Weird and Wonderful World of Indoor Farming." *ThinkProgress.* July 9. https://thinkprogress.org/the-weird-and-wonderful-world-of-indoor-farming-333b6a12cdec/

Stroud, Richard H. (1985). *National Leaders of American Conservation.* Washington, DC: Smithsonian Institution Press.

Stubenrauch, Bob. (1984). *Restore and Drive: Collectible Cars of Postwar America.* New York: Norton.

Subramaniam, R. and Lee Sing Kong. (2012). "Aeroponics: Experiences From Singapore on a Green Technology for Urban Farming." In *Environmental Leadership: A Reference Handbook.* Volume One. Ed. Deborah Rigling Gallagher. Thousand Oaks: Sage, 653–662.

Sulkunen, Pekka, John Holmwood, Hilary Radner and Gerhard Schulze, eds. (1997). *Constructing the New Consumer Society.* New York: St Martin's Press.

Swann, Russell. (2001). "Ecocentrism, Leader Compassion and Community." *Leading and Managing* 7.2: 163–180.

Sweeney, Oisin, John Turnbull, Menna Elizabeth Jones, Mike Letnic and Thomas Newsome. (2019). "We Can 'Rewild' Swathes of Australia by Focusing on What Makes It Unique." *The Conversation.* February 27. http://theconversation.com/we-can-rewild-swathes-of-australia-by-focusing-on-what-makes-it-unique-111749

Syse, Karen Lykke and Martin Lee Mueller, eds. (2015). *Sustainable Consumption and the Good Life: Interdisciplinary Perspectives.* London: Routledge.

Taylor, Nik and Richard Twine, eds. (2014). *The Rise of Critical Animal Studies: From the Margins to the Centre.* London: Routledge.

Taylor, Paul W. (1981). "The Ethics of Respect for Nature." *Environmental Ethics* 3: 197–218.

Taylor, Paul W. (1986). *Respect for Nature: A Theory of Environmental Ethics.* Princeton: Princeton University Press.

Tena, Joan Carles Membrado. (2015). "Residential Migration and Urban Sprawl in the Spanish Mediterranean." *Cuadernos de Turismo* 35: 469–472.

Thomas, Jack Ward. (1993). "Ethics for Leaders." In *Environmental Leadership: Developing Effective Skills and Styles*. Eds. John C. Gordon and Joyce K. Berry. Washington, DC: Island Press, 31–45.

Thompson, Janna. (1990). "A Refutation of Environmental Ethics." *Environmental Ethics* 12.2: 147–160.

Thompson, Michael J. (2015). "On the Ethical Dimensions of Waste." *Archives for Philosophy of Law and Social Philosophy* 101.2: 252–269.

Thompson, Richard C., Shanna H. Swan, Charles J. Moore and Frederick S. vom Saal. (2009). "Our Plastic Age." *Philosophical Transactions of the Royal Society B Biological Sciences* 364.1526. http://rstb.royalsocietypublishing.org/content/364/1526/1973

Thoreau, Henry David. (1854). *Walden, or, Life in the Woods*. Boston: Ticknor & Fields.

Thoreau, Henry David. (1962). *The Journal of Henry D. Thoreau*. Fourteen vols. Eds. Bradford Torrey and Francis H. Allen. New York: Dover.

Thornett, Alan. (2019). *Facing the Apocalypse: Arguments for Ecosocialism*. London: Resistance Books.

Tice, Ty. (1993). "Managing Conflict." In *Environmental Leadership: Developing Effective Skills and Styles*. Eds. John C. Gordon and Joyce K. Berry. Washington, DC: Island Press, 67–89.

Timberlake, Lloyd. (1992). *Environmental Politics for the 21st Century*. Reading: University of Reading (Geography Department).

Tranter, Bruce. (2009). "Leadership and Change in the Tasmanian Environmental Movement." *Leadership Quarterly* 20.5: 708–724.

Tucker, Robert C. (1968). "The Theory of Charismatic Leadership." *Daedalus* 97.3: 731–756.

Tucker, Robert C. (1977). "Personality and Political Leadership." *Political Science Quarterly* 92.3: 383–393.

Turner, James Morton. (2002). "From Woodcraft to 'Leave No Trace': Wilderness, Consumerism, and Environmentalism in Twentieth-Century America." *Environmental History* 7.3: 462–484.

Tyers, Roger. (2017). "It's Time to Wake Up to the Devastating Impact Flying Has on the Environment." *The Conversation*. January 11. https://theconversation.com/its-time-to-wake-up-to-the-devastating-impact-flying-has-on-the-environment-70953

Uhl-Bien, Mary. (2006). "Relational Leadership Theory: Exploring the Social Processes of Leadership and Organizing." *Leadership Quarterly* 17.6: 654–676.

United Nations Department of Economic and Social Affairs (UN DESA). (2019). *World Population Prospects 2019, Volume One: Comprehensive Tables*. New York: UN. https://population.un.org/wpp/Publications/Files/WPP2019_Volume-I_Comprehensive-Tables.pdf

United Nations Environmental Assembly (UNEA). (2019). *Global Environment Outlook*. www.unenvironment.org/resources/global-environment-outlook-6

United Nations Environmental Programme-World Conservation Monitoring Centre (UNEP-WCMC) and International Union for Conservation of Nature (IUCN). (2016). *Protected Planet Report 2016*. Cambridge/Gland. https://wdpa.s3.amazonaws.com/Protected_Planet_Reports/2445%20Global%20Protected%20Planet%202016_WEB.pdf

van den Bergh, Jeroen C. (2001). "Ecological Economics: Themes, Approaches, and Differences with Environmental Economics." *Regional Environmental Change* 2.1: 13–23.

van Vugt, Mark. (2004). "The Nature in Leadership: Evolutionary, Biological, and Social Neuroscience Perspectives." In *The Nature of Leadership*. Eds. John Antonakis, Anna T. Cianciolo and Robert J. Sternberg. Thousand Oaks: Sage, 141–175.

Varner, Gary E. (1995). "Can Animal Rights Activists Be Environmentalists." In *People, Penguins, and Plastic Trees: Basic Issues in Environmental Ethics*. Second ed. Eds. Christine Pierce and Donald VanDeVeer. Belmont: Wadsworth, 254–273.

Vilkka, Leena. (1997). *The Intrinsic Value of Nature*. Amsterdam: Rodopi.

Villarreal, Luis P. (2004). "Are Viruses Alive?" *Scientific American* 291.6: 100–105.

von Hardenberg, Wilko Graf, Matthew Kelly, Claudia Leal and Emily Wakild, eds. (2017). *Nature State: Rethinking the History of Conservation*. London: Routledge Taylor & Francis.

Vredenburg, Harrie and Frances Westley. (1993). "Environmental Leadership in Three Contexts: Managing for Global Competitiveness." *Proceedings of the International Association for Business and Society* 4: 979–990.

Walley, Noah and Bradley Whitehead. (1994). "It's Not Easy Being Green." *Harvard Business Review* 3: 46–52.

Warner, Keith. (2011). "Franciscan Environmental Ethics: Imagining Creation as a Community of Care." *Journal of the Society of Christian Ethics* 31.1: 143–160.

Warren, Carol and Leontine Visser. (2016). "The Local Turn: An Introductory Essay Revisiting Leadership, Elite Capture and Good Governance in Indonesian Conservation and Development Programs." *Human Ecology* 44: 277–286.

Warren, Julianne Lutz. (2012). "Leading Questions." In *Environmental Leadership: A Reference Handbook*. Volume Two. Ed. Deborah Rigling Gallagher. Thousand Oaks: Sage, 815–822.

Warren, Karen. (2000). *Ecofeminist Philosophy: A Western Perspective on What It Is and Why It Matters*. Lanham: Rowman & Littlefield.

Washington, Haydn and Michelle Maloney. (2020). "The Need for Ecological Ethics in a New Ecological Economics." *Ecological Economics* 169.

Washington, Haydn, Bron Taylor, Helen Kopnina, Paul Cryer and John J. Piccolo. (2017). "Why Ecocentrism Is the Key Pathway to Sustainability." *The Ecological Citizen* 1.1. https://openaccess.leidenuniv.nl/bitstream/handle/1887/50284/WashingtonetalWhyecocentrismisthekeypathwaytosustainability2017.pdf?sequence=1

Washington, Haydn and Paul Twomey, eds. (2016). *A Future Beyond Growth: Towards a Steady State Economy*. Abingdon: Routledge.

Watson, James E. M. and others. (2016). "Catastrophic Declines in Wilderness Areas Undermine Global Environment Targets." *Current Biology* 26.21: 2929–2934.

Weber, Max. (1947). *The Theory of Social and Economic Organization*. Trans. A. M. Henderson and Talcott Parsons. New York: Oxford University Press.

Weber, Max. (1967). *From Max Weber: Essays in Sociology*. Eds. and trans. H. H. Gerth and C. Wright Mills. New York: Oxford University Press.

Weber, Max. (1978). *Economy and Society: An Outline of Interpretive Sociology*. Volume One. Trans. Ephraim Fischoff and others. Eds. Guenther Roth and Claus Wittich. Berkeley: University of California Press.

Weber, Rachel. (2002). "Extracting Value from the City: Neoliberalism and Urban Redevelopment." *Antipode* 34.3: 519–540.

Webster, Henry H. (1993). "Lessons from State and Regional Resource Management." In *Environmental Leadership: Developing Effective Skills and Styles*. Eds. John C. Gordon and Joyce K. Berry. Washington, DC: Island Press, 104–122.

Weinberger, Mary Beth. (1987). "The Relationship Between Women's Education and Fertility: Selected Findings From the World Fertility Surveys." *International Family Planning Perspectives* 13.2: 35–46.

Weisberg, Barry. (1970). *Ecocide in Indochina: The Ecology of War.* New York: Harper and Row.

Western, Simon. (2008). *Leadership: A Critical Text.* First ed. Thousand Oaks: Sage.

Western, Simon. (2010). "Eco-Leadership: Towards the Development of a New Paradigm." In *Leadership for Environmental Sustainability.* Ed. Benjamin W. Redekop. New York: Routledge, 36–54.

Western, Simon. (2013). "The Eco-Leadership Discourse." In *Leadership: A Critical Text.* Second ed. Thousand Oaks: Sage, 243–280.

Western, Simon. (2018). "The Eco-Leadership Paradox." In *Innovation in Environmental Leadership: Critical Perspectives.* New York: Routledge, 48–60.

Westoff, Charles F. and Norman B. Ryder. (1977). *The Contraceptive Revolution.* Princeton: Princeton University Press.

Westover, Robert Hudson. (2016). *Conservation versus Preservation?* March 22. www.fs.fed.us/blogs/conservation-versus-preservation

Wheatley, Margaret J. (1992). *Leadership and the New Science: Learning About Organizations from an Orderly Universe.* San Francisco: Berrett-Koehler Publishers.

White, Lynn, Jr. (1940). "Technology and Invention in the Middle Ages." *Speculum* 15.2: 141–159.

White, Lynn, Jr. (1962). *Medieval Technology and Social Change.* Oxford: Clarendon Press.

White, Lynn, Jr. (1967). "The Historical Roots of Our Ecologic Crisis." *Science* 155.3767: 1203–1207.

White, Lynn, Jr. (1978). "The Future of Compassion." *The Ecumenical Review* 30.2: 99–109.

White, Thomas. (2019). "Philosophy Should Care About the Filthy, Excessive and Unclean." *Aeon: A World of Ideas.* https://aeon.co/ideas/philosophy-should-care-about-the-filthy-excessive-and-unclean

Whyte, Martin King, Wang Feng and Yong Cai. (2015). "Challenging Myths About China's One-Child Policy." *The China Journal* 74: 144–159.

Wielkiewicz, Richard M. and Stephen P. Stelzner. (2005). "An Ecological Perspective on Leadership Theory, Research, and Practice." *Review of General Psychology* 9.4: 326–334.

Wildavsky, Aaron B. (1984). *The Nursing Father: Moses as a Political Leader.* University: University of Alabama Press.

Wilkie, Benjamin. (2016). "Defence White Paper Shows Australian Forces Must Safeguard Nature Too." *The Conversation.* February 26. https://theconversation.com/defence-white-paper-shows-australian-forces-must-safeguard-nature-too-55386

Williams, Raymond. (1983). *Towards 2000.* Harmondsworth: Penguin.

Williams, Robert L. (2010). "Leadership and the Dynamics of Collaboration: Averting the Tragedy of the Commons." In *Leadership for Environmental Sustainability.* Ed. Benjamin W. Redekop. New York: Routledge, 67–92.

Wilson, Edward O. (2002). *The Future of Life.* New York: Alfred A. Knopf.

Wilson, Edward O. (2016). *Half-Earth: Our Planet's Fight for Life.* New York: Liveright Publishing Corporation (W. W. Norton & Co).

Wilson, George R. and Melanie J. Edwards. (2008). "Native Wildlife on Rangelands to Minimize Methane and Produce Lower-Emission Meat: Kangaroos Versus

Livestock." *Conservation Letters: A Journal of the Society for Conservation Biology* 1.3: 119–128.

Wittgenstein, Ludwig. (2009). *Philosophical Investigations*. Rev. fourth ed. Trans. G. E. M. Amscombe, P. M. S. Hacker and Joachim Schulte. Eds. P. M. S. Hacker and Joachim Schulte. Chichester: Blackwell Publishing.

Wolloch, Nathaniel. (2009). "William Smellie and Enlightenment Anti-Anthropocentrism." *Eighteenth-Century Life* 33.2: 45–63.

Wollstonecraft, Mary. (1845). *Vindication of the Rights of Women, with Strictures on Political and Moral Subjects*. New York: G. Vale.

Wood, David. (2001). "What Is Ecophenomenology?" *Research in Phenomenology* 31: 78–95.

Wood, David. (2019). *Reoccupy Earth: Notes Toward an Other Beginning*. New York: Fordham University Press.

Woodhouse, Keith Mako. (2018). *The Ecocentrists: A History of Radical Environmentalism*. New York: Columbia University Press.

World Commission on Environment and Development (WCED) [Brundtland Commission]. (1987). *Our Common Future: The Report of the World Commission on Environment and Development*. Oxford: Oxford University Press.

World Wildlife Fund (WWF). (2018). *Living Planet Report 2018: Aiming Higher*. Eds. Monique Grooten and Rosamunde E. A. Almond. Gland: WWF. www.wwf.org. uk/sites/default/files/2018-10/wwfintl_livingplanet_full.pdf

World Wildlife Fund (WWF). (n.d.). "How Many Species Are We Losing?" *WWF*. http://wwf.panda.org/our_work/biodiversity/biodiversity/

Worster, Donald. (1977). *Nature's Economy: The Roots of Ecology*. San Francisco: Sierra Club Books.

Worster, Donald. (1980). "The Intrinsic Value of Nature." *Environmental Review* 4.1: 43–49.

Wortman, Max S., Jr. (1982). "Strategic Management and Changing Leader-Follower Roles." *Journal of Applied Behavioral Science* 18.3: 371–383.

Wuerthner, George, Eileen Crist and Tom Butler, eds. (2015). *Protecting the Wild: Parks and Wilderness, the Foundation for Conservation*. Washington, DC: Island Press.

Yaeger, Patricia. (2008). Editor's Column: The Death of Nature and the Apotheosis of Trash; Or, Rubbish Ecology." *PMLA* 123.2: 321–339.

Youngblood, Ruth. (1987). "'Stop at 2' Campaign Works Too Well; Singapore Urges New Baby Boom." *Los Angeles Times*. June 21. www.latimes.com/archives/la-xpm-1987-06-21-mn-8983-story.html

Zafft, Carmen R. (2013). "Authentic, Transformational Leadership: A Phenomenological Study of the Experiences of Black/White Biracial Leaders." PhD Thesis. University of Nebraska, Lincoln.

Zalasiewicz, Jan, Mark Williams, Will Steffen and Paul Crutzen. (2010). "The New World of the Anthropocene." *Environmental Science & Technology* 44.7: 2228–2231.

Zaleznik, Abraham. (1966). *Human Dimensions of Leadership*. New York: Harper & Row.

Zaleznik, Abraham. (1977/1992). "Managers and Leaders: Are They Different?" *Harvard Business Review* 55.3: 67–78. Reprinted as an "HBR Classic." *Harvard Business Review* 70.2: 3–12.

Zierler, David. (2011). *The Invention of Ecocide: Agent Orange, Vietnam, and the Scientists Who Changed the Way We Think About the Environment*. Athens: University of Georgia Press.

Zimmerman, Michael E. (1988). "Quantum Theory, Intrinsic Value, and Panentheism." *Environmental Ethics* 10.1: 3–30.

Žižek, Slavoj. (2010a). *Living in the End Times*. London: Verso.

Žižek, Slavoj. (2010b). "O Earth, Pale Mother!" *In These Times*. June 17. http://inthe
setimes.com/article/6079/o_earth_pale_mother

Zoller, Heather M. and Gail T. Fairhurst. (2007). "Resistance Leadership: The Overlooked Potential in Critical Organization and Leadership Studies." *Human Relations*
60.9: 1331–1360.

Zukav, Gary. (1979). *The Dancing Wu Li Masters: An Overview of the New Physics*. New
York: Morrow.

INDEX

Printed in the United States
by Baker & Taylor Publisher Services